COMMON
WITNESS
TO THE
GOSPEL

COMMON WITNESS TO THE GOSPEL

DOCUMENTS ON ANGLICAN-ROMAN CATHOLIC RELATIONS 1983-1995

Edited by Jeffrey Gros, E. Rozanne Elder, and Ellen K. Wondra

United States Catholic Conference • Washington, D.C.

The National Conference of Catholic Bishops' Committee for Ecumencial and Interreligious Affairs recommended this publication, prepared in collaboration with the Episcopal Church and the Canadian Conference of Catholic Bishops. The texts have been reviewed by Bishop Alexander Brunett, chair of the NCCB Committee for Ecumenical and Interreligious Affairs, and it is authorized for publication by the undersigned.

MONSIGNOR DENNIS M. SCHNURR
General Secretary
NCCB/USCC

Cover photo: Catholic News Service

First Printing, June 1997
ISBN 1-57455-060-8

CONTENTS

PREFACE

GOD'S PURPOSE, according to Holy Scripture, is to gather into communion with himself the whole of creation under the lordship of Christ by the power of the Holy Spirit (Eph 1). In response to God's grace, we follow a pilgrimage toward full visible unity in faith, sacramental life, and witness to the Gospel in the world. For thirty years, Anglicans and Roman Catholics have been engaged 'in a serious dialogue which, founded on the Gospels and on the ancient traditions, may lead to that unity in truth, for which Christ prayed' (Pope Paul VI and Archbishop Michael Ramsey, 1966). We live within a real, if yet imperfect, communion between our two Churches. The texts assembled in this volume are designed to serve the reconciling purpose of God in Jesus Christ.

In this pilgrimage our people are called to conversion of heart and mind. Conversion to Christ entails conversion to the Church and Christ's will for its unity. This means our people are called, as Anglicans and as Roman Catholics, to a commitment and fidelity to their community. This fidelity further entails a commitment to one another in our common baptism and our common pilgrimage toward visible unity. The documents in this volume, like *The Final Report* and other texts from Canada and the United States, are meant to serve the spiritual and pastoral lives of our people as communion deepens. Some of them are also presented to our Churches to form the basis for common decision making for building the structures of communion. It is our hope that these documents will nourish the prayer, study, and pastoral life of all our people.

We have begun to evaluate the results of our common journey together in faith. We rejoice that the responses of the Roman Catholic Church and the Anglican Communion recognize in *The Final Report* a common faith in the eucharist and a new common context for the understanding of ordained ministry. The progress on authority has laid the groundwork for the next stages in the international dialogue.

In this context we were not surprised, but very gratified, when Archbishop George Carey was among the first to respond positively to Pope John Paul's invitation in *Ut Unum Sint* to review the Petrine office, to see how it might be renewed to better serve the unity of Christians.

As the earlier work of the International Commission and the dialogues in the United States and Canada have already enriched our common life of faith, so the international texts on salvation, ethics, and the sacramental nature of the Church as communion create new stages on the pilgrimage toward unity. These texts, along with the doctrinal, pastoral, and analytical documents produced by the dialogues and by bishops and individuals in Canada and the United States, are building blocks on which our full reconciliation will be constructed. May their reading and study strengthen the bonds of communion we already experience and the hopes for full communion that are central to the identity of both our Churches.

We make our own the commitment of Pope John Paul II and Archbishop Robert Runcie: 'We here solemnly recommit ourselves and those we represent to the restoration of visible unity and full ecclesial communion in the confidence that to seek anything less would be to betray Our Lord's intention for the unity of his people' *(Common Declaration*, October 2, 1989).

✠ **FRANK GRISWOLD**
✠ **JOHN SNYDER**
Cochairs
Anglican–Roman Catholic Dialogue, USA

✠ **JOHN BAYCROFT**
✠ **TERRENCE PENDERGAST**
Cochairs
Anglican–Roman Catholic Dialogue, Canada

INTRODUCTION

ANGLICANS AND ROMAN CATHOLICS SHARE REAL COMMUNION in their commitment to Scripture, baptism, the catholic structures of ministry, the mission of proclaiming the Gospel in word and deed, the historical creeds, and the visible sacramental unity of the Church. This common commitment has led our two Churches to enter into and remain in official dialogue for the express purpose of perfecting this still imperfect communion into full visible unity. This dialogue has progressed in a marvelously productive fashion since 1965.

The Anglican Communion in its Lambeth Conferences (Coleman, 1992) and the Roman Catholic Church in its Second Vatican Council (Tanner, 1990) have acknowledged the special relationship that exists between our two communions. Early in this century, contacts and dialogues developed that laid the groundwork for the official dialogue (Purdy, 1995).

In the two vast nations of North America, our two Churches first engaged in official dialogue in 1965 in the United States and in 1971 in Canada. In each country, members of the two Churches have found that they live with particular benefits and unique challenges arising from their specific location. We share common languages, live in a pluralistic context, have put behind us many Old World suspicions, and have enjoyed the benefits of religious liberty. Enormous geographical distances, great diversity of cultures and tongues within the same Church, and the development of democratic institutions and sensibilities in the surrounding society have shaped Anglican and Roman Catholic thought and practice in the United States and Canada.

The dialogues between the two Churches have thus had as their purpose both growing towards unity with each other and offering their unique North American insights and experiences to the international dialogue as well as to our Churches throughout the world. (See especially documents 15 and 19 in this volume.) ARC Canada and ARC USA have responded readily and ably to ARCIC's requests for comment and criticism, and Canadian and American statements included in this volume reflect these two purposes. Other documents from the dialogues not reproduced here are listed in Appendix I.

This collection of official documents is aimed at making Roman Catholics and Anglicans aware of how much they share in faith and structures and at removing those challenges that still remain in the pilgrimage toward full communion. In parishes, dioceses, institutions, and the interchurch homes of our people, communion is lived on a day-to-day basis. Constant thanksgiving in our hearts and in our Churches celebrates the communion that now exists and impels us to work and to pray together in realizing Christ's will for the Church.

This series of groundbreaking texts is published in one volume to provide resources for preaching, study, catechetical instruction, prayer, and reflection. The documents should encourage those who work to heal divisions. This series is also a reference work to aid leaders and scholars in giving authentic witness to the common ground these two Churches share in Christ. The documents here bring up to 1995 documentation previously collected and published (Wright/Witmer, 1985) that covers the period from 1966 to 1983. Some of these texts are available in the context of other ecumenical documents (Vischer, 1984; Burgess, 1989, 1995).

Those studying Anglican-Roman Catholic relations will know *The Final Report* (1982). An important study text, with responses and supporting documentation, is already available (Hill, 1994). Only those texts that seem essential to this process of reception and response are included in the present volume.

For the reader's convenience the material is organized by topic rather than by chronology. We are now more than thirty years into the journey together, and many people have studied all the texts as they have emerged. There are others new to dialogue for whom a synthetic or topical reading will help in seeing the breadth of the foundation already in place. Still others will find the volume a resource for handy reference.

Accordingly, the material has been arranged in three sections: (1) the Church, including texts on its nature, unity, and relation to salvation; (2) sacraments and ministry, including responses to the earlier work on eucharist, ministry, and authority; and (3) the people of God and pastoral care, including ethics, encouragement to the faithful, and possible directions for future discussion and prayer. Appendices summarize the chronology of the relationship, identify the members of the dialogues, and provide a bibliography. The notes in the text refer to this bibliography.

The documents come from a variety of sources and carry different weight in our ecumenical relationship. Statements issued by the Anglican Churches and Roman Catholic Episcopal Conferences of Canada and the United States are included along with the agreed statements of the officially commissioned national and international dialogues in hope of setting national and international concerns into context for the reader. Three official position papers of the Churches are included (nos. 8, 9, 12). Some texts resulted from the officially commissioned Anglican Roman Catholic International Commission (nos. 1, 5, 12, 16). Others were written by the ARC dialogue teams of Canada (nos. 3, 6, 10, 15, 16, 20) and the United States (nos. 4, 11, 13, 14, 17, 19). In addition, there are texts from groups of bishops (nos. 2, 16, 21). Many of the national ARC dialogue texts were written in response to ARCIC texts and are best read together with them (nos. 7, 10, 11, 12, 13, 19). The introductions to each section will point out the source and purpose of each text, when necessary.

These documents, of course, provide only a partial record of the reconciling efforts of our two Churches. Diocesan ecumenical officers of each Church regularly study and foster the relationship (Falardeau, 1990; Bird, 1995; Diocesan Officers, 1996). There are parishes and dioceses that have many years' experience of covenant relationships. The Episcopal Church has sponsored two conferences at which this relationship, among others, has been evaluated (Wright, 1979; Norgren, 1994). Bishops of our Churches meet together regularly and have traveled together on pilgrimage to Canterbury and Rome, the historic centers of our church life (Gros, 1995; *One In Christ*, 1995).

While some editorial adjustments have been made to harmonize the texts, differences in spellings have been maintained from the original.

Parish study groups are unlikely to find these materials easily adaptable to study or retreat methodologies without some assistance. If educators and lay leaders in the congregation take the time to work through the materials, however, they will find the content both spiritually nourishing and immensely illuminating within the congregation.

Pastors seeking resources for preaching will want to read and discuss some of the texts with colleagues. The international dialogues (nos. 1, 5, 12, 18) will be particularly useful for this purpose. Catechists will want to study together texts that relate to their work of encouraging conversion to the ecumenical vision (nos. 2, 3, 4, 11); of preparing Christians for a full sacramental life (nos. 11, 12, 13, 14)—especially in the light of *The Final Report* agreement on the eucharist; and of teaching the nature and structures of the Church (nos. 1, 11, 17), the doctrines of grace and faith (no. 5), and ethical positions (nos. 18, 19). Used in conjunction with the *Catechism of the Catholic Church* and Anglican catechetical materials, these documents form a particularly important aid for interpreting those sections dealing with the Church, sacraments, authority, salvation, and ethics.

Some of the texts, such as those on the Church (no. 1) and ethics (no. 18), while drawing on the particular traditions of these two Churches, provide a basis for sustained discussion among a wide range of Christians in Churches committed to full visible unity. A pair of congregations can set aside six to nine weeks for a series of meetings to which they invite their members and others to come together to pray and reflect on a text or series of texts. Topics should be outlined beforehand, and the dialogue statements tested against the participants' own understanding of the faith. By this means Christians can share with their leaders their own hopes for deeper communion. Covenanted parishes and dioceses can assign representatives of vestries and parish councils to study selected texts and to suggest practical steps that could be taken in the local situation to embody the levels of accord reached in the documents.

Some of these documents can be excerpted for reading in a liturgical context and others chosen for reflection by parish leaders as part of their personal meditation and prayer. Most lend themselves to study and discussion. Once study groups have read and evaluated selections from the documents, they may wish to send their reflections to their diocesan ecumenical officer, their bishops, or the national offices of their Churches. Responses from local groups, especially if shared with congregations and leadership, are vital to the process of reception.

Some study groups will wish to explore more deeply their own and the other tradition, possibly reading together the *Catechism of the Catholic Church* or the resolutions of the Lambeth Conferences (Coleman, 1992). The material in this series can also be related to other dialogues in which our congregations and Churches are involved, especially Lutheran-Catholic and Lutheran-Anglican documents (nos. 5, 6, 7). With the concrete proposals now before some of the Churches (Norgren, 1988, 1991; Lehmann, 1990), Lutherans, Anglicans, and Roman Catholics may welcome an opportunity to study some of this material together.

The pilgrimage toward full communion requires a deepened conversion and spiritual commitment. The theological and institutional elements are only a partial, though necessary, dimension of the renewal of ourselves and our Churches. These documents are the result of study, prayer, and hard work. We believe they are the work of the Holy Spirit given to us by God's grace. May their study and reading deepen the prayer and encourage the mission of our people as we celebrate the communion we already share.

This text is commended to the reader with a benediction from Archbishop George Carey and Pope John Paul II in their *Common Declaration* of December 5, 1996:

We look forward to the celebration of two thousand years since the Word became flesh (cf. Jn 1:14). We encourage Anglicans and Catholics, with all their Christian brothers and sisters, to pray, celebrate, and witness together in the year 2000. We make this call in a spirit of humility, recognizing that credible witness will only fully be given when Anglicans and Catholics, with all their Christian brothers and sisters, have achieved that full, visible unity that corresponds to Christ's prayer 'that they may all be one . . . so that the world may believe' (Jn 17:21).

I

THE CHURCH

IN1982, **HAVING REACHED AGREEMENT** on eucharist and ministry and remarkable consensus on authority in the Church—theological issues that had divided the two Churches for 450 years—the first Anglican Roman Catholic International Commission (ARCIC I) published its *Final Report*. By having decided at the outset in 1969 to avoid contentious terminology that had on both sides hardened into theological battle cries, ARCIC I chose a course that has borne fruit in ecumenical dialogue, not only between Anglicans and Roman Catholics but in many bilateral discussions and in such multilateral documents as *Baptism, Eucharist, and Ministry*. This remarkably succinct document of the Faith and Order Commission of the World Council of Churches, proposed to the Church at large by theologians of traditions as long divided and hence diverse as Eastern Orthodox and Anabaptists, signaled a new willingness of Christians to look through yet beyond their own history and theological terminology to reach a depth of agreement not possible without the method used by ARCIC I.

After submitting its *Final Report* to the two Churches for official evaluation and response, ARCIC I was dissolved, its task completed. Shortly afterwards, as *The Final Report* began to be evaluated by the national Churches of the Anglican Communion and by national conferences of Roman Catholic bishops, Pope John Paul II visited Canterbury Cathedral, the historic center of Anglicanism. He and the archbishop of Canterbury took the occasion to establish a second international commission 'to examine, especially in the light of our respective judgments on *The Final Report*, the outstanding doctrinal differences which still separate us, with a view towards their eventual resolution' *(Common Declaration* of Pope John Paul II and the archbishop of Canterbury, May 29, 1982, in Wright/Witmer, 1985, p. 301).

Salvation and the Church, the first Agreed Statement of ARCIC II, was published in January 1987. Its reception was overshadowed by the decision of certain provinces of the

Anglican Communion to extend the sacrament of holy orders to women and the consequent spate of official letters between Rome and Canterbury. The *Observations* of the Congregation for the Doctrine of the Faith (no. 6), published later that year, reflect heightened Roman Catholic caution towards deviations from long accepted terminology. The ARC Canada Comments (no. 7), by drawing attention to the consonance of the Agreed Statement with official Catholic teaching, recall both Churches to the real issues under discussion.

Meeting in 1988, ARCIC II began its task encouraged by Anglican approval, yet faced with a new, potentially church-dividing issue, an issue as vehemently, if less savagely, disputed as sixteenth-century debates over eucharist, ministry, and authority. The same Lambeth Conference (1988) which recognized *The Final Report* as 'consonant in substance' with Anglican teaching also resolved to 'respect the decision and attitudes of other provinces in the ordination of women to the episcopate'. In agreeing to disagree among themselves on this important step and cognizant of ecumenical reaction, Anglican bishops from around the world declared themselves committed to maintaining 'an open dialogue in the Church to whatever extent communion is impaired' by this action (Coleman, 202, 193, resolutions 1.1, 8.1).

The Church as Communion (CC) was published during the Week of Prayer for Christian Unity, 1991. Whether the coincidence of the publication of this agreed statement and public disagreement on ordination and gender proves in the end to be ironic or prophetic remains to be seen. In an atmosphere of renewed caution and much public contrasting of tradition and traditionalism, ARCIC II released for review and response a major document on the Church as *koinonia*, the communion which is given the people of God by the Holy Spirit and the fellowship that binds disparate persons with diverse ways of expressing the faith into the one body of Christ.

The commission took as its starting point the conviction that had been growing throughout two decades of dialogue: that Anglicans and Roman Catholics already are in communion to some degree, despite the existence of parallel hierarchical structures and residual ecclesiastical obstacles to sacramental communion—both now re-emphasized. The Church—the 'one, holy, catholic, and apostolic Church'—the commission wrote, 'is a dynamic reality moving towards its fulfillment' (CC, no. 3). A living organism quickened by the abiding presence of the Holy Spirit, the Church is becoming what it already is. No Church is yet what God wills the Church to be. Neither the Anglican Communion nor the Roman Catholic Church embodies the fullness of the Church; each is diminished by its separation from the other and from all the other Christians not included in this particular dialogue. Each is therefore crippled in its mission of sharing the Good News of Jesus Christ with all our fellow human beings who 'long for true community in freedom, justice, and peace and for the respect of human dignity' (CC, no. 3) and for whose reconciliation Christ prayed and died (CC, no. 22).

By their serious, candid, scriptural, and prayerful consideration of the great mystery of salvation and the Church, ARCIC II calls our two Churches and each of their members to look beyond old and newly formulated differences to the Christ in whom we are all incorporated at baptism and the faith to which we commit ourselves each time we recite the creed; to cherish the Tradition we shared for fifteen hundred years and still share in our differing expressions; to 'listen to the gifts of the other' *(Reconciling Unity and Plurality)*; to sacrifice personal and ecclesiastical preferences; and never to acquiesce to 'human sinfulness, division, and alienation' (CC, no. 19). For our vocation as redeemed members of the one mystical body of Christ is to make Christ present and visible and audible in a world torn apart by sin. Without being in communion within the body of Christ, how can Christians guide fragmented humanity to salvation?

1. CHURCH AS COMMUNION

An Agreed Statement by the Second Anglican Roman Catholic International Commission, 1991

PREFACE

During the past four years the members of the Anglican Roman Catholic International Commission have considered the mystery of communion which is given and made visible in the Church. This has not been an easy task, because of the inherent complexity and depth of the mystery. For the same reason, our study cannot be complete or perfect. We have paid particular attention to the sacramentality of the Church; that is, to the Church as a divine gift, grounded in Christ himself and embodied in human history, through which the grace of Christ is mediated for the salvation of humankind. In doing this, we believe that we have laid a necessary foundation for further work on vital topics which were broached by our predecessors in the first Anglican Roman Catholic International Commission. In particular we look forward to deeper study of the nature of the authority of Christ, the living Word of God, over his Church, and of the means through which he exercises that authority and his people respond to it.

In considering the Church as communion we have drawn upon thinking in both our Churches and in the dialogues with other Christian bodies in which both are engaged. We offer the outcome of our labours not only to our own respective Churches, but to all who are concerned with the common search for that full ecclesial unity which we believe to be God's will for all his people. We do this in the hope of study and response.

The members of the Commission have not only been engaged in theological dialogue. Their work and study have been rooted in shared prayer and common life. This in itself has given them a profound experience of communion in Christ; not indeed that full sacramental communion which is our goal, but nevertheless a true foretaste of that fullness of communion for which we pray and strive.

We are painfully aware of the difficulties which still lie in our way. Nevertheless, we are heartened and encouraged by the words of Pope John Paul II and Archbishop Robert Runcie in their Common Declaration of 2 October 1989:

Against the background of human disunity, the arduous journey to Christian unity must be pursued with determination and vigour, whatever obstacles are perceived with determination to block the path. We here solemnly recommit ourselves and those we represent to the restoration of visible unity and full ecclesial communion in the confidence that to seek anything less would be to betray our Lord's intention for the unity of his people.

The pope and the archbishop also declared: 'The ecumenical journey is not only about the removal of obstacles but also about the sharing of gifts'. That indeed has been the experience of the members of the Commission. In giving we receive. That is of the essence of communion in Christ.

✠ **CORMAC MURPHY-O'CONNOR**
✠ **MARK SANTER**
Dublin, 6 September 1990

THE STATUS OF THE DOCUMENT

The document published here is the work of the Second Anglican Roman Catholic International Commission (ARCIC II). It is a joint statement of the Commission. The authorities who appointed the Commission have allowed the statement to be published so that it may be widely discussed. It is not an authoritative declaration by the Roman Catholic Church or by the Anglican Communion, who will evaluate the document in order to take a position on it in due time.

INTRODUCTION

1. Together with other Christians, Anglicans and Roman Catholics are committed to the search for that unity in truth and love for which Christ prayed. Within this context, the purpose of the Anglican Roman Catholic International Commission is to examine and try to resolve those doctrinal differences which stand in the way of ecclesial communion between Anglicans and Roman Catholics. *The Final Report* of ARCIC I and the publication of ARCIC II's statement on *Salvation and the Church* have contributed to progress in mutual understanding and growing awareness of the need for ecclesial communion. We believe it is time now to reflect more explicitly upon the nature of communion and its constitutive elements. This will enable us to meet the requests that have been made for further clarification of the ecclesiological basis of our work.

2. This statement on communion differs from previous ARCIC reports in that it does not focus specifically on doctrinal questions that have been historically divisive. Nor does it seek to treat all the issues pertaining to the doctrine of the Church. Its purpose is to give substance to the affirmation that Anglicans and Roman Catholics are already in a real though as yet imperfect communion and to enable us to recognise the degree of communion that exists both within and between us.[1] Moreover, we believe that within the perspective of communion the outstanding difficulties that remain between us will be more clearly

understood and are more likely to be resolved; thus we shall be helped to grow into a more profound communion.

3.   There are advantages in adopting the theme of communion in an exploration of the nature of the Church. Communion implies that the Church is a dynamic reality moving towards its fulfilment. Communion embraces both the visible gathering of God's people and its divine life-giving source. We are thus directed to the life of God, Father, Son, and Holy Spirit, the life God wills to share with all people. There is held before us the vision of God's reign over the whole creation, and of the Church as the firstfruits of humankind which is drawn into that divine life through acceptance of the redemption given in Jesus Christ. Moreover this focus on communion enables us to affirm that which is already realised in the Church, the eucharistic community. It enables us also to acknowledge as a gift of God the good that is present in community life in the world: communion involves rejoicing with those who rejoice and being in solidarity with those who suffer and those who search for meaning in life. To explore the meaning of communion is not only to speak of the Church but also to address the world at the heart of its deepest need, for human beings long for true community in freedom, justice, and peace and for the respect of human dignity.

4.   Furthermore to understand the Church in terms of communion confronts Christians with the scandal of our divisions. Christians' disunity obscures God's invitation to communion for all humankind and makes the Gospel we proclaim harder to hear. But the consideration of communion also enables Christians to recognise that certain yet imperfect communion they already share. Christians of many traditions are coming to acknowledge the central place of communion in their understanding of the nature of the Church and its unity and mission. This is the communion to the study of which this document is devoted.

5.   After a survey of how communion is unfolded in Scripture, we explore the way in which the Church as communion is sacrament of the merciful grace of God for all humankind. Then follows a treatment of the relationship of communion to the apostolicity, catholicity, and holiness of the Church and the consideration of the necessary elements required for unity and ecclesial communion. Finally, we affirm the existing communion between our two Churches and outline some of the remaining issues which continue to divide us.

I. COMMUNION UNFOLDED IN SCRIPTURE

6.   The relationship between God and his creation is the fundamental theme of Holy Scripture. The drama of human existence, as expounded in Scripture, consists in the formation, breakdown, and renewal of this relationship. The biblical story opens with God establishing this relationship by creating human beings in his image and likeness; God blesses and honours them by inviting them to live in communion both with him and with one another as stewards of his creation. In the unfolding saga of Genesis the disobedience of Adam and Eve undermines both their relation with God and their relation with each other:

they hide from God; Adam blames Eve; they are expelled from the garden; their relationship with the rest of creation is distorted. What ensues in Genesis illustrates this recurrent pattern in human history.

7.   In the variety of literary styles and theological traditions coming from every period of the long history of the people of Abraham, the books of the Old Testament bear witness to the fact that God wants his people to be in communion with him and with each other. God's purpose is reaffirmed in covenant with his people. Through Abraham God gives the promise of blessing to all the nations (Gn 12:1-3). Through Moses God establishes a people as his own possession, a community in a covenant relationship with him (Ex 19:5-6). In the Promised Land the Temple becomes the place where God chooses to set his name, where he dwells with his people (Dt 12:5). The prophets consistently denounce the community's faithlessness as threatening this relationship. Nevertheless, God's fidelity remains constant and he promises through the prophets that his promise will be accomplished. Although division and exile follow upon the sins of the chosen people, reconciliation of the scattered people of God will spring from a radical transformation within a new covenant (Jer 31:3ff). God will raise up a servant to fulfil his purpose of communion and peace for his chosen people and also for all the nations (Is 49:6; also Mi 4:1-4).

8.   In the fullness of time, God sends his Son, born of a woman, to redeem his people and bring them into a new relationship as his adopted children (cf. Gal 4:4-5). When Jesus begins his ministry he calls together a band of disciples with whom he shares his mission (Mk 3:14; cf. Jn 20:21). After Easter they are to be witnesses to his life, teaching, death, and resurrection. In the power of the Spirit given at Pentecost they proclaim that God's promises have been fulfilled in Christ. For the apostolic community the baptism of repentance and faith bestowed in this New Covenant does more than restore that which was lost: by the Spirit believers enter Christ's own communion with the Father. In the eucharist, the memorial of the New Covenant, believers participate in the body and blood of Christ (1 Cor 11:23-27) and are made one body in him (1 Cor 10:16-17). It is communion with the Father, through the Son, in the Holy Spirit which constitutes the people of the New Covenant as the Church, 'a people still linked by spiritual ties to the stock of Abraham'.[2]

9.   On Calvary the hideous nature of sin and evil is clearly exposed. In the Cross are found God's judgement upon the world and his gift of reconciliation (2 Cor 5:14-19). Through the paschal victory all estrangement occasioned by differences of culture, class, privilege and sex is overcome. All those who are united with the death and resurrection of Christ have equal standing before God. Moreover, because Christ is the one in whom and through whom all things are created and reconciled, the proper relationship between humanity and the rest of creation is restored and renewed in him (Col 1:15-20; Gal 3:27-29).

10. However, the life of communion is still impaired by human sin (1 Cor 1:10ff). The failure of Christians to respond to the demands of the Gospel gives rise to divisions among

Christians which obscure the Church's witness. The New Testament affirms that there is a constant need for recourse to the repentance and reconciliation offered by Christ through the Church (Mt 18:15-20; cf. 1 Jn 1:5-10).

11. In the writings of the New Testament the failures of the disciples and the divisions among them are fully recognised. Nevertheless the reign of God is already perceived as a reality in the world (Mk 1:15; Lk 11:20), even though it will be perfectly realised only in the fullness of the Kingdom of God. Its culmination is described as a feast, 'the wedding supper of the Lamb' (Rev 19:9), a vivid image of communion deeply rooted in human experience. This feast is spoken of by Jesus in the parables (Mt 22:1-10), and foreshadowed in the feeding of the multitudes (Jn 6). The celebration of the eucharist prefigures and provides a foretaste of this messianic banquet (Lk 22:30). In the world to come, such signs will cease since the sacramental order will no longer be needed, for God will be immediately present to his people. They will see him face to face and join in endless praise (Rev 22:3-4). This will be the perfection of communion.

12. In the New Testament the word *koinonia* (often translated 'communion' or 'fellowship') ties together a number of basic concepts such as unity, life together, sharing, and partaking. The basic verbal form means 'to share', 'to participate', 'to have part in', 'to have something in common', or 'to act together'. The noun can signify fellowship or community. It usually signifies a relationship based on participation in a shared reality (e.g., 1 Cor 10:16). This usage is most explicit in the Johannine writings: 'We proclaim to you what we have seen and heard, so that you also may have fellowship with us. And our fellowship is with the Father and with his Son Jesus Christ' (1 Jn 1:3; cf. 1 Jn 1:7).[3]

13. In the New Testament the idea of communion is conveyed in many ways. A variety of words, expressions, and images points to its reality: the people of God (1 Pt 2:9-10); flock (Jn 10:14; Acts 20:28-29; 1 Pt 5:2-4); vine (Jn 15:5); temple (1 Cor 3:16-17); bride (Rev 21:2); body of Christ (1 Cor 12:27; 1 Cor 10:17; Rom 12:4-5; Eph 1:22-23). All these express a relationship with God and also imply a relationship among the members of the community. The reality to which this variety of images refers is communion, a shared life in Christ (1 Cor 10:16-17; cf. Jn 17) which no one image exhaustively describes. This communion is participation in the life of God through Christ in the Holy Spirit, making Christians one with each other.

14. It is characteristic of the Apostle Paul to speak of the relationship of believers to their Lord as being 'in Christ' (2 Cor 5:17; Col 1:27-28; Gal 2:20; cf. also Jn 15:1-11) and Christ being in the believer through the indwelling of the Holy Spirit (Rom 8:1-11). This relationship Paul also affirms in his description of the Church as the one body of Christ. This description is integrally linked with the presence of Christ in the eucharist. Those who share in the supper of the Lord are one body in Christ because they all partake of the one bread (1 Cor 10:16-17). This description underlines the intimate, organic relationship which exists between the Risen Lord and all those who receive new life through communion with

him. Equally it emphasises the organic relationship thus established among the members of the one body, the Church. All who share in the 'holy things' of the sacramental life are made holy through them: because they share in them together they are in communion with each other.

15. The New Testament reflects different dimensions of communion as experienced in the life of the Church in apostolic times.

At the centre of this communion is life with the Father, through Christ, in the Spirit. Through the sending of his Son the living God has revealed that love is at the heart of the divine life. Those who abide in love abide in God and God in them; if we, in communion with him, love one another, he abides in us and his love is perfected in us (cf. 1 Jn 4:7-21). Through love God communicates his life. He causes those who accept the light of the truth revealed in Christ rather than the darkness of this world to become his children. This is the most profound communion possible for any of his creatures.

Visibly, this communion is entered through baptism and nourished and expressed in the celebration of the eucharist. All who are baptised in the one Spirit into one body are united in the eucharist by this sacramental participation in this same one body (1 Cor 10:16-17; 12:13). This community of the baptised, devoted to the apostolic teaching, fellowship, breaking of bread and prayer (cf. Acts 2:42), finds its necessary expression in a visible human community. It is a community which suffers with Christ in anticipation of the revelation of his glory (Phil 3:10; Col 1:24; 1 Pt 4:13; Rom 8:17). Those who are in communion participate in one another's joys and sorrows (Heb 10:33; 2 Cor 1:6-7); they serve one another in love (Gal 5:13) and share together to meet the needs of one another and of the community as a whole. There is a mutual giving and receiving of spiritual and material gifts, not only between individuals but also between communities, on the basis of a fellowship that already exists in Christ (Rom 15:26-27; 2 Cor 8:1-15). The integrity and building up of that fellowship require appropriate structure, order, and discipline (cf. 1 Cor 11:17-34 and the Pastoral Epistles *passim*).

Communion will reach its fulfilment when God will be all in all (1 Cor 15:28). It is the will of God for the whole creation that all things should be brought to ultimate unity and communion in Christ (Eph 1:10; Col 1:19-20).

Already in the New Testament these different dimensions of communion are discernible, together with a striving towards their ever more faithful realisation.

II. COMMUNION: SACRAMENTALITY AND THE CHURCH

16. God's purpose is to bring all people into communion with himself within a transformed creation (cf. Rom 8:19-21). To accomplish this the eternal Word became incarnate. The life and ministry of Jesus Christ definitively manifested the restored humanity God intends. By who he was, by what he taught, and by what he accomplished through the cross and resurrection, he became the sign, the instrument, and the firstfruits of

God's purpose for the whole of creation (Col 1:15-17). As the new Adam, the Risen Lord is the beginning and guarantor of this transformation. Through this transformation, alienation is overcome by communion, both between human beings and above all between them and God. These two dimensions of communion are inseparable. This is the mystery of Christ (Eph 2:11-3.12).

17. Communion with God through Christ is constantly established and renewed through the power of the Holy Spirit. By the power of the Spirit, the incomparable riches of God's grace are made present for all time through the Church. Those who are reconciled to God form 'one body in Christ and are individually members one of another' (Rom 12:5). By the action of the same Spirit, believers are baptised into the one Body (1 Cor 12:13) and in the breaking of the bread they also participate in that one Body (1 Cor 10:16-17; 11:23-29). Thus the Church 'which is Christ's body, the fullness of him who fills all in all', reveals and embodies 'the mystery of Christ' (cf. Eph 1:23; 3:4, 8-11). It is therefore itself rightly described as a visible sign which both points to and embodies our communion with God and with one another; as an instrument through which God effects communion; and as a foretaste of the fullness of communion to be consummated when Christ is all in all. It is a 'mystery' or 'sacrament'.

18. The Church as a communion of believers with God and with each other is a sign of the new humanity God is creating and a pledge of the continuing work of the Holy Spirit. Its vocation is to embody and reveal the redemptive power of the Gospel, signifying reconciliation received through faith and participation in the new life in Christ. The Church is the sign of what God has done in Christ, is continuing to do in those who serve him, and wills to do for all humanity. It is a sign of God's abiding presence, and of his eternal faithfulness to his promises, for in it Christ is ever present and active through the Spirit. It is the community where the redemptive work of Jesus Christ has been recognised and received, and is therefore being made known to the world. Because Christ has overcome all the barriers of division created by human sin, it is the mission of the Church as God's servant to enter into struggle to end those divisions (cf. Eph 2:14-18; 5:1-2).

19. The Holy Spirit uses the Church as the means through which the word of God is proclaimed afresh, the sacraments are celebrated, and the people of God receive pastoral oversight, so that the life of the Gospel is manifested in the life of its members. The Church is both the sign of salvation in Christ, for to be saved is to be brought into communion with God through him, and at the same time the instrument of salvation, as the community through which this salvation is offered and received. This is what is meant when the Church is described as an 'effective sign', given by God in the face of human sinfulness, division, and alienation.[4]

20. Human sinfulness and Christian division obscure this sign. However, Christ's promise of his abiding presence in the midst of his people (Mt 18, 20; 28:20) gives the assurance that the Church will not cease to be this effective sign. In spite of the frailty and sinfulness

of its members, Christ promises that powers of destruction will never prevail against it (Mt 16:18).

21. Paradoxically it is pre-eminently in its weakness, suffering, and poverty that the Church becomes the sign of the efficacy of God's grace (cf. 2 Cor 12:9; 4:7-12). It is also paradoxical that the quality of holiness is rightly attributed to the Church, a community of sinners. The power of God to sanctify the Church is revealed in the scandal of the cross where Christ in his love gave himself for the Church so that it might be presented to him without spot or wrinkle, holy and without blemish (Eph 5:26-27). God was in Christ reconciling the world to himself, making him who knew no sin to be sin for us so that in him we might become the righteousness of God (cf. 2 Cor 5:19-21).

22. The communion of the Church demonstrates that Christ has broken down the dividing wall of hostility, so as to create a single new humanity reconciled to God in one body by the cross (cf. Eph 2:14-16). Confessing that their communion signifies God's purpose for the whole human race, the members of the Church are called to give themselves in loving witness and service to their fellow human beings.

This service is focused principally in the proclaiming of the Gospel in obedience to the command of Christ. Having received this call, the Church has been entrusted with the stewardship of the means of grace and with the message of salvation. In the power of Christ's presence through the Spirit it is caught up in the saving mission of Christ. The mandate given to the Church to bring salvation to all the nations constitutes its unique mission. In this way the Church not only signifies the new humanity willed by God and inaugurated by Christ. It is itself an instrument of the Holy Spirit in the extension of salvation to all human beings in all their needs and circumstances to the end of time. To speak of the Church as sacrament is to affirm that in and through the communion of all those who confess Jesus Christ and who live according to their confession, God realises his plan of salvation for all the world. This is not to say that God's saving work is limited to those who confess Christ explicitly. By God's gift of the same Spirit who was at work in the earthly ministry of Christ Jesus, the Church plays its part in bringing his work to its fulfilment.

23. To be united with Christ in the fulfilment of his ministry for the salvation of the world is to share his will that the Church be one, not only for the credibility of the Church's witness and for the effectiveness of its mission, but supremely for the glorification of the Father. God will be truly glorified when all peoples with their rich diversity will be fully united in one communion of love. Our present communion with God and with each other in the Holy Spirit is a pledge and foretaste here and now of the ultimate fulfilment of God's purpose for all, as proclaimed in the vision of 'a great multitude which none could number, from every nation, from all tribes and peoples and tongues . . . crying out with a loud voice, "Salvation belongs to our God who sits upon the throne, and to the Lamb!"' (Rev 7:9-10).

24. The sacramental nature of the Church as sign, instrument, and foretaste of communion is especially manifest in the common celebration of the eucharist. Here, celebrating the memorial of the Lord and partaking of his body and blood, the Church points to the origin of its communion in Christ, himself in communion with the Father; it experiences that communion in a visible fellowship; it anticipates the fullness of the communion in the world.

III. COMMUNION: APOSTOLICITY, CATHOLICITY, AND HOLINESS

25. The Church points to its source and mission when it confesses in the Creed, 'We believe in one holy catholic and apostolic Church'. It is because the Church is built up by the Spirit upon the foundation of the life, death, and resurrection of Christ as these have been witnessed and transmitted by the apostles that the Church is called *apostolic*. It is also called apostolic because it is equipped for its mission by sharing in the apostolic mandate.

26. The content of the faith is the truth of Christ Jesus as it has been transmitted through the apostles. This God-given deposit of faith cannot be dissociated from the gift of the Holy Spirit. Central to the mission of the Spirit is the safeguarding and quickening of the memory of the teaching and work of Christ and of his exaltation, of which the apostolic community was the first witness. To safeguard the authenticity of its memory the Church was led to acknowledge the canon of Scripture as both test and norm. But the quickening of its memory requires more than the repetition of the words of Scripture. It is achieved under the guidance of the Holy Spirit by the unfolding of revealed truth as it is in Jesus Christ. According to the Johannine Gospel the mission of the Holy Spirit is intimately linked with all that Christ Jesus said, did, and accomplished. Christ promised that the Father will send the Holy Spirit in his name to teach the disciples all things and to bring to remembrance all that he has said (cf. Jn 14:26). To keep alive the memory of Christ means to remain faithful to all that we know of him through the apostolic community.

27. Such faithfulness must be realised in daily life. Consequently in every age and culture authentic faithfulness is expressed in new ways and by fresh insights through which the understanding of the apostolic preaching is enriched. Thus the Gospel is not transmitted solely as a text. The living word of God, together with the Spirit, communicates God's invitation to communion to the whole of his world in every age. This dynamic process constitutes what is called the living tradition, the living memory of the Church. Without this the faithful transmission of the Gospel is impossible.

28. The living memory of the mystery of Christ is present and active within the Church as a whole; it is at work in the constant confession and celebration of the apostolic faith and in the insights, emphases, and perspectives of faithful members of the Church. And since faith seeks understanding, this includes an examination of the very foundations of faith. As the social setting of the Christian community changes, so the questions and challenges posed both from within and from without the Church are never entirely the

same. Even within the period covered by the New Testament this process is evident when new images and fresh language are used to express the faith as it is handed on in changing cultural contexts.

29. If the Church is to remain faithfully rooted and grounded in the living truth and is to confess it with relevance, then it will need to develop new expressions of the faith. Diversity of cultures may often elicit a diversity in the expression of the one Gospel; within the same community distinct perceptions and practices arise. Nevertheless these must remain faithful to the tradition received from the apostles (cf. Jude 3). Since the Holy Spirit is given to all the people of God, it is within the Church as a whole, individuals as well as communities, that the living memory of the faith is active. All authentic insights and perceptions, therefore, have their place within the life and faith of the whole Church, the temple of the Holy Spirit.

30. Tensions inevitably appear. Some are creative of healthy development. Some may cause loss of continuity with apostolic tradition, disruption within the community, estrangement from other parts of the Church. Within the history of Christianity, some diversities have become differences that have led to such conflict that ecclesial communion has been severed. Whenever differences become embodied in separated ecclesial communities, so that Christians are no longer able to receive and pass on the truth within the one community of faith, communion is impoverished and the living memory of the Church is affected. As Christians grow apart, complementary aspects of the one truth are sometimes perceived as mutually incompatible. Nevertheless the Church is sustained by Christ's promise of its perseverance in the truth (cf. Mt 16:18), even though its unity and peace are constantly vulnerable. The ultimate God-given safeguard for this assurance is the action of the Spirit in preserving the living memory of Christ.

31. This memory, realised and freshly expressed in every age and culture, constitutes the apostolic tradition of the Church. In recognising the canon of Scripture as the normative record of the revelation of God, the Church sealed as authoritative its acceptance of the transmitted memory of the apostolic community. This is summarised and embodied in the creeds. The Holy Spirit makes this tradition a living reality which is perpetually celebrated and proclaimed by word and sacrament, pre-eminently in the eucharistic memorial of the once-for-all sacrifice of Christ, in which the Scriptures have always been read. Thus the apostolic tradition is fundamental to the Church's communion which spans time and space, linking the present to past and future generations of Christians.

32. Responsibility for the maintenance of the apostolic faith is shared by the whole people of God. Every Christian has a part in this responsibility. The task of those entrusted with oversight, acting in the name of Christ, is to foster the promptings of the Spirit and to keep the community within the bounds of the apostolic faith, to sustain and promote the Church's mission, by preaching, explaining, and applying its truth. In responding to the insights of the community, and of the individual Christian, whose conscience is also

moulded by the same Spirit, those exercising oversight seek to discern what is the mind of Christ. Discernment involves both heeding and sifting in order to assist the people of God in understanding, articulating, and applying their faith. Sometimes an authoritative expression has to be given to the insights and convictions of the faithful. The community actively responds to the teaching of the ordained ministry, and when, under the guidance of the Spirit, it recognises the apostolic faith, it assimilates its content into its life.

33. Succession in the episcopal ministry is intended to assure each community that its faith is indeed the apostolic faith, received and transmitted from apostolic times. Further, by means of the communion among those entrusted with the episcopal ministry the whole Church is made aware of the perceptions and concerns of the local churches; at the same time the local churches are enabled to maintain their place and particular character within the communion of all the Churches.

34. In the Creeds the Church has always confessed its *catholicity*: 'I believe in . . . the holy catholic Church'. It gets this title from the fact that by its nature it is to be scattered throughout the world, from one end of the earth to the other, from one age to the next. The Church is also catholic because its mission is to teach universally and without omission all that has been revealed by God for the salvation and fulfilment of humankind; and also because its vocation is to unite in one eucharistic fellowship men and women of every race, culture, and social condition in every generation. Because it is the fruit of the work of Christ upon the cross, destroying all barriers of division, making Jews and Gentiles one holy people, both having access to the one Father by the one Spirit (cf. Eph 2:14–18), the Church is catholic.

35. In the mystery of his will God intends the Church to be the re-creation in Christ Jesus of all the richness of human diversity that sin turns into division and strife (cf. Eph 1:9–10). Insofar as this re-creation is authentically demonstrated in its life, the Church is a sign of hope to a divided world that longs for peace and harmony. It is the grace and Gospel of God that brings together this human diversity without stifling or destroying it; the Church's catholicity expresses the depth of the wisdom of the Creator. Human beings were created by God in his love with such diversity in order that they might participate in that love by sharing with one another both what they have and what they are, thus enriching each other in their mutual communion.

36. Throughout its history the Church has been called to demonstrate that salvation is not restricted to particular cultures. This is evident in the variety of liturgies and forms of spirituality, in the variety of disciplines and ways of exercising authority, in the variety of theological approaches, and even in the variety of theological expressions of the same doctrine. These varieties complement one another, showing that, as the result of communion with God in Christ, diversity does not lead to division; on the contrary, it serves to bring glory to God for the munificence of his gifts. Thus the Church in its catholicity is the place where God brings glory to his name through the communion of those created in his

own image and likeness, so diverse yet profoundly one. At every eucharistic celebration of Christian communities dispersed throughout the world, in their variety of cultures, languages, social and political contexts, it is the same one and indivisible body of Christ reconciling divided humanity that is offered to believers. In this way the eucharist is the sacrament of the Church's catholicity in which God is glorified.

37. In the eucharist the Church also manifests its solidarity with the whole of humanity. This is given expression in intercession and thanksgiving, and in the sending out of the people of God to serve and to proclaim the message of salvation to the world. The Church's concern for the poor and oppressed is not peripheral but belongs to the very heart of its mission (cf. 2 Cor 8:1-9).

Moreover, for the Church effectively to carry out its ministry of reconciliation, it is necessary that its members and communities display in their common life the fruits of Christ's reconciling work. As long as Christians are divided, they do not fully manifest the catholic nature of the Church.

38. Catholicity is inseparable from holiness, as is evident from the early liturgical traditions which often speak of 'the holy catholic Church', and from early forms of the Creed which include the words 'We believe in the Holy Spirit in the holy Catholic Church'. The Church is *holy* because it is 'God's special possession' (1 Pt 2:9-10), endowed with his Spirit (Eph 2:21-22), and it is his special possession since it is there that 'the mystery of his will, according to his good pleasure' is realised, 'to bring all things in heaven and on earth together under one head, Christ' (Eph 1:9-10).

Being set apart as God's special possession means that the Church is the communion of those who seek to be perfect as their Heavenly Father is perfect (Mt 5:48). This implies a life in communion with Christ, a life of compassion, love, and righteousness. The holiness of the Church does not mean that it is to be cut off from the world (Jn 17:15ff). Its vocation is to be, through its holiness, salt of the earth, light of the world (Mt 5:13-16). In this way the Church declares the praises of him who called his people out of darkness into his marvelous light (cf. 1 Pt 2:9).

39. The catholicity of God's purpose requires that all the diverse gifts and graces given by God to sanctify his people should find their proper place in the Church. Every Christian is called to be consecrated to the life and service of the communion (1 Pt 4:10 ff; 1 Cor 12:4 ff). And what is true of the individual is equally true of the local churches. Communion with other local churches is essential to the integrity of the self-understanding of each local church, precisely because of its catholicity. Life in self-sufficient isolation, which rejects the enrichment coming from other local churches as well as the sharing with them of gifts and resources, spiritual as well as material, is the denial of its very being. It is the particular ministry of oversight to affirm and order the diverse gifts and graces of individuals and communities; to effect and embody the unity of the local church and its unity with the wider communion of the Churches. By the example of their lives those who bear oversight

are to witness to the holiness of the Church and in their ministry foster holiness amongst its members.

Amid all the diversity that the catholicity intended by God implies, the Church's unity and coherence are maintained by the common confession of the one apostolic faith, a shared sacramental life, a common ministry of oversight, and joint ways of reaching decisions and giving authoritative teaching.

40. The catholicity of the Church is threatened, in the first place, when the apostolic faith is distorted or denied within the community. It is also threatened whenever the faith is obscured by attitudes and behaviour in the Church which are not in accord with its calling to be the holy people of God, drawn together by the Spirit to live in communion. Just as the Church has to distinguish between tolerable and intolerable diversity in the expression of the apostolic faith, so in the area of life and practice the Church has to discover what is constructive and what is disruptive of its own communion. Catholicity and holiness are also impaired when the Church fails to confront the causes of injustice and oppression which tear humanity apart or when it fails to hear the cries of those calling for sustenance, respect, peace, and freedom.

41. When the Creed speaks of the Church as holy, catholic, and apostolic, it does not mean that these attributes are distinct and unrelated. On the contrary, they are so interwoven that there cannot be one without the others. The holiness of the Church reflects the mission of the Spirit of God in Christ, the Holy One of God, made known to all the world through the apostolic teaching. Catholicity is the realisation of the Church's proclamation of the fullness of the Gospel to every nation throughout the ages. Apostolicity unites the Church of all generations and in every place with the once-for-all sacrifice and resurrection of Christ, where God's holy love was supremely demonstrated.

IV. UNITY AND ECCLESIAL COMMUNION

42. The Church, since apostolic times, has always included belief in its unity among the articles of faith (e.g., 1 Cor 12:12 ff; Eph 4:4-6). Because there is only one Lord, with whom we are called to have communion in the one Spirit, God has given his Church one Gospel, one faith, one baptism, one eucharist, and one apostolic ministry through which Christ continues to feed and guide his flock.

43. For a Christian the life of *communion* means sharing in the divine life, being united with the Father, through the Son, in the Holy Spirit, and consequently to be in fellowship with all those who share in the same gift of eternal life. This is a spiritual communion in which the reality of the life of the world to come is already present. But it is inadequate to speak only of an invisible spiritual unity as the fulfilment of Christ's will for the Church; the profound communion fashioned by the Spirit requires visible expression. The purpose of the visible ecclesial community is to embody and promote this spiritual communion with God (cf. paras. 16-24).

For a local community to be a *communion* means that it is a gathering of the baptised brought together by the apostolic preaching, confessing the one faith, celebrating the one eucharist, and led by an apostolic ministry. This implies that this local church is in communion with all Christian communities in which the essential constructive elements of ecclesial life are present.

For all the local churches to be *together in communion*, the one visible communion which God wills, it is required that all the essential constitutive elements of ecclesial communion are present and mutually recognised in each of them. Thus the visible communion between these Churches is complete and their ministers are in communion with each other. This does not necessitate precisely the same canonical ordering: diversity of canonical structures is part of the acceptable diversity which enriches the one communion of all the Churches.

44. The *constitutive elements* essential for the visible communion of the Church are derived from and subordinate to the common confession of Jesus Christ as Lord. In the picture of the Jerusalem Church in the Acts of the Apostles we can already see in nascent form certain necessary elements of ecclesial communion which must be present in the Church in every age (cf. para. 15).

45. In the light of all that we have said about communion it is now possible to describe what constitutes ecclesial communion. It is rooted in the confession of the one apostolic faith, revealed in the Scriptures, and set forth in the Creeds. It is founded upon one baptism. The one celebration of the eucharist is its pre-eminent expression and focus. It necessarily finds expression in shared commitment to the mission entrusted by Christ to his Church. It is a life of shared concern for one another in mutual forbearance, submission, gentleness, and love; in the placing of the interests of others above the interests of self; in solidarity with the poor and the powerless; and in the sharing of gifts both material and spiritual (cf. Acts 2:44). Also constitutive of life in communion is acceptance of the same basic moral values, the sharing of the same vision of humanity created in the image of God and recreated in Christ, and the common confession of the one hope in the final consummation of the Kingdom of God.

For the nurture and growth of this communion, Christ the Lord has provided a ministry of oversight, the fullness of which is entrusted to the episcopate, which has the responsibility of maintaining and expressing the unity of the Churches (cf. paras. 33 and 39 and *The Final Report, Ministry and Ordination*). By shepherding, teaching, and celebrating the sacraments, especially the eucharist, this ministry holds believers together in the communion of the local church and in the wider communion of all the Churches (cf. para. 39). This ministry of oversight has both collegial and primatial dimensions. It is grounded in the life of the community and is open to the community's participation in the discovery of God's will. It is exercised so that unity and communion are expressed, preserved, and fostered at every level—locally, regionally, and universally. In the context of the communion of all the Churches the episcopal ministry of a universal primate finds its role as the visible focus of unity.

Throughout history different means have been used to express, preserve, and foster this communion between bishops: the participation of bishops of neighbouring sees in episcopal ordinations; prayer for bishops of other dioceses in the liturgy; exchanges of episcopal letters. Local churches recognised the necessity of maintaining communion with the principal sees, particularly with the See of Rome. The practice of holding synods and councils, local, provincial, ecumenical, arose from the need to maintain unity in the one apostolic faith (cf. *The Final Report*, *Authority in the Church*, I.19-23, II.12).

46. All these interrelated elements and facets belong to the visible communion of the universal Church. Although their possession cannot guarantee the constant fidelity of Christians, neither can the Church dispense with them. They need to be present in order for one local church to recognise another canonically. This does not mean that a community in which they are present expresses them fully in its life.

47. Christians can never acquiesce with complacency in disunity without impairing further their communion with God. As separated Churches grow towards ecclesial communion it is essential to recognise the profound measure of communion they already share through participation in spiritual communion with God and through those elements of a visible communion of shared faith and sacramental life they can already recognise in one another. If some element or important facet of visible communion is judged to be lacking, the communion between them, though it may be real, is incomplete.

48. Within the pilgrim Church on earth, even when it enjoys complete ecclesial communion, Christians will be obliged to seek even deeper communion with God and one another. This is also expressed through faith in the 'Communion of Saints', whereby the Church declares its conviction that the eucharist community on earth is itself a participation in a larger communion which includes the martyrs and confessors and all who have fallen asleep in Christ throughout the ages. The perfection of full communion will only be reached in the fullness of the Kingdom of God.

V. COMMUNION BETWEEN ANGLICANS AND ROMAN CATHOLICS

49. The convictions which this Commission believes that Anglicans and Roman Catholics share concerning the nature of communion challenge both our Churches to move forward together towards visible unity and ecclesial communion. Progress in mutual understanding has been achieved. There exists a significant degree of doctrinal agreement between our two communions even upon subjects which previously divided us. In spite of past estrangements, Anglicans and Roman Catholics now enjoy a better understanding of their long-standing shared inheritance. This new understanding enables them to recognise in each other's Church a true affinity.

50. Thus we already share in the communion founded upon the saving life and work of Christ and his continuing presence through the Holy Spirit. This was acknowledged jointly in the Common Declaration of Pope John Paul II and Archbishop Robert Runcie of 2 October 1989.

> We also urge our clergy and faithful not to neglect or undervalue that certain yet imperfect communion we already share. This communion already shared is grounded in faith in God our Father, in our Lord Jesus Christ, and in the Holy Spirit; our common baptism into Christ; our sharing of the Holy Scriptures, of the Apostles' and Nicene Creeds; the Chalcedonian definition and the teaching of the Fathers; our common Christian inheritance for many centuries. This communion should be cherished and guarded as we seek to grow into the fuller communion Christ wills. Even in the years of our separation we have been able to recognise gifts of the Spirit in each other. The ecumenical journey is not only about the removal of obstacles but also about the sharing of gifts.

51. One of the most important ways in which there has already been a sharing of gifts is in spirituality and worship. Roman Catholics and Anglicans now frequently pray together. Alongside common participation in public worship and in private prayer, members of both Churches draw from a common treasury of spiritual writing and direction. There has been a notable convergence in our patterns of liturgy, especially in that of the eucharist. The same lectionary is used by both Churches in many countries. We now agree on the use of the vernacular language in public worship. We agree also that communion in both kinds is the appropriate mode of administration of the eucharist. In some circumstances, buildings are shared.

52. In some areas there is collaboration in Christian education and in service to local communities. For a number of years, Roman Catholic and Anglican scholars have worked together in universities and other academic institutions. There is closer co-operation in ministerial formation and between parochial clergy and religious communities. The responsibility for the pastoral care of inter-church families is now increasingly entrusted to both Churches. Meetings of Roman Catholic and Anglican bishops are becoming customary, engendering mutual understanding and confidence. This often results in joint witness, practical action, and common statements on social and moral issues. The growing measure of ecclesial communion experienced in these ways is the fruit of the communion we share with the Father, through the Son, in the Holy Spirit.

53. We cannot, however, ignore the effects of our centuries of separation. Such separation has inevitably led to the growth of divergent patterns of authority accompanied by changes in perceptions and practices. The differences between us are not only theological. Anglicans and Roman Catholics have now inherited different cultural traditions. Such dif-

ferences in communities which have become isolated from one another have sometimes led to distortions in the popular perceptions which members of one Church have of the other. As a result visible unity may be viewed as undesirable or even unattainable. However, a closer examination of the developments which have taken place in our different communities shows that these developments, when held in complementarity, can contribute to a fuller understanding of communion.

54. In recent years each communion has learnt from its own and each other's experiences, as well as through contact with other Churches. Since the Second Vatican Council, the principle of collegiality and the need to adapt to local cultural conditions have been more clearly recognised by the Roman Catholic Church than before. Developing liturgical diversity, the increasing exercise of provincial autonomy, and the growing appreciation of the universal nature of the Church have led Anglicans to develop organs of consultation and unity within their own communion. These developments remind us of the significance of mutual support and criticism, as together we seek to understand ecclesial communion and to achieve it.

55. Developments in the understanding of the theology of communion in each of our Churches have provided the background for the Commission's reflections on the nature of communion. This Statement intends to be faithful to the doctrinal formulations to which Anglican and Roman Catholics are each committed without providing an exhaustive treatment of the doctrine of the Church.

56. Grave obstacles from the past and of recent origin must not lead us into thinking that there is no further room for growth towards fuller communion. It is clear to the Commission, as we conclude this document, that, despite continuing obstacles, our two Communions agree in their understanding of the Church as communion. Despite our distinct historical experiences, this firm basis should encourage us to proceed to examine our continuing differences.

57. Our approach to the unresolved matters we must now face together will be shaped by the agreed understanding of communion we have elaborated.

An appreciation both of the existing degree of communion between Anglicans and Roman Catholics as well as the complete ecclesial communion to which we are called will provide a context for the discussion of the long-standing problem of the reconciliation of ministries which forms part of ARCIC II's mandate. This will build upon ARCIC I's work on *Ministry and Ordination*, which provides a new context for discussion of the consequences of the Bull *Apostolicæ Curæ* (1896).

In the light of our agreement we must also address the present and future implications of the ordination of women to the priesthood and episcopate in those Anglican provinces which consider this to be a legitimate development within the catholic and apostolic tradition. The Lambeth Conference of 1988, while resolving that 'each Province respect the decision and attitudes of other Provinces in the ordination or consecration of women to the episcopate', also stressed the importance of 'maintaining the highest possible degree of communion with the Provinces that differ' (Resolution 1,1).

Writing to the Archbishop of Canterbury shortly after the Lambeth Conference, Pope John Paul II said of the ordination of women that 'The Catholic Church, like the Orthodox Church and the Ancient Oriental Churches, is firmly opposed to this development, viewing it as a break with Tradition of a kind we have no competence to authorise'. Referring to ARCIC's work in the reconciliation of ministries the pope said that 'the ordination of women to the priesthood in some provinces of the Anglican Communion, together with the recognition of the right of individual provinces to proceed with the ordination of women to the episcopacy appears to preempt this study and effectively block the path to the mutual recognition of ministries' (Letter of Pope John Paul II to the Archbishop of Canterbury, 8 December 1988).

Another area which the Commission is currently engaged in studying is that of moral issues. Our distinct cultural inheritances have sometimes led us to treat of moral questions in different ways. Our study will explore the moral dimension of Christian life and seek to explain and assess its significance for communion as well as the importance of agreement or difference on particular moral questions.

It is evident that the above issues are closely connected with the question of authority. We continue to believe that an agreed understanding of the Church as communion is the appropriate context in which to continue the study of authority in the Church begun by ARCIC I. Further study will be needed of episcopal authority, particularly of universal primacy, and of the office of the Bishop of Rome; of the question of provincial autonomy in the Anglican Communion; and the role of the laity in decision-making within the Church. This work will take into account the response of the Roman Catholic Church to *The Final Report* of ARCIC I.

58. Serious as these remaining obstacles may seem, we should not overlook the extent of the communion already existing between our two Churches, which we have described in the last part of this Statement. Indeed, awareness of this fact will help us to bear the pain of our differences without complacency or despair. It should encourage Anglicans and Roman Catholics locally to search for further steps by which concrete expression can be given to this communion which we share. Paradoxically, the closer we draw together the more acutely we feel those differences which remain. The forbearance and generosity with which we seek to resolve these remaining differences will testify to the character of the fuller communion for which we strive. Together with all Christians, Anglicans and Roman Catholics are called by God to continue to pursue the goal of complete communion of faith and sacramental life. This call we must obey until all come into the fullness of that Divine Presence, to whom, Father, Son, and Holy Spirit, be ascribed all honour, thanksgiving, and praise to the ages of ages. Amen.

NOTES

1 Cf. *Common Declaration*, Pope John Paul II and the Archbishop of Canterbury, Robert Runcie, 2 October 1989.

2 Second Vatican Council, *Nostra Aetate*, 4.

3 Communion has been treated in many ecumenical documents including *The Final Report* of ARCIC I (Introduction). Cf. also *Communion-Koinonia: A Study by the Institute for Ecumenical Research*, Strasbourg, 1990.

4 The language of 'effective sign' and 'instrument' is known to Anglicans in the [Church of England] *Catechism of the Book of Common Prayer* and in the Articles of Religion, in which baptism and the eucharist are said to be 'not only a sign . . . but rather . . . a sacrament', 'sure witness, and effectual signs of grace', 'as a means whereby we receive' grace, 'as by an instrument', and which 'be effectual because of Christ's institution and promise' (*The Catechism*; Articles 25, 26, 27, 28). For the Roman Catholic Church, similarly, instrumental language was largely developed in relation to the sacraments rather than the Church. But reflection on the mystery of Christ and the Church led to the development of its self-understanding in terms of itself being 'in Christ . . . in the nature of sacrament—a sign and instrument, that is, of communion with God and of unity among all people', 'as the universal sacrament of salvation' (*Lumen Gentium*, 1, 48).

2. RECONCILING UNITY AND PLURALITY

Episcopal Chairs of the Bishops' Committee for Ecumenical and Interreligious Affairs and the Standing Commission on Ecumenical Relations, 1993

Now there are varieties of gifts, but the same Spirit; and there are varieties of services, but the same Lord; and there are varieties of activities, but it is the same God who activates all of them in everyone. To each is given the manifestation of the Spirit for the common good. (1 Cor 12:4-7)

Sisters and brothers in Christ, we would bring before you the gifts God has given us in our relationship to one another as Roman Catholic and Episcopal Churches in the United States and between our two communions worldwide.

The greatest gift we share is the unity in which all Christians participate by virtue of our baptism into Christ Jesus, who has died, risen, and ascended in behalf of the whole creation. Through common baptism we are at the deepest level already one in Christ and, hence, with each other.

As we rejoice in this fundamental gift of God, we know that we need to live into the promise of our common baptism by seeking to find and appreciate the distinctive gifts God has bestowed upon each of our Churches and by responding to the Spirit of Christ as he works in and through this mutual adventure in new ways.

The Lord has blessed us with twenty-five years of fruitful relationships, including theological dialogue grounded in a commitment to perfect the real, if yet imperfect, communion that already joins our Churches in Christ. The blessings of this relationship have borne pastoral fruit in mutual collaboration in mission and witness, cooperation in education and social action, the testimony and nurture of interchurch families, and covenants in many dioceses and parishes that give concrete local form to this commitment to full communion. As the gradual process of our reconciliation unfolds, we take heart in the amazing progress that has been made and encourage all in each place to take leadership in fostering unity. We realize honestly that the closer we come to one another the clearer will be the marks of our four hundred years of estrangement.

For some of us, Anglican and Roman Catholic, movement toward reunion has been much too slow to satisfy our longing for unity and our experience of real communion. Yet we know that for many, both in our country and throughout the world, this longing has yet to be ignited. This conversion to the ecumenical vision is only possible by the grace of the Holy Spirit, and so it is for this conversion and the commitment of all of our people that we pray. Such a conviction about God's will for the Church demands patience and active engagement. What is needed most by all of us, including ourselves as leaders as well as all of the Christian people, is a willingness to listen and to pray.

We are called to listen to the gifts of the other, to those elements in the life of the other Church that may seem most different from our own experience of Christian living. We are called to listen to the four hundred years of Christian living carried out in separation, where we have been nurtured, often, on the pain of division. Above all we are called to listen to the quarter-century of dialogue and its results. We realize we are entering the initial stages of laying the groundwork in common faith, worship, and mutual accountability on which true sacramental communion can develop.

We know that evaluations of the results of these conversations will be challenging and sometimes disappointing to those hoping for more tangible results more readily. However, in God's good time the care of these conversations and the attentiveness to our reservations about one another are essential to our listening to the Spirit's voice in the Church.

Indeed, as we hope for more signs of institutional unity we also pray that the opportunity to know one another and appreciate the gifts we have to receive from one another may become the experience of all of our people. Both of our Churches experience the wounds of separation, though many of our members have become complacent in their divisions.

We recognize that in our division we continue to act in our internal life and in our separate understandings of what the Christian faith demands of us in society in ways that continue to cause pain. We recognize that this is a common pain, the healing of which is a common task. We cannot know how these painful differences will be resolved or comprehended as communion deepens, but by the power of the Holy Spirit we commit ourselves and call our people to commit themselves to facing honestly and sensitively these painful moments in our pilgrimage together. We do not yet know what plurality of gifts is finally compatible with full communion.

Not only are the fostering of unity and the fostering of plurality not opposed to each other, they also enrich each other to the extent that they both aim at building up the one body of Christ which is the Church through love, which is the bond of perfection. We have not yet developed a full appreciation of those elements of diversity that will enrich our lives when full communion is restored. However, it is this plurality that is the concrete testimony to the catholicity of the Church we confess together in the creed.

We realize that deepened levels of communion represent deeper levels of honesty and therefore are a challenge on this journey toward full communion. As we know one another better, we know how we differ in more detail. As our international dialogue, the Anglican Roman Catholic International Commission, notes, 'Separation has inevitably led to the growth of divergent patterns of authority accompanied by changes in perceptions and practices'. As we attempt to minister to our people in the midst of the changing world, the contemporary sexual revolution, and the new roles of women in ministry, we realize that our theological decisions and pastoral approaches will continue to differ, short of full communion. Indeed, we respect the integrity of each other's faithful development while recognizing the burden it places on our relationship with one another. We encourage our people to respect and to come to understand the different heritage and identity we bring to the journey and to support one another in these times of stress in the relationship. Surely the Holy Spirit will bring healing where our own honest development brings challenges to our unity in Christ.

'Communion implies that the Church is a dynamic reality moving toward its fulfillment. Communion embraces both the visible gathering of God's people and its divine life-giving source. We are thus directed to the life of God, Father, Son, and Holy Spirit, the life God wills to share with all people'. For this reason we are encouraged even in the new challenges history places before us, assured that God will give us the strength. Our commitment is central to our identity as Roman Catholics and Anglicans. It will provide us with the resources to continue on the journey.

We make our own the call of Archbishop Runcie and Pope John Paul II: 'We also urge our clergy and faithful not to neglect or undervalue that certain yet imperfect communion we already share. . . . This communion should be cherished and guarded as we seek to grow into the fuller communion Christ wills. Even in the years of our separation we have been able to recognize gifts of the Spirit in each other. The ecumenical journey is not only about the sharing of gifts', and we trust that the Holy Father and the new Archbishop of Canterbury, George Carey, will continue to work together in the same spirit.

☩ **REMBERT WEAKLAND, ARCHBISHOP OF MILWAUKEE**
Chairman of the U.S. Roman Catholic Bishops' Committee for Ecumenical and Interreligious Affairs

☩ **THEODORE EASTMAN, BISHOP OF BALTIMORE**
Chairman of the Episcopal Church's Standing Commission on Ecumenical Relations

January 16, 1993

3. A CALL TO PERSEVERANCE IN ECUMENISM:
OBSERVATIONS OF THE ANGLICAN-ROMAN CATHOLIC DIALOGUE IN CANADA ON THE MEETING OF THE ARCHBISHOP OF CANTERBURY AND POPE JOHN PAUL II

Anglican–Roman Catholic Dialogue, Canada, 1990

We, the members of the Anglican-Roman Catholic Dialogue in Canada, recognize in the recent visit of the archbishop of Canterbury to the bishop of Rome a moment of grace for our respective Churches. We see in their declarations on that occasion a challenge to our fellow Anglicans and Roman Catholics to persevere on the road to unity despite historic and recent obstacles that stand before us. We rejoice in their statement that 'We here solemnly recommit ourselves and those we represent to the restoration of visible unity and full ecclesial communion in the confidence that to seek anything less would be to betray Our Lord's intention for the unity of his people'.

In the twenty-five years since the Second Vatican Council's Decree on Ecumenism (*Unitatis Redintegratio*) successive archbishops of Canterbury and bishops of Rome have met, so that mutual understanding has been fostered, and their frank and open exchanges are seen as the foundation for wider consultations at national and international levels.

The several meetings that occurred between September 28 and October 2, 1989 were characterized by Archbishop Runcie and Pope John Paul as a celebration of the common history that links the sees of Canterbury and Rome. Invoking the memory of Pope St. Gregory's sending St. Augustine of Canterbury to evangelize England, both leaders stressed the importance of Christian unity for the contemporary re-evangelization of Europe and the healing of divisions exported by European missionaries to the rest of the world.

In addition, the pope and the archbishop made reference in their public statements to the unity between the two Churches that already exists, for example, in the holiness of their members, in the recent collaboration between missionaries of their respective communions, and in the modern witness of the martyrs of each Church. It was noted that the divisions between us, however great, do not reach to heaven and, here below, do not preclude our cooperation in those areas where common action, worship, and witness are possible even before we achieve full ecclesial communion.

While our divisions remain a stumbling-block for a fully credible evangelization of our world, there are centers of unity as well: the Gospels as the unifying force of our lives, our

While our divisions remain a stumbling-block for a fully credible evangelization of our world, there are centers of unity as well: the Gospels as the unifying force of our lives, our links from our past history and our present-day awareness that there are legitimately diverse ways of inculturating the Christian faith which do not hinder unity. Both the archbishop and the pope touched on the possible role of the bishop of Rome as a focus of unity in terms such as a 'presiding in love' or as a primacy of action for mission and of 'initiative in favor of unity'.

We must not, nor do we, minimize the difficulties that lie in the way, such as the ordination of women as priests and bishops and the structures of authority in the Church. Still, we see ourselves on a pilgrimage towards unity, not knowing fully all the stages ahead, but confident that where God leads we wish to follow. And so we welcome the challenge of our leaders to persevere and we invite our brothers and sisters to join us in the ecumenical task.

March 30, 1990

4. A RECOMMITMENT TO FULL COMMUNION

Anglican–Roman Catholic Dialogue in the United States, 1992

We the members of the Anglican-Roman Catholic Consultation, meeting in Baltimore June 14–17, 1992, as representatives of our two Churches, recommit ourselves to the restoration of visible unity to and full ecclesial communion between our two Churches.

In 1965 the first Anglican Roman Catholic International Commission (ARCIC I) came into being under the auspices of Pope Paul VI and the Archbishop of Canterbury, Michael Ramsey. At the same time the ARC dialogue began to meet in this country. ARCIC I ended its work in 1981 with the publication of its *Final Report*, in which delegates of both of our Churches affirmed that they had reached 'substantial agreement' on such formerly divisive issues as the eucharist and the nature of the ordained ministry, and also a degree of convergence on authority in the Church. This *Report* was then submitted to the authorities of both Churches for evaluation.

The Lambeth Conference of bishops of the Anglican Communion in 1988 judged the ARCIC statements on eucharist and ministry to be 'consonant in substance with the faith of Anglicans' and welcomed the authority statement as 'a firm basis for the direction and agenda of the continuing dialogue'.

The Vatican Response published in December 1991 gave a warm welcome to *The Final Report* and commended its achievements, but it was not able to endorse the affirmation that substantial agreement on the eucharist and ordained ministry had been reached.

We here acknowledge that there has been a widespread disappointment with the official Roman Catholic *Response* to *The Final Report*, and we note the concern of some theologians about the language and methodology of the *Response*. And yet we also note and underline that in its *Response* the Vatican acknowledges that 'notable progress' has been achieved in *The Final Report* in respect to eucharistic doctrine and that 'significant consensus' has been achieved on the understanding of ordained ministry. And above all we rejoice that the *Response* reaffirms the ecumenical goal of our two Churches as 'the restoration of visible unity and full ecclesial communion'.

We ourselves take up this mission in the United States once again in full knowledge of the discouragement with which many view the slow progress of Christian reconciliation. We do so because, in the words of the 1989 Common Declaration of the pope and the archbishop of Canterbury, 'to seek anything less would be to betray Our Lord's intention for the unity of his people'. We do so because the united witness of Christians makes an important contribution to the development of peace and justice at this time of heightened tension and conflict in our society. We pledge to the members of our two Churches that we will continue to explore the problems that divide us and the opportunities that lie before us. During the next few years we intend to offer to our Churches pastoral, liturgical, and theological initiatives through which we all may move to new levels of common life. In recording this determination we recall the words of Holy Scripture used by Pope Paul VI and Archbishop Michael Ramsey in their original mandate instituting the first Anglican-Roman Catholic Conversation: 'Forgetting those things which are behind, and reaching forth unto those things which are before, I press towards the mark for the prize of the high calling of God in Christ Jesus' (Phil 3:13-14).

5. SALVATION AND THE CHURCH

Anglican Roman Catholic International Commission, 1986

THE STATUS OF THE DOCUMENT

The document published here is the work of the Second Anglican Roman Catholic International Commission (ARCIC II). It is simply a joint statement of the Commission. The authorities who appointed the Commission have allowed the statement to be published so that it may be discussed and improved by the suggestions received. It is not an authoritative declaration by the Roman Catholic Church or by the Anglican Communion, who will evaluate the document in order to take a position on it in due time.

The Commission will be glad to receive observations and criticisms made in a constructive and fraternal spirit. Its work is done to serve the progress of the two communions towards unity. It will give responsible attention to every serious comment which is likely to help in improving or completing the result so far achieved. This wider collaboration will make its work to a greater degree work in common, and by God's grace will 'lead us to the full unity to which he calls us' (*Common Declaration* of Pope John Paul II and the Archbishop of Canterbury, Pentecost 1982).

PREFACE BY THE CO-CHAIRMEN

The 29th of May 1982, the Eve of the Feast of Pentecost, was a day of great significance for the Anglican and Roman Catholic Churches on their path towards unity. In the footsteps of St. Augustine of Canterbury whom his predecessor Pope Gregory the Great had sent from Rome to convert the English, Pope John Paul II visited Canterbury. There, in the Church founded by Augustine, he and the present Archbishop of Canterbury, Dr. Robert Runcie, along with representatives of the English Churches and of the whole Anglican Communion, proclaimed and celebrated the one baptismal faith which we all share. The pope and the archbishop also gave thanks to God for the work of the first Anglican Roman Catholic International Commission (ARCIC I) whose *Final Report* had just been published and agreed to the establishment of a new commission (ARCIC II) to continue its work.

The primary task of ARCIC II is to examine and try to resolve those doctrinal differences which still divide us. Accordingly, at the request of the Anglican Consultative Council (Newcastle, England, September 1981), we addressed ourselves to the doctrine of justification, which at the time of the Reformation was a particular cause of contention. This request sprang out of a widespread view that the subject of justification and salvation is so central to the Christian faith that, unless there is assurance of agreement on this issue, there can be no full doctrinal agreement between our two Churches.

We have spent more than three years on this task. The doctrine of justification raises issues of great complexity and profound mystery. Furthermore it can be properly treated only within the wider context of the doctrine of salvation as a whole. This in turn has involved discussion of the role of the Church in Christ's saving work. Hence the title of our agreed statement: *Salvation and the Church*. We do not claim to have composed a complete treatment of the doctrine of the Church. Our discussion is limited to its role in salvation.

In our work, particularly on the doctrine of justification as such, we have been greatly helped by the statement *Justification by Faith* agreed in 1983 by the Lutheran-Roman Catholic Consultation in the USA (Augsburg Publishing House, Minneapolis, 1985). This illustrates the interdependence of all ecumenical dialogues—an interdependence which is an expression of the growing communion which already exists between the Churches. For the search for unity is indivisible.

A question not discussed by the Commission, though of great contemporary importance, is that of the salvation of those who have no explicit faith in Christ. This has not been a matter of historical dispute between us. Our ancestors, though divided in Christian faith, shared a world in which the questions posed by people of other faiths, or none, could scarcely arise in their modern form. Today this is a matter for theological study in both our Communions.

Although our first concern has been to state our common faith on the issues in the doctrine of salvation which have proved problematic in the past, we believe that the world, now as much as ever, stands in need of the Gospel of God's free grace. Part of the challenge of Christians is this: how can we bear true witness to the good news of a God who accepts us, unless we can accept one another?

The purpose of our dialogue is the restoration of full ecclesial communion between us. Our work has recalled for us still wider perspectives—not only the unity of all Christian people but the fulfilment of all things in Christ.

We trust that God who has begun this good work in us will bring it to completion in Christ Jesus our Lord.

✠ **CORMAC MURPHY-O'CONNOR**
✠ **MARK SANTER**
Llandaff, Wales, 3 September 1986
Feast of St. Gregory the Great

INTRODUCTION

1.   The will of God, Father, Son, and Holy Spirit, is to reconcile to himself all that he has created and sustains, to set free the creation from its bondage to decay, and to draw all humanity into communion with himself. Though we, his creatures, turn away from him through sin, God continues to call us and opens up for us the way to find him anew. To

bring us to union with himself, the Father sent into the world Jesus Christ, his only Son, in whom all things were created. He is the image of the invisible God; he took flesh so that we in turn might share the divine nature and so reflect the glory of God. Through Christ's life, death, and resurrection, the mystery of God's love is revealed, we are saved from the powers of evil, sin, and death, and we receive a share in the life of God. All this is pure unmerited gift. The Spirit of God is poured into the hearts of believers—the Spirit of adoption, who makes us sons and daughters of God. The Spirit unites us with Christ and, in Christ, with all those who by faith are one with him. Through baptism we are united with Christ in his death and resurrection, we are by the power of the Spirit made members of one body, and together we participate in the life of God. This fellowship in one body, sustained through word and sacrament, is in the New Testament called *koinonia* (communion). '*Koinonia* with one another is entailed by our *koinonia* with God in Christ. This is the mystery of the Church' (ARCIC I, *The Final Report*, Introduction 5). The community of believers, united with Christ, gives praise and thanksgiving to God, celebrating the grace of Christ as they await his return in glory, when he will be all in all and will deliver to the Father a holy people. In the present age the Church is called to be a sign to the world of God's will for the healing and re-creation of the whole human race in Jesus Christ. As the Church proclaims the good news which it has received, the heart of its message must be salvation through the grace of God in Christ.

2. The doctrine of salvation has in the past been a cause of some contention between Anglicans and Roman Catholics. Disagreements, focusing on the doctrine of justification, were already apparent in the Church of the later Middle Ages. In the sixteenth century these became a central matter of dispute between Roman Catholics and continental Reformers. Though the matter played a less crucial role in the English Reformation, the Church of England substantially adopted the principles expressed in the moderate Lutheran formulations of the Augsburg and Württemberg Confessions. The Decree on Justification of the Council of Trent was not directed against the Anglican formularies, which had not yet been compiled. Anglican theologians reacted to the decree in a variety of ways, some sympathetic, others critical at least on particular points.[1] Nevertheless in the course of time Anglicans have widely come to understand that decree as a repudiation of their position. Since the sixteenth century, various debates on the doctrine of justification and on related issues (such as predestination, original sin, good works, sanctification) have been pursued within each of our Communions.

3. In the area of the doctrine of salvation, including justification, there was much agreement. Above all it was agreed that the act of God in bringing salvation to the human race and summoning individuals into a community to serve him is due solely to the mercy and grace of God, mediated and manifested through Jesus Christ in his ministry, atoning death, and rising again. It was also no matter of dispute that God's grace evokes an authentic human response of faith which takes effect not only in the life of the individual but

also in the corporate life of the Church. The difficulties arose in explaining how divine grace related to human response, and these difficulties were compounded by a framework of discussion that concentrated too narrowly upon the individual.

4.   *One* difficulty concerned the understanding of the *faith* through which we are justified, insofar as this included the individual's confidence in his or her own final salvation. Everyone agreed that confidence in God was a mark of Christian hope, but some feared that too extreme an emphasis on assurance, when linked with an absolute doctrine of divine predestination, encouraged a neglect of the need for justification to issue in holiness of life. Catholics thought that this Protestant understanding of assurance confused faith with a subjective state and would actually have the effect of undermining hope in God. Protestants suspected that Catholics, lacking confidence in the sufficiency of Christ's work and relying overmuch on human efforts, had lapsed either into a kind of scrupulosity or into a mere legalism and so lost Christian hope and assurance.

5.   A *second* difficulty concerned the understanding of *justification* and the associated concepts, righteousness and justice. Fearing that justification might seem to depend upon entitlement arising from good works, Reformation theologians laid great emphasis on the imputation to human beings of the righteousness of Christ. By this they meant that God declared the unrighteous to be accepted by him on account of the obedience of Christ and the merits of his passion. Catholics took them to be implying that imputed righteousness was a legal fiction, that is, a merely nominal righteousness that remained only external to the believer. They objected that this left the essential sinfulness of the individual unchanged, and excluded the imparted, or habitual and actual, righteousness created in the inner being of the regenerate person by the indwelling Spirit. Anglican theologians of the sixteenth and seventeenth centuries saw imputed and imparted righteousness as distinct to the mind, but indissoluble in worship and life. They also believed that, while we are made truly righteous because we are forgiven, we know ourselves to be in continuing need of forgiveness.

6.   A *third* difficulty concerned the bearing of *good works* on salvation. Reformation theologians understood the Catholic emphasis on the value of good works and religious practices and ceremonies to imply that justification in some degree depended upon them in such a way as to compromise the sovereignty and unconditional freedom of God's grace. Catholics, on the other hand, saw the Reformation's understanding of justification as implying that human actions were of no worth in the sight of God. This, in their judgement, led to the negation of human freedom and responsibility, and to the denial that works, even when supernaturally inspired, deserved any reward. The Anglican theologians of the Reformation age, taking 'by faith alone' to mean 'only for the merit of Christ', also held good works to be not irrelevant to salvation, but imperfect and therefore inadequate. They saw good works as a necessary demonstration of faith, and faith itself as inseparable from hope and love.

7.   Although the sixteenth-century disagreements centered mainly on the relation-ship of faith, righteousness, and good works to the salvation of the individual, *the role of the Church* in the process of salvation constituted a *fourth* difficulty. As well as believing that Catholics did not acknowledge the true authority of Scripture over the Church, Prot-estants also felt that Catholic teaching and practice had interpreted the mediatorial role of the Church in such a way as to derogate from the place of Christ as 'sole mediator between God and man' (1 Tm 2:5). Catholics believed that Protestants were abandoning or at least devaluing the Church's ministry and sacraments, which were divinely appointed means of grace; also that they were rejecting its divinely given authority as guardian and interpreter of the revealed word of God.

8.   The break in communion between Anglicans and Roman Catholics encouraged each side to produce caricatures of the other's beliefs. There were also extremists on both sides whose words and actions seemed to confirm the anxieties of their opponents.

The renewal of biblical scholarship, the development of historical and theological stud-ies, new insights gained in mission, and the growth of mutual understanding within the ecumenical movement enable us to see our divisions in a new perspective. We have explored our common faith in the light of these shared experiences and are able in what follows to affirm that the four areas of difficulty outlined above need not be matters of dispute between us.

SALVATION AND FAITH

9.   When we confess that Jesus Christ is Lord, we praise and glorify God the Father, whose purpose for creation and salvation is realised in the Son, whom he sent to redeem us and to prepare a people for himself by the indwelling of the Holy Spirit. This wholly un-merited love of God for his creatures is expressed in the language of grace, which embraces not only the once for all death and resurrection of Christ, but also God's continuing work on our behalf. The Holy Spirit makes the fruits of Christ's sacrifice actual within the Church through word and sacrament: our sins are forgiven, we are enabled to respond to God's love, and we are conformed to the image of Christ. The human response to God's initiative is itself a gift of grace, and is at the same time a truly human, personal response. It is through grace that God's new creation is realised. Salvation is the gift of grace; it is by faith that it is appropriated.

10.   The gracious action of God in Christ is revealed to us in the Gospel. The Gospel, by proclaiming Christ's definitive atoning work, the gift and pledge of the Holy Spirit to every believer, and the certainty of God's promise of eternal life, calls Christians to faith in the mercy of God and brings them assurance of salvation. It is God's gracious will that we, as his children, called through the Gospel and sharing in the means of grace, should be confi-dent that the gift of eternal life is assured to each of us. Our response to this gift must come from our whole being. Faith, therefore, not only includes an assent to the truth of the

Gospel but also involves commitment of our will to God in repentance and obedience to his call; otherwise faith is dead (Jas 2:17). Living faith is inseparable from love, issues in good works, and grows deeper in the course of a life of holiness. Christian assurance does not in any way remove from Christians the responsibility of working out their salvation with fear and trembling (Phil 2:12-13).

11. Christian assurance is not presumptuous. It is always founded upon God's unfailing faithfulness and not upon the measure of our response. God gives to the faithful all that is needed for their salvation. This is to believers a matter of absolute certitude. The word of Christ and his sacraments give us this assurance. Throughout the Christian tradition there runs the certainty of the infinite mercy of God, who gave his Son for us. However grave our sins may be, we are sure that God is always ready to forgive those who truly repent. For the baptised and justified may still sin. The New Testament contains warnings against presumption (e.g., Col 1:22 ff; Heb 10:36 ff). Christians may never presume on their perseverance but should live their lives with a sure confidence in God's grace. Because of what God has revealed of his ultimate purpose in Christ Jesus, living faith is inseparable from hope.

SALVATION AND JUSTIFICATION

12. In baptism, the 'sacrament of faith' (cf. Augustine *Ep.* 98:9), together with the whole Church, we confess Christ, enter into communion with him in his death and resurrection, and through the gift of the Holy Spirit are delivered from our sinfulness and raised to new life. The Scriptures speak of this salvation in many ways. They tell of God's eternal will fulfilled in Christ's sacrifice on the cross, his decisive act in overcoming the power of evil and reconciling sinners who believe. They also speak of the abiding presence and action of the Holy Spirit in the Church, of his present gifts of grace, and of our continuing life and growth in this grace as we are transformed into the likeness of Christ. They also speak of our entry with all the saints into our eternal inheritance, of our vision of God face to face, and of our participation in the joy of the final resurrection.

13. In order to describe salvation in all its fullness, the New Testament employs a wide variety of language. Some terms are of more fundamental importance than others: but there is no controlling term or concept; they complement one another. The concept of salvation has the all-embracing meaning of the deliverance of human beings from evil and their establishment in that fullness of life which is God's will for them (e.g., Lk 1:77; Jn 3:16-17; cf. Jn 10:10). The idea of reconciliation and forgiveness stresses the restoration of broken relationships (e.g., 2 Cor 5:18 ff; Eph 2:13-18). The language of expiation or propitiation (*hilasterion*, etc.), drawn from the context of sacrifice, denotes the putting away of sin and the reestablishment of right relationship with God (e.g., Rom 3:2; Heb 2:17; 1 Jn 2:2, 4, 10). To speak of redemption or liberation is to talk of rescue from bondage so as to become God's own possession, and of freedom bought for a price (e.g., Mk 10:45; Eph 1:7;

1 Pt 1:18 ff). The notion of adoption refers to our new identity as children of God (e.g., Rom 8:15–17, 23; Gal 4:4 ff). Terms like regeneration, rebirth, and new creation speak of God's work of re-creation and the beginning of new life (e.g., Jn 3:3; 2 Cor 5:17; 1 Pt 1:23). The theme of sanctification underlines the fact that God has made us his own and calls us to holiness of life (e.g., Jn 17:15 ff; Eph 4:25 ff; 1 Pt 1:15 ff). The concept of justification relates to the removal of condemnation and to a new standing in the eyes of God (e.g., Rom 3:22 ff, 4:5, 5:1 ff; Acts 13:39). Salvation in all these aspects comes to each believer as he or she is incorporated into the believing community.

14. Roman Catholic interpreters of Trent and Anglican theologians alike have insisted that justification and sanctification are neither wholly distinct from nor unrelated to one another. The discussion, however, has been confused by differing understandings of the word justification and its associated words. The theologians of the Reformation tended to follow the predominant usage of the New Testament, in which the verb *dikaioun* usually means 'to pronounce righteous'. The Catholic theologians, and notably the Council of Trent, tended to follow the usage of patristic and medieval Latin writers, for whom *justificare* (the traditional translation of *dikaioun*) signified 'to make righteous'. Thus the Catholic understanding of the process of justification, following Latin usage, tended to include elements of salvation which the Reformers would describe as belonging to sanctification rather than justification. As a consequence, Protestants took Catholics to be emphasising sanctification in such a way that absolute gratuitousness of salvation was threatened. On the other side, Catholics feared that Protestants were so stressing the justifying action of God that sanctification and human responsibility were gravely depreciated.

15. Justification and sanctification are two aspects of the same divine act (1 Cor 6:11). This does not mean that justification is a reward for faith or works: rather, when God promises the removal of our condemnation and gives us a new standing before him, this justification is indissolubly linked with his sanctifying recreation of us in grace. This transformation is being worked out in the course of our pilgrimage, despite the imperfections and ambiguities of our lives. God's grace effects what he declares: his creative word imparts what it imputes. By pronouncing us righteous, God also makes us righteous. He imparts a righteousness which is his and becomes ours.[2]

16. God's declaration that we are accepted because of Christ together with his gift of continual renewal by the indwelling Spirit is the pledge and first instalment of the final consummation and the ground of the believer's hope. In the life of the Church, the finality of God's declaration and the continuing movement towards our ultimate goal are reflected in the relation between baptism and the eucharist. Baptism is the unrepeatable sacrament of justification and incorporation into Christ (1 Cor 6:11, 12:12–13; Gal 3:27). The eucharist is the repeated sacrament by which the life of Christ's body is constituted and renewed, when the death of Christ is proclaimed until he comes again (1 Cor 11:26).

17. Sanctification is that work of God which actualises in believers the righteousness and holiness without which no one may see the Lord. It involves the restoring and perfecting in humanity of the likeness of God marred by sin. We grow into conformity with Christ, the perfect image of God, until he appears and we shall be like him. The law of Christ has become the pattern of our life. We are enabled to produce works which are the fruit of the Holy Spirit. Thus the righteousness of God our Saviour is not only declared in a judgement made by God in favour of sinners, but also bestowed as a gift to make them righteous. Even though our acceptance of this gift will be imperfect in this life, Scripture speaks of the righteousness of believers as already effected by God through Christ: 'he raised us up with him and seated us with him in the heavenly realms in Christ Jesus' (Eph 2:6).

18. The term justification speaks of a divine declaration of acquittal, of the love of God manifested to an alienated and lost humanity prior to any entitlement on our part. Through the life, death, and resurrection of Christ, God declares that we are forgiven, accepted, and reconciled to him. Instead of our own strivings to make ourselves acceptable to God, Christ's perfect righteousness is reckoned to our account. God's declaration is sometimes expressed in the New Testament in the language of law, as a verdict of acquittal of the sinner. The divine court, where the verdict is given, is the court of the judge who is also Father and Saviour of those whom he judges. While in a human law-court an acquittal is an external, even impersonal act, God's declaration of forgiveness and reconciliation does not leave repentant believers unchanged but establishes with them an intimate and personal relationship. The remission of sins is accompanied by a present renewal, the rebirth to newness of life. Thus the juridical aspect of justification, while expressing an important facet of the truth, is not the exclusive notion in the light of which all other biblical ideas and images of salvation must be interpreted. For God sanctifies as well as acquits us. He is not only the judge who passes a verdict in our favour, but also the Father who gave his only Son to do for us what we could not do for ourselves. By virtue of Christ's life and self-oblation on the cross we are able with him to say through the Holy Spirit, 'Abba, Father' (Rom 8:15; Gal 4:6).

SALVATION AND GOOD WORKS

19. As justification and sanctification are aspects of the same divine act, so also living faith and love are inseparable in the believer. Faith is no merely private and interior disposition, but by its very nature is acted out: good works necessarily spring from a living faith (Jas 2:17 ff). They are truly good because, as the fruit of the Spirit, they are done in God, in dependence on God's grace.

The person and work of Christ are central to any understanding of the relation between salvation and good works. God has brought into being in the person of his Son a renewed humanity, of Jesus Christ himself, the 'last Adam' or 'second man' (cf. 1 Cor

15:45, 47). He is the firstborn of all creation, the prototype and source of our new human-ity, so as to live the human life now as God has refashioned it in Christ (cf. Col 3:10). This understanding of our humanity as made new in Christ by God's transforming power throws light on the New Testament affirmation that, while we are not saved *because of* works, we are created in Christ *for* good works (Eph 2:8 ff). 'Not because of work': nothing even of our best achievement or good will can give us any claim to God's gift of renewed humanity. God's recreating deed originates in himself and nowhere else. 'For good works': good works are the fruit of the freedom God has given us in his Son. In restoring us to his likeness, God confers freedom on fallen humanity. This is not the natural freedom to choose between alternatives, but the freedom to do his will: 'the law of the Spirit of life in Christ Jesus has set me free from the law of sin and death . . . in order that the just requirement of the law might be fulfilled in us' (Rom 8:2, 4). We are freed and enabled to keep the commandments of God by the power of the Holy Spirit, to live faithfully as God's people and to grow in love within the discipline of the community, bringing forth the fruit of the Spirit.[3]

Inasmuch as we are recreated in his 'own image and likeness', God involves us in what he freely does to realise our salvation (Phil 2:12 ff). In the words of Augustine: 'The God who made you without you, without you does not make you just' (Sermons 169:13). Thus from the divine work follows the human work: it is we who live and act in a fully human way, yet never on our own or in a self-sufficient independence. This fully human life is possible if we live in the freedom and activity of Christ who, in the words of St. Paul, 'lives in me' (Gal 2:20).

20. To speak thus of freedom in Christ is to stress that it is in Jesus Christ that the shape of human life lived in total liberty before God is decisively disclosed. Our libera-tion commits us to an order of social existence in which the individual finds fulfilment in relationship with others. Thus freedom in Christ does not imply an isolated life, but rather one lived in a community governed by mutual obligations. Life in Christ sets us free from the demonic forces manifested not only in individual but also in social egotism.

21. The growth of believers to maturity, and indeed the common life of the Church, are impaired by repeated lapses into sin. Even good works, done in God and under the grace of the Spirit, can be flawed by human weakness and self-centredness, and therefore it is by daily repentance and faith that we reappropriate our freedom from sin. This insight has sometimes been expressed by the paradox that we are at once just and sinners.[4]

22. The believer's pilgrimage of faith is lived out with the mutual support of all the people of God. In Christ all the faithful, both living and departed, are bound together in a communion of prayer. The Church is entrusted by the Lord with authority to pronounce forgiveness in his name to those who have fallen into sin and repent. The Church may also help them to a deeper realisation of the mercy of God by asking for practical amends for

what has been done amiss. Such penitential disciplines, and other devotional practices, are not in any way intended to put God under obligation. Rather, they provide a form in which one may more fully embrace the free mercy of God.

23. The works of the righteous performed in Christian freedom and in the love of God which the Holy Spirit gives us are the object of God's commendation and receive his reward (Mt 6:4; 2 Tm 4:8; Heb 10:35, 11:6). In accordance with God's promise, those who have responded to the grace of God and consequently borne fruit for the kingdom will be granted a place in that kingdom when it comes at Christ's appearing. They will be one with the society of the redeemed in rejoicing in the vision of God. This reward is a gift depending wholly on divine grace. It is in this perspective that the language of 'merit'[5] must be understood, so that we can say with Augustine: 'When God crowns our merits it is his own gifts that he crowns' (Ep 194.5.19). Christians rest their confidence for salvation on the power, mercy, and loving-kindness of God and pray that the good work which God has begun he will in grace complete. They do not trust in their own merits but in Christ's. God is true to his promise to 'render to everyone according to his works' (Rom 2:6); yet when we have done all that is commanded we must still say: 'We are unprofitable servants, we have only done our duty' (Lk 17:10).

24. The language of merit and good works, therefore, when properly understood, in no way implies that human beings, once justified, are able to put God in their debt. Still less does it imply that justification itself is anything but a totally unmerited gift. Even the very first movements which lead to justification, such as repentance, the desire for forgiveness, and even faith itself, are the work of God as he touches our hearts by the illumination of the Holy Spirit.

THE CHURCH AND SALVATION

25. The doctrine of salvation is intimately associated with the doctrine of the Church, which 'is the community of those reconciled with God and with each other because it is the community of those who believe in Jesus Christ and are justified through God's grace' (*The Final Report*, Introduction, 8). The Church proclaims the good news of our justification and salvation by God in Christ Jesus. Those who respond in faith to the Gospel come to the way of salvation through incorporation by baptism into the Church. They are called to witness to the Gospel as members of the Church.

26. The Church is itself a *sign* of the Gospel, for its vocation is to embody and reveal the redemptive power contained within the Gospel. What Christ achieved through his cross and resurrection is communicated by the Holy Spirit in the life of the Church. In its life the Church signifies God's gracious purpose for his creation and his power to realise this purpose for sinful humanity. It is thus a sign and foretaste of God's kingdom. In fulfiling this vocation the Church is called to follow the way of Jesus Christ, who being the image of the Father took the form of a servant and was made perfect by suffering. When for Christ's

sake the Church encounters opposition and persecution, it is then a sign of God's choice of the way of the cross to save the world.

27. This once-for-all atoning work of Christ, realised and experienced in the life of the Church and celebrated in the eucharist, constitutes the free gift of God which is proclaimed in the Gospel. In the service of this mystery the Church is entrusted with a responsibility of *stewardship*. The Church is called to fulfil this stewardship by proclaiming the Gospel and by its sacramental and pastoral life. The Church is required to carry out this task in such a way that the Gospel may be heard as good news in differing ages and cultures, while at the same time seeking neither to alter its content nor minimise its demands. For the Church is servant and not master of what it has received. Indeed, its power to affect the hearer comes not from our unaided efforts but entirely from the Holy Spirit, who is the source of the Church's life and who enables it to be truly the steward of God's design.

28. The Church is also an *instrument* for the realisation of God's eternal design, the salvation of humanity. While we recognise that the Holy Spirit acts outside the community of Christians, nevertheless it is within the Church, where the Holy Spirit gives and nurtures the new life of the kingdom, that the Gospel becomes a manifest reality. As this instrument, the Church is called to be a living expression of the Gospel, evangelised and evangelising, reconciled and reconciling, gathered together and gathering others. In its ministry to the world the Church seeks to share with all people the grace by which its own life is created and sustained.

29. The Church is therefore called to be, and by the power of the Spirit actually is, a *sign*, *steward*, and *instrument* of God's design. For this reason it can be described as *sacrament* of God's saving work. However, the credibility of the Church's witness is undermined by the sins of its members, the shortcomings of its human institutions, and not least by the scandal of division. The Church is in constant need of repentance and renewal so that it can be more clearly seen for what it is: the one, holy body of Christ. Nevertheless the Gospel contains the promise that despite all failures the Church will be used by God in the achievement of his purpose: to draw humanity into communion with himself and with one another, so as to share his life, the life of the Holy Trinity.

30. The Church which in this world is always in need of renewal and purification is already here and now a foretaste of God's kingdom in a world still awaiting its consummation—a world full of suffering and injustice, division and strife. Thus Paul speaks of a fellowship which is called to transcend the seemingly insuperable divisions of the world; where all, because of their equal standing before the Lord, must be equally accepted by one another; a fellowship where, since all are justified by the grace of God, all may learn to do justice to one another; where racial, ethnic, social, sexual, and other distinctions no longer cause discrimination and alienation (Gal 3:28). Those who are justified by grace, and who are sustained in the life of Christ through word and sacrament, are liberated from self-

centeredness and thus empowered to act freely and live at peace with God and with one another. The Church, as the community of the justified, is called to embody the good news that forgiveness is a gift to be received from God and shared with others (Mt 6:14–15). Thus the message of the Church is not a private pietism irrelevant to contemporary society, nor can it be reduced to a political or social programme. Only a reconciled and reconciling community, faithful to its Lord, in which human divisions are being overcome, can speak with full integrity to an alienated, divided world, and so be a credible witness to God's saving action in Christ and a foretaste of God's kingdom. Yet, until the kingdom is realised in its fullness, the Church is marked by human limitation and imperfection. It is the beginning and not yet the end, the first fruits and not yet the final harvest.

31. The source of the Church's hope for the world is God, who has never ceased to work within it. It is called, empowered, and sent by God to proclaim this hope and to communicate to the world the conviction on which this hope is founded. Thus the Church participates in Christ's mission to the world through the proclamation of the Gospel of salvation by its words and deeds. It is called to affirm the sacredness and dignity of the person, the value of natural and political communities, and the divine purpose for the human race as a whole; to witness against the structures of sin in society, addressing humanity with the Gospel of repentance and forgiveness and making intercession for the world. It is called to be an agent of justice and compassion, challenging and assisting society's attempts to achieve just judgement, never forgetting that in the light of God's justice all human solutions are provisional. While the Church pursues its mission and pilgrimage in the world, it looks forward to 'the end, when Christ delivers the kingdom to God the Father after destroying every rule and every authority and power' (1 Cor 15:24).

CONCLUSION

32. The balance and coherence of the constitutive elements of the Christian doctrine of salvation had become partially obscured in the course of history and controversy. In our work we have tried to rediscover that balance and coherence and to express it together. We are agreed that this is not an area where any remaining differences of theological interpretation or ecclesiological emphasis, either within or between our Communions, can justify our continuing separation. We believe that our two Communions are agreed on the essential aspects of the doctrine of salvation and on the Church's role within it. We have also realised the central meaning and profound significance which the message of justification and sanctification, within the whole doctrine of salvation, continues to have for us today. We offer our agreement to our two Communions as a contribution to reconciliation between us, so that together we may witness to God's salvation in the midst of the anxieties, struggles, and hopes of our world.

NOTES

1 The Council of Trent's Decree on Justification was issued after seven months' work on 13 January 1547 and should be read as a whole. It is printed in Denzinger Schönmetzer *Enchiridion Symbolorum Definitionum et Declarationum* (=DS) (Herder, Freiburg, 1965), 1520-1583. English translation in H. Schroeder, ed., *The Canons and Decrees of the Council of Trent* (Tan Books and Publishers, USA, 1978); extracts in J. Meuner and J. Dupuis, eds., *The Christian Faith in the Doctrinal Documents of the Catholic Church* (Collins, 1983), nos. 1924-83. The principal documents and authors for Anglican consideration of the subject in the period before 1661 are the *Thirty Nine* Articles (1571); Cranmer's *Homily 'Of Salvation'* (1547), to which Article 11 refers; Richard Hooker's *Learned Discourse of Justification* (1586); Richard Field, *Of the Church* III, Appendix, chapter 11 (1606); John Davenant, *Disputatio de Iustitia habituali et actuali* (1631, translated by Allport, 1844 as *Treatise on Justification*); William Forbes, *Considerationes Modestae et Pacificae* I (posthumously published 1658, translated 1850 as *Calm Considerations*).

2 For Richard Hooker, 'we participate Christ partly by imputation, as when those things which he did and suffered for us are imputed unto us for righteousness; partly by habitual and real infusion, as when grace is inwardly bestowed while we are on earth, and afterwards more fully both our souls and bodies made like unto his in glory' (*Laws of Ecclesiastical Polity*, V. lVI. 11).

3 Cf. Article 10 of the *Thirty Nine Articles*: 'We have no power to do good works pleasant and acceptable to God, without the grace of God by Christ preventing us, that we may have a good will, and working with us (*cooperante*), when we have that good will'. This echoes Augustine's language about 'prevenient' and 'co-operating' grace (*De Gratia et libero arbitro*, 17.33).

4 *Simul iustus et peccator* is a Lutheran not a characteristically Anglican expression. It does not appear in Trent's Decree on Justification. The Second Vatican Council (*Lumen Gentium*, 8) speaks of the Church as 'holy and at the same time always in need of purification' (*sancta simul et semper purificanda*). The paradox is ultimately of Augustinian inspiration (cf. En. in Ps 140.14 f and Ep 185.40).

5 Misunderstanding has been caused by the fact that the Latin *mereor* has a range of meanings, from 'deserve' to 'be granted' and 'obtain'. This range is reflected in patristic and medieval Christian Latin usage. By 'merit' the Council of Trent (DS 1545) did not mean the exact equality between achievement and reward, except in the case of Christ, but the value of goodness, as being, in the divine liberality, pleasing to God who is not so unjust as to overlook this work and love of the justified (Heb 6:10).

6. OBSERVATIONS ON *SALVATION AND THE CHURCH*

The [Vatican] Congregation for the Doctrine of the Faith, 1987

PREFACE

The following observations constitute an authoritative doctrinal judgment which is offered to the members of the Commission for the furthering of the dialogue. They have been prepared by the Congregation for the Doctrine of the Faith within the framework of its contacts with the Secretariat for Christian Unity.

1. GENERAL JUDGMENT

Taken as a whole, even though it does not present a complete teaching on this question and even though it contains several ambiguous formulations, the document of the second Anglican Roman Catholic International Commission (ARCIC II) titled *Salvation and the Church* can be interpreted in a way that conforms with Catholic faith. It contains a number of satisfying elements, notably on points that have been classically controversial.

The judgment of the Congregation for the Doctrine of the Faith on this report is therefore substantially positive. We are not, however, at the point of being able to ratify the final affirmation (no. 32), according to which the Catholic Church and the Anglican Communion 'are agreed on the essential aspects of the doctrine of salvation and on the Church's role within it'.

2. PRINCIPAL OBSERVATIONS

(a) The document is written in a language which we might describe as symbolic, and it is therefore difficult to interpret it univocally. Such an interpretation is necessary given that the purpose is to reach a definitive declaration of agreement.

(b) On the chapter 'Salvation and the Faith':
- Because of the importance in discussion with Protestants of the whole problem of *sola fides*, a more extended discussion of this controversial point would be desirable.
- It would be good to have further precision on the relationship between grace and faith as *initium salutis* (cf. no. 9).
- The relationship *fides quæ-fides qua*, together with the distinction between *assurance* and *certitude* or *certainty* needs to be better developed.

(c) Concerning the chapter 'Salvation and Good Works':

- It would be appropriate to give more precision on the doctrine of grace and merit in relation to the distinction between justification and sanctification.
- If the formulation *simul iustus et peccator* is to be retained, it should be explained more fully so as to avoid all ambiguity.
- In general, the sacramental economy of grace in the regaining of freedom out of sin should be put more in evidence (cf., e.g., nos. 21 and 22).

(d) Concerning the chapter 'The Church and Salvation':

- The role of the Church in salvation is not only to bear witness to it, but also and above all, to be the effective instrument—notably by means of the seven sacraments—of justification and salvation: This essential point needs to be further elaborated, especially in relation to *Lumen Gentium*.
- It is particularly important to draw more clearly the distinction between the holiness of the Church as universal sacrament of salvation on the one hand and its members, who in some measure are still given to sin, on the other (cf. no. 29).

3. CONCLUSION

The divergences which, in the light of this document, still exist between the Catholic Church and the Anglican Communion principally concern certain aspects of ecclesiology and of sacramental doctrine.

The vision of the Church as sacrament of salvation and the specifically sacramental dimension of man's justification and sanctification are too vague and too weak to allow us to affirm that ARCIC II has arrived at substantial agreement.

COMMENTARY ON THE OBSERVATIONS
The Nature of the Observations and the Purpose of the Present Commentary

The publication last year [1986] of *Salvation and the Church*, the (first) document of the second Anglican Roman Catholic International Commission, was accompanied by a preliminary note which explained its status. Among other things, it explained that 'it is not an authoritative declaration by the Roman Catholic Church or by the Anglican Communion, who will evaluate the document in order to take a position on it in due time'. For their part, the authors declared that 'the Commission will be glad to receive observations and criticisms made in a constructive and fraternal spirit'.

The publication today, with the authority of a text approved by the Holy Father, of the observations of the Congregation for the Doctrine of the Faith on the above-mentioned document of ARCIC II takes place with this in mind. The present commentary on these observations is intended to facilitate understanding the document and the observations themselves, and consequently it is also intended to encourage the members of the Commission, especially the Catholic ones, in the continuation of the dialogue, which began in 1982.

A Point Emphasized in the Document

In the introduction the authors sketch out a kind of typology of their respective positions and maintain that they can identify an important cause of disunion in the different explanations of the relation between divine grace and human response. Leaving aside the inevitable oversimplifications in this sketch, one point emphasized in the document can be concentrated on: the interior transformation of the human person achieved by the presence of the Holy Spirit.

Salvation really is, according to the document, a 'gift of grace' (no. 9), the 'gift and pledge of the Holy Spirit to every believer' (no. 10), who accomplishes in the believer his 'abiding presence and action' (no. 12). Properly speaking, it is in this 'indwelling of the Holy Spirit' (no. 9) that consists the presence of the God who justifies through the gift of a righteousness, 'which is his and becomes ours' (no. 15), and who realizes in us 'deliverance from evil', 'putting away of sin', 'rescue from bondage', and 'removal of condemnation'(no. 13). This is not a title or a purely exterior imputation, but a gift which, by making them partakers of the divine nature, inwardly transforms human persons (cf. *Lumen Gentium*, 40).

Seeking to express the different understandings of the verb *dikaioun*, the document speaks of a 'divine declaration of acquittal' (no. 18), but first emphasizes that God's 'grace effects what he declares: His creative word imparts what it imputes. By pronouncing us righteous, God also makes us righteous' (no. 15). This is followed by the specification, 'the righteousness of God our Saviour is not only declared in a judgment made by God in favor of sinners, but is also bestowed as a gift to make them righteous' (no. 17). From a juridical perspective, righteousness represents the 'verdict of acquittal' of sinners, but at the ontological level it is necessary to say that 'God's declaration of forgiveness and reconciliation does not leave repentant believers unchanged, but establishes with them an intimate and personal relationship' (no. 18).

On this subject, we point out incidentally the ambiguity of the reference to the Lutheran expression *simul iustus et peccator* (no. 21), which in any case does not belong to the Anglican tradition. If one really wishes to maintain this formula, it would then be necessary to state what exactly is intended: not the existence of two states in the baptized person contradictory to one another (that of grace and that of mortal sin), but the possible presence, in the righteous one who possesses sanctifying grace, of that 'sin which does not lead to death' (1 Jn 5:17).

The Problem of Faith

As regards baptism, 'the unrepeatable sacrament of justification and incorporation into Christ' (no. 16), the document underlines, and not without reason, the importance of faith. *Sacramentium fidei*: This expression of St. Augustine, who is referred to here (no. 12), was repeated as is noted by the Council of Trent (Denzinger Schönmetzer, 1529). Baptism is indeed a sacrament of faith, as is witnessed by the Scriptures and the Fathers. However, the document from the beginning strongly accentuates the subjective dimension of the faith (*fides qua*), explained primarily as a 'a truly human, personal response' (no. 9) and 'commitment of our will' (no. 10), but only mentions 'assent to the truth of the Gospel' in passing (no. 10). Even if the *fides fiducialis* is thus to a certain extent completed by the aspect of *assensus intellectus* in the relationship between *fides qua* and *fides quæ*, there nevertheless remains an imbalance to which the Congregation for the Doctrine of the Faith draws attention in its observations.

That faith is necessary for justification is a truth which cannot be questioned, but which must be properly understood. According to the Council of Trent, 'we are called justified through faith because faith is the beginning point of the salvation of the human person, the foundation and the root of every justification, "without which it is impossible to be pleasing to God" (Heb 11:6) or to come to share the destiny of his children' (Denzinger Schönmetzer, 1532).

The affirmation 'it is by faith that it [salvation, the gift of grace] is appropriated' (no., 9) takes on its full weight only in this light. If justification is above all the objective gift of God, which the sacraments communicate as principal instrument, faith does not cease to have, in reality, a decisive, even if subordinate, role. Only faith can, in fact, recognize the reality of this gift and prepare the spirit to receive it; only faith assures that inward participation in the sacraments which renders their action efficacious in the soul of the believer. At the same time faith, by itself, is not capable of justifying the sinner. Furthermore, in order better to clarify this point, it would have been useful also to treat the question of faith in the case of the baptism of children.

In order to take fully into account the incapacity of *sola fides* to justify the human person, the distinction between *assurance* and *certitude* or *certainty* with respect to salvation should have been better explained. The authentic 'assurance of salvation' (no. 10; cf. no. 11) which the human person possesses, is founded on the certainty of faith that God wishes 'to have mercy on all' (Rom 11:32) and has offered to them, in the sacraments, the means of salvation. This cannot mean a personal certainty of one's own salvation or of one's own state of grace, since the fragility and sinfulness of the human person can always be an obstacle to God's love.

The Sacramental Dimension of Sanctification

The traditional Protestant fear referred to in the document (cf. no. 14) that the Catholic understanding of sanctification threatens the absolute gratuity of salvation does not seem well founded, since one is quite aware that the totally free communication of grace comes from above (cf. Jn 3:7).

But it must be pointed out that the document does not sufficiently keep in mind the sacramental dimension of sanctification, alluding as it does only briefly to the post-baptismal sacraments, which are the privileged means of the communication of grace. In addition to the eucharist, to which only passing allusion is made and without much doctrinal rigor (cf. nos. 16 and 27), emphasis should have been given in particular to the significance and the necessity of the sacrament of penance, of which—according to Catholic doctrine—'repentance' (no. 21) is, although fundamental, only an aspect, and not reducible, moreover, to 'penitential disciplines' (no. 22).

Above all, the affirmation of the document, 'it is by daily repentance and faith that we reappropriate our freedom from sin' (no. 21), deserved more precise explanation further on. It is true that repentance (and the faith which is a presupposition of it) constitutes the nucleus of conversion from sin and that perfect contrition reconciles with God. But on this matter the Council of Trent makes the following decisive specification in this context: 'Although it sometimes happens that contrition is perfected by charity, and reconciles the human person with God before the effective reconciliation of the sacrament, nevertheless this reconciliation must not be attributed to the contrition itself apart from the desire for the sacrament (*votum sacramenti*), which is included in it' (Denzinger Schönmetzer, 1677). In fact, the human person is freed from the 'sin which leads to death' (1 Jn 5:16) by means of sacramental contact with the Redeemer or at least by means of the desire to be cleansed by a sacramental grace which no one can give to oneself.

Freedom and Merit

With good reason the document seeks to address the question of good works beginning with a reflection on freedom, but the approach adopted remains insufficient from many points of view. The pre-eminent gift of that freedom which resulted from the redemption is properly underlined: 'In restoring us to his likeness, God confers freedom on fallen humanity'. But the explanation which follows provokes puzzlement. 'This is not the natural freedom to choose between alternatives, but the freedom to do his will' (no. 19). Such an opposition between two kinds of freedom could in fact refer to a conception of human freedom which does not take full account of its created nature. According to Catholic doctrine, the deprivation of original righteousness which followed upon the sin of Adam makes human persons incapable of tending, with the powers that remain to them, toward the supernatural end for which they were created. Nevertheless, as the Council of Trent adds in this perspective, sin does not totally corrupt human nature without taking away its original capacity of pleasing God (cf. Denzinger Schönmetzer, 1555, 1557, etc.).

With these premises in mind, it is now possible to address the problem of merit. For the purpose of excluding, correctly, an unacceptable understanding of salvation 'because of works', which would suppose the possibility of human persons attaining salvation through their own effort, the document turns to the Pauline expression, 'for the purpose of good works' (Eph 2:10; cf. also 2 Cor 9:8). The main section dedicated to this theme (no. 19 ff) endeavors to reconcile the teachings of St. Paul (Gal 2:16) and St. James (Jas 2:17ff) on works. But a more exact placement of these teachings in their respective contexts would have contributed to a better grasp of the point which the Congregation for the Doctrine of the Faith makes in this regard. St. James affirms that we are justified by means of work and not by faith alone (Jas 2:24), while St. Paul strongly emphasizes that works carried out prior to faith are not meritorious, without hesitating, however, to invite the believer 'to be adorned with good deeds' (1 Tm 2:10). This means that human persons cannot merit fundamental justification, that is, cannot pass by their own effort from the state of sin to the state of grace, but that they are called and made able to 'multiply good works of every sort' (Col 1:10); not producing them 'from self' (Jn 15:4), but while 'living in the love' of Christ (Jn 15:9-10), love which 'has been poured out in our hearts through the Holy Spirit who has been given to us' (Rom 5:5).

In this sense, to say that Christians cannot 'put God in their debt' (no. 24) is to limit oneself to an overly extrinsic affirmation with respect to inward cooperation with grace, such as the Church eminently contemplates it in the cooperation of Mary in the work of salvation. Such cooperation is not the condition of our being approved of in the eyes of God or of his forgiveness; it is rather a grace that Christ confers freely and with absolute generosity. It is the fruit of the 'faith which expresses itself through love' (Gal 5:6).

The Role of the Church in Salvation

The Commission presents a rather vague conception of the Church, which seems to lie at the base of all the difficulties that have been pointed out. Certainly one can only be delighted by the fact that, in describing the Church, the notions of *sign* (no. 26), *instrument*, and *sacrament* (no. 29) are explicitly taken up, notions which the Second Vatican Council itself proposed (*Lumen Gentium*, 1, 9, 48). By the expression *stewardship* (no. 27), its structural dimension is also emphasized. Indeed, the Church is not only a spiritual communion, but is also constitutively a 'visible organism', a 'society structured with hierarchical organs', through which Christ 'communicates truth and grace to all' (*Lumen Gentium*, 8).

This aspect, which the Commission will still have to explore in greater depth—with particular reference to the observations of the Congregation for the Doctrine of the Faith on the *Final Report* of ARCIC I[1]—attains however its authentic significance only because the Church is also and first of all a mystery of faith, '*ecclesiae sanctæ mysterium*' (*Lumen Gentium*, 5). This point is truly decisive, and only it permits a way out from the dead end of a primarily functional ecclesiology, at the mercy of human dispositions.

Moreover, only this point allows a true understanding of the foundation of the intrinsic relationship of the Church with salvation. This relationship is not absent in the document, particularly when the Holy Spirit is mentioned (no. 28) or when the eucharist is examined (no. 27). Here also, however, some clarifications are necessary.

For example, it is said that in the eucharist 'is celebrated' the 'once-for-all atoning work of Christ, realized and expressed in the life of the Church' (no. 27). Does this expression really indicate recognition of the 'propitiatory value' of the eucharistic sacrifice?[2] And does the term *realize* imply therefore an authentic actualization of this sacrifice through the mediation of an ordained minister,[3] whose priesthood differs essentially from the common priesthood of the faithful (cf. *Lumen Gentium*, 10)? The importance of these questions will be readily grasped, because when this doctrine is not fully accepted, the role of the Church in the furtherance of salvation risks being limited to witnessing to a truth that it is incapable of efficaciously making present, a truth which then risks being reduced to a subjective 'experience' which does not bear within itself the guarantee of its redemptive power.

As for the doctrinal content, the Congregation perceives finally a certain equivocation on the nature of the *ecclesia mater*, connected with the stress on the idea, not erroneous in itself, of the Church 'in constant need of repentance' (no. 29) and 'of renewal and purification' (no. 30). It is true that the council, while dwelling upon the specific nature of the Church, wanted to correct what one could call a certain ecclesial 'monophysitism', discreetly cautioning against an excessive assimilation of the Church into Christ. The Church is the immaculate bride whom the spotless Lamb has purified (*Lumen Gentium*, 6), but the Church is also made up of human persons and as such 'is called by Christ to that continual reformation of which, as a human and earthly institution, she always has need' (*Unitatis Redintegratio*, 6).

This entirely human aspect of the Church is real, but must not be taken in isolation. In her most inward essence, the Church is 'holy and immaculate' (Eph 5:27), and precisely for this reason she truly is the 'universal sacrament of salvation' (*Lumen Gentium*, 48, cf. 52), and her members are 'holy' (1 Cor 1:2, 2 Cor 1:1). The fact that she, as a pilgrim, 'clasps sinners to her bosom' (*Lumen Gentium*, 8) and is thus 'imperfect' (*Lumen Gentium*, 48) does not keep her from being 'on earth already endowed with real holiness' (*Lumen Gentium*, 48) and 'necessary for salvation' (*Lumen Gentium*, 14). In fact, she carries out her salvific mission not only 'through the proclamation of the Gospel of salvation by her words and deeds' (no. 31), but also, as mystery through communications of divine life to human persons and casting the light which shines forth from this divine life into the whole world (cf. *Gaudium et Spes*, 40).

Substantial Agreement?

The preceding analysis has shown that the document of ARCIC II contains many satisfying elements concerning a traditionally controversial subject. One can only congratulate the members of the Commission for having sought to highlight the 'balance and coherence of the constitutive elements' of Christian doctrine of salvation (no. 32). The criticisms which have been expressed do not in any way deny the fact that they have been partially successful. But one cannot affirm that full and substantial agreement on the essential aspects of this doctrine has been achieved, primarily because of deficiencies concerning the role of the Church in salvation. To the concern of trying to attain unity on such a central point, what one could call, based on St. Irenaeus, 'the patience of growth into maturity' would have been preferable.

Already in its observations on *The Final Report* of ARCIC I, the Congregation for the Doctrine of the Faith cautioned against the ambiguity of common texts which leave open the 'possibility of twofold interpretation'.[4] The same observation can be made today concerning *Salvation and the Church*. The language used is strongly symbolic as is shown for example by the image of *stewardship* to indicate responsibility in the Church. Thanks to its expressive qualities, the document has been successful not only in strengthening in its readers an eager search for unity in the faith, but also in suitably placing it within the hermeneutical horizon of biblical language, along the lines of Vatican II and some recent encyclicals of Pope John Paul II.

Nevertheless, it should be recognized that the symbolic nature of the language makes difficult, if not impossible, a truly univocal agreement where, as is the case here, questions are treated which are decisive from the dogmatic point of view and figure among the historically most controversial articles of faith. By using more rigorous doctrinal formulations, though not necessarily scholastic ones, the document would better have avoided the doubts which surface in dialogue if one does not always seek a rigorous comparison between the respective positions or if one is sometimes satisfied with a consensus which is almost entirely verbal, the fruit of reciprocal compromises.

Without disavowing anything in a method which has produced incontestable results, one could still ask if it would not be opportune to perfect the procedure in such a way as to permit a more precise determination of the doctrinal content of the formulas employed to express a common faith. Would it not be suitable along these lines also to point out, possibly in a separate protocol, the elements on which divergences remain?

Likewise, it would be desirable to see more attention devoted to the tradition, particularly to the Fathers and to the magisterium of the Catholic Church, as well as to the official acts of the Anglican Communion, for example the 'Thirty Nine Articles of Religion'.[5]

The questions and the considerations raised in the observations of the Congregation for the Doctrine of the Faith have the sole purpose of encouraging the members of ARCIC II to move forward along the road they have been following since 1982 when, instituting this second commission, Pope John Paul II and the Anglican primate Dr. Robert Runcie conferred on them the specific task to 'examine, especially in the light of our respective judgments on the *Final Report* (ARCIC I), the outstanding doctrinal differences which still separate us, with a view toward their eventual resolution'.[6]

NOTES

1   'Observations on *The Final Report* of ARCIC by the Congregation for the Doctrine of the Faith', *Acta Apostolicæ Sedis*, 74 (1982) 1063–1074.

2   Ibid., 1066. 'The propitiatory value that Catholic dogma attributes to the eucharist, which is not mentioned by ARCIC, is precisely that of [the] sacramental offering' (B, I, 1).

3   Ibid., 'Through him [the priest] the Church offers sacramentally the sacrifice of Christ' (B, II, 1), '(t)he real presence of the sacrifice of Christ [is] accomplished by the sacramental words, that is to say, by the ministry of the priest saying *in persona Christi* the words of the Lord' (B, I, 1).

4   Ibid., 1064–1065. 'Certain formulations in the report are not sufficiently explicit and hence can lend themselves to a twofold interpretation in which both parties can find unchanged the expression of their own position. This possibility of contrasting and ultimately incompatible readings of formulations which are apparently satisfactory to both sides gives rise to a question about the real consensus of the two Communions, pastors and faithful alike. In effect, if the formulation which has received the agreement of the experts can be diversely interpreted, how could it serve as a basis for reconciliation on the level of church life and practice?' (A, 2, iii).

5   Ibid., 1065, 'It would have been useful—in order to evaluate the exact meaning of certain points of agreement—had ARCIC indicated their position in reference to the documents which have contributed significantly to the formulation of the Anglican identity (*The Thirty Nine Articles of Religion*, Book of Common Prayer, Ordinal) in those cases where the assertions of *The Final Report* seem incompatible with these documents. The failure to take a stand on these texts can give rise to uncertainty about the exact meaning of the agreements reached' (A, 2, iii).

6   Common Declaration, 3, in AAS, 74 (1982), 925.

7. COMMENTS OF THE ANGLICAN-ROMAN CATHOLIC DIALOGUE OF CANADA ON THE OBSERVATIONS OF THE CONGREGATION OF THE DOCTRINE OF THE FAITH ON *SALVATION AND THE CHURCH*

Anglican–Roman Catholic Dialogue, Canada, 1990

We are grateful for the 'substantially positive' assessment which the Congregation for the Doctrine of the Faith (CDF) makes of *Salvation and the Church* (SC). The CDF puts before us in unmistakable terms elements of convergence between Anglicans and Roman Catholics on salvation and the Church,[1] but as in a similar CDF document reacting to *The Final Report* of ARCIC I, it is not ready to endorse the substantial agreement laid out in the document.

The actual Observations of the Congregation (Obs) are brief and succinct. The accompanying fourteen page typed commentary (Comm), which does not purport to have the same official status, offers a rationale for the Obs and a more detailed critique of SC. This Commentary does not have the authority of a text approved by the Holy Father, whereas the Obs do.[2]

The status of the Obs as a church document is not totally clear. On the one hand we are told that the Obs constitute an 'authoritative doctrinal judgement',[3] but on the other the very title 'Observations' chosen for this document indicates a lesser degree of definitiveness, and the observations are offered to the members of the Commission with a view to helping them further their dialogue, in response to the request of ARCIC II for observations and criticisms. Indeed this response of the CDF can be counted among new tools of expression whose development the ecumenical dialogue of the last century has occasioned. These tools are helpful, even indispensable, but understandably confusion at times exists about their status and intent.

The Anglican-Roman Catholic Dialogue of Canada, as a number of other national dialogues, is intimately involved in the work of ARCIC II, and has chosen to enter in the conversation which the CDF wishes to foster on the agreed statement *Salvation and the Church*. The issues raised by the CDF are quite pertinent to the continuing dialogue of ARCIC II on *koinonia* and the steps our two Churches need to take towards full communion. They also have a bearing on how our two Churches receive *The Final Report* of ARCIC I.

In order to justify its unwillingness to acknowledge that SC expresses a substantial agreement on the doctrine of salvation and the Church's role within it, Obs makes a number of points. The first, on the allegedly symbolic language of SC, and the last, on the role of Church and sacraments in salvation, are of greater substance than the observations which suggest improvements to SC when it deals with its main topic, the classic areas of sixteenth century controversy.[4]

In our comments on the CDF document, we shall begin with the less substantive points which CDF makes regarding SC. We will then deal with the two crucial issues, that of the Church and salvation and that of the language used by SC. We will base these comments not only on the observations themselves but also on the accompanying commentary, which is intended as a support and an elucidation.

THE CLASSICAL ISSUES OF JUSTIFICATION, SANCTIFICATION, SALVATION

In relation to *Simul Justus et Peccator*: The Commentary on page 3 makes a great deal about the incidental use of this formula in no. 21 of SC. But SC evokes this formula only to tell us that it was often used to express the main point made in no. 21. The *simul justus et peccator* formula is subordinate to the main point, and not the reverse. This phrase is not found in any Anglican formularies of faith.

The main point of SC no. 21, which has to do with the need of Christian believers to constantly seek freedom from sin, is expressed in impeccably orthodox terms. Nowhere does SC intimate the ontological coexistence of sanctifying grace and moral sin in the justified person. The ontological transformation of those justified is not expressed in those exact words, but the reality is abundantly expressed in SC 17 and 18, which takes pains to reflect not only the 'not yet' but also the 'already now' of God's salvific action, in terms drawn mainly from Paul's major epistles.[5] In sum, the CDF Commentary seems to have misconstrued the sense of SC on this point.[6]

In relation to *fides qua* and *fides quæ* (p. 3): Obs claims that the reference to *fides quæ* is only made in passing. This appears to reflect a concern that Anglicans in fact subscribe to the position that faith is purely fiducial, without any cognitive dimension. In the sentence to which the Comm refers in SC no. 10, the point about cognitive faith is made quite clearly, even though the main clause of the sentence is to assert that faith implies more than a cognitive dimension, a point which needs to be made in the classical Catholic tradition as well. In addition, that section of SC abounds in references to the assurance and certitude, not that I am saved, but that the mercy of God is infinite and that the means of salvation are available to all. The cognitive dimension is present, but appears to have been missed by the CDF assessors.

In relation to assurance and certitude: The CDF Commentary reads SC on assurance and certitude as if SC were open to the views on assurance and certitude condemned at Trent (p. 5, top). It is very clear that SC no. 11 rejects the understanding condemned by Trent that I must have certitude of my own salvation in order to be saved. The first sentence, 'Christian assurance is not presumptuous' reflects the first sentence of Chapter 12 of the Decree on Justification (DS 805) which makes that point with regards to predestination. SC clearly states that this assurance is based on God's faithfulness and not on the measure of our response, and that Christians may never presume on their perseverance. The concerns of the CDF are not based on the text of SC, which expresses a sound and balanced doctrine on this point.

In relation to *sola fides*: The Comm is particularly difficult to understand where it appears to seek traces in SC of the doctrine of *sola fides* as it was condemned at Trent. It fails to recognize that the justifying faith which SC speaks of is a living faith 'inseparable from love' (no. 10) and 'inseparable from hope' (no. 11). On the one hand it admits that for Paul faith is the foundation and root of justification, but then implies that this role is subordinate, without explaining how something foundational can be subordinate. SC does state that baptism is the sacrament of faith (no. 12) and implies that it is the sacrament by which justification is normally imparted (no. 16).[7] Yet at this point the Comm appears to subordinate the reality of which the sacraments are efficacious signs to the efficacious signs themselves. Moreover it does not advert to God's ability to impart the transforming grace of justification apart from the normal sacramental means. In effect it appears to subordinate the gift of faith to the objective grace of justification imparted by baptism, as if that gift of faith—remember that by faith SC means living faith which includes love and hope—were distinct from the grace of justification imparted by baptism.

The Comm asks for a reference of faith in the case of the baptism of children (presumably infants rather than children are meant here). In that case justification takes place with faith as a habitual gift but without faith as an explicit act. The gift of faith is no less foundational within the grace of baptism for the one incapable of a deliberate human act than it is for the adult.

In relation to the gratuity of salvation: SC in no. 14 alludes to the traditional Protestant fear that Catholic doctrine threatens the absolute gratuity of salvation. This allusion is part of the structure of the document, which mentions both Catholic and Protestant fears and considers both unjustified in terms of the newer understandings reached in recent scholarly and ecumenical dialogue. SC mentions that fear as a fact, but in order to show that it is not well-grounded. The reaction of the Comm (middle of page 5) is particularly sensitive on this point. The very mention of the Protestant position by SC seems for Obs to imply that the SC endorses it.

In relation to freedom and merit: The puzzlement of the CDF Commentary (p. 6) is itself puzzling, since it appears not to recognize the reliance of ARCIC II on the theology of Augustine and his role as the common doctor of grace in the Western tradition. Augustine draws a clear distinction between the different forms of freedom, the *liberum arbitrium*, the foundational power of free choice which is not destroyed but weakened by sin, and the *libertas arbitrii*, the power effectively to say yes to God, which is taken away by sin and restored by grace.[8] When SC speaks of a natural freedom to choose between alternatives, a freedom not taken away by sin and underlying our free response to God's grace (no. 19, second paragraph), and the freedom to do God's will, it is simply echoing the basic Augustinian distinction. SC uses the term 'natural' for the freedom to choose between alternatives, and does not imply that this freedom is taken away by sin. This section of SC is not an attempt to paper over what the Comm sees as an unsatisfactory Anglican understanding of these matters but rather faithfully reflects the doctrine of Augustine and finds its meaning in that doctrine.

The point which Obs goes on to make about merit and indebtedness suggests another misunderstanding of SC. The point about not putting God in one's debt in SC, no. 24 is a summary of what is developed in SC, no. 23. If no. 23 is an overly extrinsic statement, as the Commentary asserts, so too is the scriptural passage about the unprofitable servant on which it is based. Indeed, SC, no. 23 expresses a balanced doctrine of merit based on Augustine. Our free cooperation under grace is adequately expressed in SC: cf. the last paragraph of no. 19. Freedom does not entail that we can do good works 'on our own or in a self-sufficient independence'. It does entail that we ourselves do them in a fully human way, activating the freedom to choose between alternatives which is part of our natural endowment.[9]

THE ROLE OF THE CHURCH AND SALVATION

It is not clear that for the CDF the above criticisms of SC would by themselves have sufficiently supported its judgement that SC fails to reach a substantial agreement between Anglicans and Catholics on salvation and the Church. It does seem clear that the deficiencies that the CDF claims to find in SC with regards to the sacramental and ecclesial dimensions of salvation do constitute their grounds for this judgement.[10]

The first point that must be made is that SC did not intend to offer a complete doctrine on the sacramental dimension of salvation. SC was elaborated in response to questions arising out of the sixteenth century disputes on justification, and it makes quite clear that on these questions nothing need keep us apart.

The CDF Commentary offers a clear summary of the agreement which *Salvation and the Church* arrived at in response to its mandate under the heading of 'A Point Emphasized in the Document'. While SC did not consider the sacramental dimension to lie within its mandate, and thus does not develop it fully, it does make clear allusions to it as required in its text, with regard to baptism and eucharist which are organically linked with justification and sanctification, and with regard to penance. In this regard, the Comm missed a clear reference to the sacrament of penance in no. 22: 'The Church is entrusted by the Lord with authority to pronounce forgiveness in his name to those who have fallen into sin and repent'. The sacrament of penance is not reduced to optional 'penitential disciplines': that term refers to the 'practical amends for what has been done amiss' which is only part of the sacrament of penance. Admittedly SC does not present a full doctrine of the sacrament of penance. Nonetheless SC recognized that this was an important cognate area and referred to it in an appropriate way. To presume that lack of full development on a point of doctrine hides some disagreement is unjustified. The same point can be made with respect to the eucharist. The reference SC makes to the eucharist (no. 16) amounts to more than a 'passing allusion'. In brief and precise terms it lays out for us the structural relationship between baptism and eucharist in the context of God's work of justification and our response.[11]

This perception by the CDF that the absence of a full treatment of the sacramental aspects of our salvation might vitiate the agreement achieved by SC is related to its concern for a proper doctrine of the Church as the sacrament of salvation. Is the Church simply a witness to a grace which it cannot efficaciously make present, or is it an authentic actualization of that grace (p. 10)? Is it nothing more than a community of those who are in constant need of repentance, or is it endowed in its inmost essence with a holiness it can communicate to human persons (p. 11)?

The language of efficacious actualization is not used by SC, but the reality is amply present: the Church embodies as well as reveals the redemptive power of the Gospel (no. 26); the once-for-all atoning work of Christ is realized as well as experienced in the life of the Church (no. 27); in the Church the Gospel 'becomes a manifest reality' (no. 28); the Church is used by God for the achievement of his purpose (no. 29). SC evidences a careful attempt to balance the noetic and the ontological aspects of God's work. Its language might not be that of scholastic theology, but the reality to which we agree is expressed quite adequately.

SC is careful to maintain yet another foundational equilibrium in its text. The Church not only is called to be but already is a sign, a steward, and an instrument of God's design (no. 29). Repentance and renewal are needed (the 'not yet' aspect) so that the Church might more clearly be seen for what it 'already now' is: the one, holy body of Christ (no. 29). The Church which in this world is always in need of renewal and purification (no. 30) is already here and now a foretaste of God's kingdom in a world still awaiting its consummation (no. 30).[12] What SC does at this point is carefully reflect the delicate balance between the holy Church and the Church of sinners, between the 'already now' and the 'not yet' aspects of God's kingdom, between God's action which we proclaim and celebrate and our own human action which is the constant object of *paranesis*.[13] This balance was established by Paul and was reflected by Vatican II. The use of less familiar scriptural language should not lead to doubts about the reality which is affirmed.

Over and over again on the points we have examined the criticisms and suggestions made in the Obs and in the Comm are based upon what appears to be misconstrual of the text. The point of SC is to establish a careful balance between possible excesses on both sides, and to express in succinct terms an understanding of our common tradition, one that does justice, especially on the basis of Augustine, to the positive contributions of both Trent and Reformers. One easily gathers, by contrast, that from the outset the Obs and the Comm seek to confirm an impression that what SC is really doing is to slide into Protestant excess under the guise of a balanced approach.

THE LANGUAGE OF SALVATION AND THE CHURCH

According to the Comm, SC fails to find sufficiently univocal formulations that can guarantee that Anglicans mean the same thing as Catholics when they agree to them. In sum, SC is insufficiently rigorous. Our comment on this point will be developed under three headings: (1) language and mystery, (2) dialogue and trust, and (3) plentitude and truth.

Language and Mystery: The broader issue of the role to be played by symbolic and analogical language has been dealt with earlier in the response of the Canadian dialogue to the CDF observations on *The Final Report*, and needs no lengthy elaboration here.[14] The interesting point that emerges here is the lament in the Comm that

> the symbolic nature of the language [of SC] makes difficult, if not impossible, a truly univocal agreement, where, as is the case here, questions are treated here which are decisive from the dogmatic point of view, and figure among the historically most controversial articles of faith. . . (p. 12).

This approach is not easy to square with the traditional theological view that statements about God and the things of God are not univocal but analogical. Mystery will never be exhausted by language. Language can point to it, can put us on the path to it, but will never allow us to control it through formulas that exclude ambiguity as if they comprehended the mystery in all its facets.

Analogy does not mean imprecision. The Ecumenical Councils strove with might and main to achieve clarity in the exposition of controverted areas of doctrine, but none of them achieved a clarity that rendered further interpretation and discussion unnecessary.[15] When language is used to speak about mystery, only a continuing community of interpretation and dialogue guided by the Spirit will preserve and foster our path towards the fullness of truth. Issues will continue to arise, but they can be dealt with in the course of time. Substantial agreement does not mean that we have reached eschatological transparency but that in faith and in trust we are able to state that in our common quest for the truth a significant meeting of minds has taken place, a meeting of minds which to the extent that it has taken place situates us in a community of dialogue by which we can further test and clarify our agreement, and expand it to other areas. That dialogue requires patience as we struggle for each successive increment of clarity.

Dialogue and Trust: Just as the indispensable condition of progression towards the truth is dialogue, so too the indispensible condition of all dialogue is trust. Trust can be betrayed, but such betrayal will eventually come to light in the course of time, and the ensuing dialogue designed to restore trust can only be carried out under the renewed presumption of trust. Not to trust is to make all dialogue, all progression towards a common sharing of the truth, impossible. The presupposition of all conversation between Christian partners is that others say what they really mean, and that indeed human minds can meet.[16]

That partners in dialogue express agreement on some matter of substance does not imply that their substantial agreement comes out of identical perspectives and experiences. Each partner in the dialogue has a unique standpoint on reality, and this standpoint is especially operative in dealing with the realm of mystery. Hence the genuine agreement which results from a dialogue is always accompanied by different perspectives on the same truth. These perspectives can to some extent be articulated and brought to the light, thus generating more clarity about the truth that is sought, but their distinctiveness will never disappear. With patience and trust, genuine agreement can be forged, an agreement which is not simply lips repeating a prescribed formula—by itself this would have little significance—but which is the fruit of hearts and minds at one within Christ's body.[17] The language of such agreements will be at once analogous, symbolic, and precise. In such language has the Church hammered out its definitions, not in a spirit of partisanship by which a set of precise theological formulations (considered orthodox by their proponents) are to supplant another set (considered heretical),[18] but in a spirit which above all treasures that fragile space in which genuine dialogue between different perspectives and ever more fruitful articulation of the mystery are possible.[19]

The following question can help us apply this point to the issue at hand: Had SC simply reexpressed the decrees of the Council of Trent—and the Comm seems to find fault with SC especially in its failure to re-echo the magisterial and theological formulations with which it is familiar—would that have offered the CDF the guarantee that it seems to be looking for? It is just as easy to suspect dialogue partners of dissembling under the guise of formulas totally acceptable to the other partner as it is to suspect them of deliberately wishing to cover up disagreement. If we are looking for an agreement which goes beyond the purely verbal and formal, we cannot bypass trust, dialogue, and the gradual unfolding of the truth within a human community which is essentially inserted in space and time; to do so would be akin to seeking salvation apart from the One who became incarnate, entered into the limitations of space and time, found fulfillment by becoming vulnerable unto death.[20]

The CDF does point out cognate questions which emerge out of SC, and offers helpful points for further dialogue between Anglicans and Roman Catholics. If what we say about dialogue and trust is correct, the fact that there is an unfinished dialogue agenda beyond SC does not preclude a genuine substantial agreement on the matters examined by SC. Indeed it is precisely that agreement which will strengthen and authenticate the community of discourse between Anglicans and Roman Catholics and will facilitate our further dialogue toward full communion in the truth.

Still the way in which the text of SC has been read by CDF does raise some serious issues. Obviously CDF was operating out of its commitment to safeguard the integral Catholic tradition. Our experience in dialogue suggests that a genuine agreement which respects the tradition is more readily achieved in an atmosphere free of any hint of suspicion or polemics.

Plentitude and Truth: A *leitmotif* that runs throughout the Obs is that in many areas it deals with SC ought to have developed cognate points much more fully. For instance the CDF seems to suggest that unless there is substantial agreement on this or that additional point (e.g., the sacramental dimension of justification) the substantial agreement claimed by SC in each area is not trustworthy. The methodology of ARCIC, however, is that of dealing with issues one by one. That substantial agreement has not been reached on every issue relating to the petrine ministry, for instance, does not exclude substantial agreement on more precise and limited points relating to the role of authority within the Church. The strategy entailed here is one of establishing beachheads of shared agreement. If we have achieved breakthroughs in certain precise areas of controverted doctrine, and as a result have established a genuine community of dialogue, then the resolution of thornier and more difficult issues becomes more feasible.

The CDF approach is less clear. Pushed to its logical limits, a refusal in each instance to recognize substantial agreement because there are unresolved issues in cognate areas would imply that we will never have substantial agreement on any doctrine unless there is substantial agreement on every doctrine. To come to the precise point at hand, the CDF seems to want SC to deal explicitly with a broad range of ecclesiological and sacramental issues, whereas the authors of SC, in response to their mandate, have dealt with the precise issue of salvation and of the role of the Church within it, entrusting unresolved cognate issues to further dialogue and further agreed statements. Indeed the major work of ARCIC II on the mystery of the Church is a task that lies ahead of it, not behind it. To know that the work of SC in the precise frame of reference in which it was conceived is recognized as sound by both Anglican and Roman Catholic Churches is to give a solid impetus to the work that lies ahead. We wish to avoid the extremes of gullibility and suspicion. We advocate a middle ground, that of a trust which is realistic, alert to difficulties along the way, able to deal with them constructively, a trust that flows from the love which Paul so eloquently praises in 1 Corinthians 13.

This point can be put in still broader terms. The Pauline 'now through a glass darkly, then face to face' applies to all Christians without exception, including those who have official teaching functions in our different Churches. We cannot demand of ourselves or of others a total state of cognitive transparency before God which is impossible to achieve in our condition of 'not yet'. As pilgrims we do receive from time to time intimations of the truth we do not yet see. Moments of agreement such as those achieved by the dialogue partners who produced the statement *Salvation and the Church* are evidences of the 'already now' present in our midst. We should celebrate them and make use of the opportunities they afford us.

NOTES

1   This is especially true in the section of the CDF Commentary entitled *A Point Emphasized in the Document*, pp. 1 and 2. 'Observations on *Salvation and the Church*'. *Origins*, 18:27 (December 15, 1988), 429-434.

2   Cf. Comm, p. 1.

3   The status of 'authoritative doctrinal judgement' was not given to the *Observation of the CDF* on *The Final Report* of ARCIC I. The term 'authoritative doctrinal judgement' requires clarification. Is this a judgement emanating from the Congregation in particular or from the Holy See as such?

4   This point is expressed more clearly towards the end of both the CDF observations and the accompanying commentary.

5   One might also comment on the understanding which the Comm has of Luther's *simul justus et peccator*. He was not speaking of the simultaneous existence of contradictory ontological states in the Christian as much as alluding to the justified person's experience of being a sinner while at the same time trusting in God's forgiving mercy. According to Otto Pesch, Luther is operating in an existential mode (dealing with grace as it affects my own personal quest for salvation), whereas classical Roman Catholic theology is operating in a sapiential mode (contemplating the mystery of grace as part of the objective economy of salvation). To interpret Luther's positions from the sapiential perspective would be to do them an injustice; cf. Otto Pesch's *Theologie der Rechtfertigung bei Martin Luther und Thomas von Aquin* (Mainz, Germany: Grünewald, 1967). A similar approach is taken in the dialogue between American Lutherans and Roman Catholics: cf. H. G. Anderson, T. A. Murphy, and J. A. Burgess, eds., *Justification by Faith: Lutherans and Catholics in Dialogue*: VII (Minneapolis: Augsburg, 1985), pp. 49-52.

6   The third paragraph on p. 45 of Comm expresses the drift of SC succinctly and accurately. That God declares our acquittal implies ontological change because God's word is creative.

7   This is abundantly reflected in Article 27 of the *Thirty Nine Articles*, and, what is more important for the adjudication of Anglican belief, in the formularies for the sacrament of baptism. What is expressed there is the ontological transformation which is imparted through the sacrament of baptism.

8   This distinction, and the supporting texts, are ably presented in M. Huftier, 'Libre arbitre, liberté et péché chez S. Augustin', *Recherches de Théologie Ancienne et Médiévale*, 33 (1966), 187-281.

9   More important than the *Thirty Nine Articles* in determining Anglican belief are the liturgical formularies of the Book of Common Prayer. Many of the Sunday Collects are translations of Roman Collects of the time of Augustine, and in this way the basic Augustinian understanding is part of the *lex orandi* as well as the *lex credendi* of the Anglican Communion. The Collect to be

used in the last Sunday before Advent (the Sunday next before Advent) admirably expresses the points SC makes in more technical language: 'Stir up, we beseech thee, O Lord, the wills of thy faithful people; that they, plenteously bringing forth the fruit of good works, may of thee be plenteously rewarded; through Jesus Christ our Lord'.

10   Cf. the Comm, p. 48: 'The Commission presents a rather vague conception of the Church which seems to lie at the base of all the difficulties which have been pointed out'.

11   Indeed one of the statements drawn up by ARCIC I deals with *Eucharistic Doctrine*.

12   'Foretaste' relates to the Pauline doctrine of our possessing here below not the fullness but the first-fruits, the down-payment, of salvation.

13   One might briefly refer at this point to the distinctive aspects of the Church found in *Lumen Gentium* 6 and in *Unitatis Redintegratio* 6, and to the sharp contrast between Paul's injunction to work out our salvation in fear and trembling with the triumphal ending of Romans 8.

14   Cf. *One in Christ* 20 (1984), 257-284.

15   The centuries of continuing debate and conciliar clarification which followed the Council of Nicaea are an outstanding example of this. The Nicene Fathers tried to achieve a clear and definitive settlement, but the clarity they sought emerged only later, for instance on the implications of *homoousia*.

16   This form of courtesy in dialogue relating to spiritual matters finds a classical expression in Ignatius Loyola's *Spiritual Exercises* (no. 22): 'one must presuppose that all good Christians should be more ready to put a good interpretation on another's statement than to condemn it as false'.

17   Such agreement is a result of a process described at Vatican II: 'At the same time, Catholic belief needs to be explained more profoundly and precisely, in ways and in terminology which our separated brethren too can readily understand' (*Unitatis Redintegratio*, 11).

18   This is a noteworthy aspect of the Council of Trent, which was very careful not to give primacy to one or other of the clearly delineated schools of theology current at that time in the Catholic Church. The result was a set of documents expressed in a language which was precise, yet very much impregnated with the symbolic and analogical ways of speaking found in Holy Scripture.

19   Here one might allude to the helpful remarks made in the preface to the study edition of *Salvation and the Church* (London: Catholic Truth Society/Church House Publishing, 1989), pp. 3 and 4: '. . . Human language is never wholly adequate to express the mysteries of God. Its range of meaning becomes even more narrow and limited in times of controversy when carefully defined terms are used to safeguard essential truths. Sadly these terms become the symbols of division. The policy explicitly adopted by ARCIC requires that vital truths be re-expressed in less "loaded" language. Because of the absence of theological terms associated with particular traditions, the ecumenical expression of doctrinal agreement might appear to some to lack rigour and precision. In fact the partners in dialogue hammer out their language during long and often painful debate . . . the language of an Agreed Statement should be interpreted in the context of the joint theological discussion which has produced it'. The upshot of this last statement is that the reliable

way to interpret words and phrases in a document such as SC is to begin by referring to the context set by the document itself.

20 A more pointed parallel in the life of Christ may be found in the temptations in the desert. In sum, the temptations urged Jesus to take the short-cuts which would win the superficial acclaim of the multitudes, playing on their short-sighted expectations of liberation, impressing them with magical deeds. The messianic path to which Jesus committed himself was that of gaining the deep adherence of faith of a few by taking the risks inherent in any personal dialogue and accepting the full consequences of this vulnerability. The contrast here is between the mere repetition of a formula and the personal appropriation of a truth.

II

SACRAMENTS AND MINISTRY

THE DOCTRINES OF THE SACRAMENTS AND MINISTRY are two of the three areas over which the Anglican and Roman Catholic Churches divided in the sixteenth century (*Malta Report*, 1968). These issues have, therefore, occupied much of Anglican-Roman Catholic dialogue over the past three decades. They are also subjects on which teaching has seen recent developments, especially during and since Vatican II. Agreement in these two areas marked a historic breakthrough in the first decade of dialogue and provided clarification for the third of these disputed doctrines: authority, where crucial work still remains to be done.

When ARCIC I issued its *Final Report* in 1982, it claimed to have reached 'substantial agreement' on the subjects of eucharist and ministry, and to have achieved 'a certain convergence' in the area of authority, where significant issues remained to be discussed. ARCIC I asked our two Churches to study *The Final Report* and to assess whether its statements are 'consonant in substance with the faith' of the two Churches (*Emmaus Report*, 1987; NCCB Evaluation, 1984). Each of the two Churches followed its own particular procedures in making its judgment. The Churches within the Anglican Communion were asked by the Anglican Consultative Council to evaluate *The Final Report* by province (national churches); nineteen of the then twenty-nine provinces had done so when the responses were published in 1987 as *The Emmaus Report*. In the Roman Catholic Church, Cardinal Willebrands (then president of the Secretariat for Promoting Christian Unity) asked national episcopal conferences to prepare assessments; some of these responses were published. All were collated by the Secretariat (now Council) for Promoting Christian Unity prior to the release of the official Vatican response in 1991 (Hill and Yarnold, 1994, pp. 4, 94-110). Various official and expert analyses of *The Final Report* have also been published. (A number of these are included in Hill and Yarnold, 1994. See also Wright, 1991; Wright, 1994; Yarnold, 1994; Tavard, 1995; and Tavard, 1996.)

Each of the two Churches has now formulated its official response to *The Final Report*, and it is with these that this section of the present volume begins.

The 1988 Lambeth Conference of Anglican bishops found that, in the areas where ARCIC I claimed substantial agreement, *The Final Report* is 'consonant in substance with the faith of Anglicans' despite misgivings in some provinces. Lambeth encouraged ARCIC II to continue its work in areas of continuing disagreement or unclarity. The official response of the Roman Catholic Church expressed certain reservations about the degree of agreement ARCIC I had reached and requested further clarification on some points. ARCIC II issued elucidations in reply to this response of the Holy See and in them addressed Vatican concerns directly. Cardinal Edward Cassidy, president of the Pontifical Council for Promoting Christian Unity, responded that the 'clarifications have indeed thrown new light on the questions concerning *Eucharist and Ministry* . . . and no further study would seem to be required at this stage'.

National dialogues in the United States and Canada also provided some elucidations in areas where clarification had been requested. Both ARC Canada and ARC USA also produced agreed statements responding to the responses to *The Final Report*. ARC Canada gave a very close reading of the Roman Catholic response, raised specific concerns, and made particular clarifications. ARC USA took a different approach, articulating underlying methodological issues and concerns raised by both Lambeth and the Vatican in their responses.

Each of the North American ARC dialogues has also taken initiative in addressing areas of particular concern within the American context, not only to foster local relations but also to further the international dialogues. ARC USA examined newly released archival evidence and the historic context of Pope Leo XIII's 1896 Bull *Apostolicæ Curæ*, which declared Anglican orders 'absolutely null and utterly void'. This, taken with subsequent developments in the theology of ministry in both Churches, they suggest, may warrant Roman Catholic reconsideration of the judgment and open a new door to the reconciliation of ministries despite challenges that remain or have developed (Franklin, 1996).

ARC Canada approaches one of these challenges in its study of the ministry of women. The experience of the two Churches in Canada has shaped the ministry of women and of men in unique ways that may be instructive to Christians in other places. Having discerned a broad range of commonality between the two Churches' experience and their understanding of women's ministries, ARC Canada poses some difficult questions about the chief remaining area of disagreement—ordination of women—and suggests that the topic must be approached as part of the larger question of the relationship between Gospel and culture.

ARC Canada has also produced a brief joint statement that touches on one of the most problematic aspects of authority: papal infallibility. This statement follows the theological structure of ARCIC I's *Final Report* and its suggestions on how the question may helpfully be addressed in dialogue between the two Churches.

The ongoing dialogue between Canadian Roman Catholic and Anglican bishops has also applied the two Churches' agreement on the doctrine of ministry to a very practical, pastoral concern: the movement of persons, particularly clergy, between the two Churches.

The documents in this section underscore ARCIC I's claim to have reached 'substantial agreement' in these areas.

The materials from the national dialogues are evidence that this agreement is not merely asserted at the international level; it is also received and deepened at the national and local levels. Far from being the highly controverted and even church-dividing matters they once were, sacraments and ministry are now areas where the two Churches share a real, though imperfect, communion. It is to be hoped that the communion will continue to grow as our two Churches face together those areas in which we are still divided.

8. THE 1988 LAMBETH CONFERENCE: RESOLUTION 8 AND EXPLANATORY NOTE REGARDING ARCIC I

This Conference:[1]

1. Recognises the Agreed Statements of ARCIC I on *Eucharistic Doctrine, Ministry and Ordination*, and their *Elucidations*, as consonant in substance with the faith of Anglicans and believes that this agreement offers a sufficient basis for taking the next step towards the reconciliation of our Churches grounded in agreement in faith.
2. Welcomes the assurance that, within an understanding of the Church as communion, ARCIC II is to explore further the particular issues of the reconciliation of ministries; the ordination of women; moral questions; and continuing questions of authority, including the relation of Scripture to the Church's developing Tradition and the role of the laity in decision-making within the Church.
3. Welcomes *Authority in the Church* (*I* and *II*) together with the *Elucidation*, as a firm basis for the direction and agenda of the continuing dialogue on authority and wishes to encourage ARCIC II to continue to explore the basis in Scripture and Tradition of the concept of a universal primacy, in conjunction with collegiality, as an instrument of unity, the character of such a primacy in practice, and to draw upon the experience of other Christian Churches in exercising primacy, collegiality, and conciliarity.
4. In welcoming the fact that the ordination of women is to form part of the agenda of ARCIC II, recognises the serious responsibility this places upon us to weigh the possible implications of action on this matter for the unity of the Anglican Communion and for the universal Church.
5. Warmly welcomes the first Report of ARCIC II, *Salvation and the Church* (1987), as a timely and significant contribution to the understanding of the Churches' doctrine of salvation and commends this Agreed Statement about the heart of Christian faith to the Provinces for study and reflection.

EXPLANATORY NOTE

This Conference has received the official responses to *The Final Report* of the Anglican Roman Catholic International Commission (ARCIC I) from the member Provinces of the Anglican Communion. We note the considerable measure of consensus and convergence which the Agreed Statements represent. We wish to record our grateful thanks to

Almighty God for the very significant advances in understanding and unity thereby expressed.

In considering *The Final Report*, the Conference bore two questions in mind:
- (i) Are the Agreed Statements consonant with Anglican faith?
- (ii) If so, do they enable us to take further steps forward?

EUCHARISTIC DOCTRINE

The Provinces gave a clear 'yes' to the statement on *Eucharistic Doctrine*. Comments have been made that the style and language used in the statement are inappropriate for certain cultures. Some Provinces asked for clarification about the meaning of *anamnesis* and bread and wine 'becoming' the body and blood of Christ. But no Province rejected the statement and many were extremely positive.

While we recognise that there are hurts to be healed and doubts to be overcome, we encourage Anglicans to look forward with the new hope which the Holy Spirit is giving to the Church as we move away from past mistrust, division, and polarisation.

While we respect the continuing anxieties of some Anglicans in the area of 'sacrifice' and 'presence', they do not appear to reflect the common mind of the Provincial responses, in which it was generally felt that the *Elucidation* of *Eucharistic Doctrine* was a helpful clarification and reassurance. Both are areas of 'mystery' which ultimately defy definition. But the Agreed Statement on the Eucharist *sufficiently* expresses Anglican understanding.

MINISTRY AND ORDINATION

Again, the Provinces gave a clear 'yes' to the statement on *Ministry and Ordination*. The language and style have, however, been a difficulty for some Provinces, especially in the Far East. Wider representation has also been called for from Africa. Though this has now been partially remedied in ARCIC II, there is still currently no representation from Latin America, a subcontinent with very large Roman Catholic populations.

An ambivalent reply came from one Province which has traditionally experienced a difficult relationship with the Roman Catholic Church. This seems to reflect the need for developing deeper links of trust and friendship as ecumenical dialogue goes forward.

While some Provinces asked for a clarification of 'priesthood' the majority believed this had been dealt with sufficiently—together with the doctrine of the eucharist—to give grounds for hope for a fresh appraisal of each other's ministries and thus to further the reconciliation of ministries and growth towards full communion.

AUTHORITY IN THE CHURCH

The responses from the Provinces to the two statements on *Authority in the Church* were generally positive.

Questions were, however, raised about a number of matters, especially primacy, jurisdiction and infallibility, collegiality, and the role of the laity. Nevertheless, it was generally felt that *Authority in the Church* (*I* and *II*), together with the *Elucidation*, give us real grounds for believing that fuller agreement can be reached, and that they set out helpfully the direction and agenda of the way forward.

NOTE

1   The bishops at the 1988 Lambeth Conference had before them a report which collated the responses of the Provinces to ARCIC—The *Emmaus Report* (Anglican Consultative Council, London: Church House Publishing, 1987). The bishops passed the [above] Resolution at the Lambeth Conference.

9. THE OFFICIAL ROMAN CATHOLIC RESPONSE TO THE FINAL REPORT OF ARCIC I

Pontifical Council for Promoting Christian Unity, 1991

GENERAL EVALUATION

1.   The Catholic Church gives a warm welcome to the Final Report of ARCIC I and expresses its gratitude to the members of the International Commission responsible for drawing up this document. The Report is a result of an in-depth study of certain questions of faith by partners in dialogue and witnesses to the achievement of points of convergence and even of agreement which many would not have thought possible before the Commission began its work. As such, it constitutes a significant milestone not only in relations between the Catholic Church and the Anglican Communion but in the ecumenical movement as a whole.

2.   The Catholic Church judges, however, that it is not yet possible to state that substantial agreement has been reached on all the questions studied by the Commission. There still remain between Anglicans and Catholics important differences regarding essential matters of Catholic doctrine.

3.   The following Explanatory Note is intended to give a detailed summary of the areas where differences or ambiguities remain which seriously hinder the restoration of full communion in faith and in the sacramental life. This Note is the fruit of a close collaboration between the Congregation for the Doctrine of the Faith and the Pontifical Council for Promoting Christian Unity, which is directly responsible for the dialogue—a dialogue which, as is well known, continues within the framework of ARCIC II.

4.   It is the Catholic Church's hope that its definitive response to the results achieved by ARCIC I will serve as an impetus to further study, in the same fraternal spirit that has characterized this dialogue in the past, of the points of divergence remaining, as well as of those other questions which must be taken into account if the unity willed by Christ for his disciples is to be restored.

EXPLANATORY NOTE

5.   Before setting forth for further study those areas of *The Final Report* which do not satisfy fully certain elements of Catholic doctrine and which thereby prevent our speaking of the attainment of substantial agreement, it seems only right and just to mention some other areas in which notable progress has been achieved by those responsible for the redaction of the *Report*. The members of the Commission have obviously given a great deal of

time, prayer, and reflection to the themes which they were asked to study together and they are owed an expression of gratitude and appreciation for the manner in which they carried out their mandate.

6. It is in respect of *Eucharistic Doctrine* that the members of the Commission were able to achieve the most notable progress toward a consensus. Together they affirm 'that the Eucharist is a sacrifice in the sacramental sense, provided that it is clear that this is not a repetition of the historical sacrifice' (*Eucharistic Doctrine: Elucidation*, para. 5); and areas of agreements are also evident in respect of the real presence of Christ: 'before the eucharistic prayer, to the question 'What is that?', the believer answers: 'It is bread'. After the eucharistic prayer, to the same question he answers: 'It is truly the body of Christ, the Bread of Life' (*Eucharistic Doctrine: Elucidation*, para. 6). The Catholic Church rejoices that such common affirmations have become possible. Still, as will be indicated further on, it looks for certain clarifications which will assure that these affirmations are understood in a way that conforms to Catholic doctrine.

7. With regard to *Ministry and Ordination*, the distinction between the priesthood common to all the baptized and the ordained priesthood is explicitly acknowledged: 'These are two distinct realities which relate, each in its own way, to the high priesthood of Christ' (*Ministry and Ordination: Elucidations*, para. 2). The ordained ministry 'is not an extension of the common Christian priesthood but belongs to another realm of the gifts of the Spirit' (*Ministry and Ordination*, para. 13). Ordination is described as a 'sacramental act' (*Ministry and Ordination*, para. 15) and the ordained ministry as being an essential element of the Church: 'The New Testament shows that ministerial office played an essential part in the life of the Church in the first century, and we believe that the provision of a ministry of this kind is part of God's design for his people' (*Ministry and Ordination*, para. 6). Moreover, 'it is only the ordained minister who presides at the eucharist' (*Ministry and Ordination: Elucidation*, para. 2). These are all matters of significant consensus and of particular importance for the future development of Anglican-Roman Catholic dialogue.

8. On both the eucharist and the ordained ministry, the *sacramental* understanding of the Church is affirmed, to the exclusion of any purely 'congregational' presentation of Christianity. The members of the Commission are seen as speaking together out of a continuum of faith and practice which has its roots in the New Testament and has developed under the guidance of the Holy Spirit throughout Christian history.

9. When it comes to the question of *Authority in the Church*, it must be noted that *The Final Report* makes no claim to substantial agreement. The most that has been achieved is a certain convergence, which is but a first step along the path that seeks consensus as a prelude to unity. Yet even in this respect, there are certain signs

of convergence that do indeed open the way to further progress in the future. As the Congregation for the Doctrine of the Faith pointed out in its *Observations* of 1982 on *The Final Report*: 'It is necessary to underline the importance of the fact that Anglicans recognize that a "primacy of the Bishop of Rome is not contrary to the New Testament, and is a part of God's purpose regarding the Church's unity and catholicity"' (cf. *Authority II*, para. 7). If this is taken with the statement made by His Grace Archbishop Runcie during his visit to Pope John Paul II in 1989 and with reference to infallibility in *Authority II*, para. 29, then one can rejoice in the fact that centuries of antagonism have given way to reasoned dialogue and theological reflection undertaken together.

10. Despite these very consoling areas of agreement or convergence on questions that are of great importance for the faith of the Catholic Church, it seems clear that there are still other areas that are essential to Catholic doctrine on which complete agreement or even at times convergence has eluded the Anglican-Roman Catholic Commission.

11. In fact, the *Report* itself acknowledges that there are such matters, and this is particularly true in respect of the Catholic dogma of papal infallibility, to which reference has just been made. In the section *Authority in the Church II*, it is stated that 'In spite of our agreement over the need for a universal primacy in a united Church, Anglicans do not accept the guaranteed possession of such a gift of divine assistance in judgement necessarily attached to the office of the bishop of Rome by virtue of which his formal decisions can be known to be wholly assured before their reception by the faithful' (para. 31).

12. *The Final Report* recalls the conditions set down for an infallible definition by the First Vatican Council, but goes on to give a different understanding of this question on the part of Catholics and Anglicans: 'When it is plain that all these conditions have been fulfilled, Roman Catholics conclude that the judgement is preserved from error and the proposition true. If the definition proposed for assent were not manifestly a legitimate interpretation of biblical faith and in line with orthodox tradition, Anglicans would think it a duty to reserve the reception of the definition for study and discussion' (*Authority II*, para. 29).

13. Similarly, the Commission has not been able to record any real consensus on the Marian dogmas. For while *Authority in the Church II*, para. 30, indicates that 'Anglicans and Roman Catholics can agree in much of the truth that the dogmas of the Immaculate Conception and Assumption are designed to affirm', under the same heading it is stated: 'The dogmas of the Immaculate Conception and the Assumption raise a special problem for those Anglicans who do not consider that the precise definitions given by these dogmas are sufficiently supported by Scripture. For many Anglicans the teaching authority of the bishop of Rome, independent of a council, is not recommended by the fact that through it these Marian doctrines were proclaimed as dogmas binding on all the faithful. Anglicans would also ask whether, in any future union between our two Churches, they would be required to subscribe to such dogmatic statements'.

14. This statement and several others in *The Final Report* illustrate the need for much further study to be done in respect of the Petrine ministry in the Church. The following quotations from *The Final Report*, while reflecting the more positive approach of Anglicans in recent times in this connection, also illustrate the reservations that still exist on the part of the Anglican community:

Much Anglican objection has been directed against the manner of the exercise and particular claims of the Roman primacy rather than against universal primacy as such (*Authority: Elucidation*, para. 8).

Relations between our two communions in the past have not encouraged reflection by Anglicans on the positive significance of the Roman primacy in the life of the universal Church. Nonetheless, from time to time Anglican theologians have affirmed that, in changed circumstances, it might be possible for the Churches of the Anglican Communion to recognize the development of the Roman primacy as a gift of divine providence—in other words, as an effect of the guidance of the Holy Spirit in the Church (*Authority II*, para. 13).

In spite of our agreement over the need for a universal primacy in a united Church, Anglicans do not accept the guaranteed possession of such a gift of divine assistance in judgement necessarily attached to the office of the bishop of Rome by virtue of which his formal decisions can be known to be wholly assured before their reception by the faithful (*Authority II*, para. 31).

15. With regard to the magisterial authority of the Church, there is a very positive presentation in *Authority in the Church II*, paras. 24-27. We read that 'at certain moments the Church can in a matter of essential doctrine make a decisive judgement which becomes part of its permanent witness. . . . The purpose of this service cannot be to add to the content of revelation, but to recall and emphasize some important truth'. A clear statement is made, moreover, in *Authority in the Church: Elucidation*, para. 3, to the effect that reception of a defined truth by the People of God 'does not create truth nor legitimize the decision'. But as has just been noted with regard to the primacy, it would seem that elsewhere *The Final Report* sees the 'assent of the faithful' as required for the recognition that a doctrinal decision of the pope or of an ecumenical council is immune from error (*Authority II*, paras. 27 and 31). For the Catholic Church, the certain knowledge of any defined truth is not guaranteed by the reception of the faithful that such is in conformity with Scripture and Tradition, but by the authoritative definition itself on the part of the authentic teachers.

16. Dealing with the authority of the ecumenical councils (*Authority II*, para. 3), ARCIC I describes the scope of doctrinal definitions by the councils as being concerned with 'fun-

damental doctrines' or 'central truths of salvation'. The Catholic Church believes that the councils or the pope, even when acting alone, are able to teach, if necessary in a definitive way, within the range of all truth revealed by God.

17. A further point of difficulty emerges in the position taken regarding the relationship of the ecclesial character of a Christian community and its incorporation into Catholic communion through union with the See of Rome. With references to *Lumen Gentium*, no. 8 and *Unitatis Redintegratio*, no. 13, which are not fully accurate, the *Report* states: 'The Second Vatican Council allows it to be said that a Church out of communion with the Roman See may lack nothing from the viewpoint of the Roman Catholic Church except that it does not belong to the visible manifestation of full Christian communion which is maintained in the Roman Catholic Church' (*Authority II*, para. 12). It is the teaching of the Second Vatican Council that a Church outside of communion with the Roman Pontiff lacks more than just the visible manifestation of unity with the Church of Christ which subsists in the Roman Catholic Church.

18. The manner in which ARCIC I writes in respect of the role of Peter among the twelve—'a special position' (*Authority II*, para. 3), 'a position of special importance' (*Authority II*, para. 5)—does not express the fullness of the Catholic faith in this regard. The dogmatic definition of the First Vatican Council declares that the primacy of the Bishop of Rome belongs to the divine structure of the Church; the Bishop of Rome inherits the primacy from Peter who received it 'immediately and directly' from Christ (DS 3055; cf. *Lumen Gentium*, no. 22). From a Catholic viewpoint, it is not possible then to accept the interpretation given in *Authority in the Church II* concerning the *Jus divinum* of the First Vatican Council, namely that it 'need not be taken to imply that the universal primacy as a permanent institution was directly founded by Jesus during his life on earth' (para. 11). The Catholic Church sees rather in the primacy of the successors of Peter something positively intended by God and deriving from the will and institution of Jesus Christ.

19. As is obvious, despite considerable convergence in this regard, full agreement on the nature and the significance of the Roman primacy has not been reached. As Pope John Paul II pointed out during his visit to the World Council of Churches on June 12, 1984, the Petrine ministry must be discussed 'in all frankness and friendship', because of the importance of this from the Catholic point of view and the difficulty that it poses for other Christians.

20. It is clear, as already affirmed, that on the questions of eucharist and the ordained ministry, greater progress has been made. There are, however, certain statements and formulations in respect of these doctrines that would need greater clarification from the Catholic point of view.

21. With regard to the eucharist the faith of the Catholic Church would be even more clearly reflected in *The Final Report* if the following points were to be explicitly affirmed:

that in the eucharist, the Church, doing what Christ commanded his apostles to do at the Last Supper, makes present the sacrifice of Calvary. This would complete, without contradicting it, the statement made in *The Final Report*, affirming that the eucharist does not repeat the sacrifice of Christ, nor add to it (*Eucharistic Doctrine*, para. 5, *Elucidation*, para. 5);

that the sacrifice of Christ is made present with all its effects, thus affirming the propitiatory nature of the eucharistic sacrifice, which can be applied also to the deceased. For Catholics 'the whole Church' must include the dead. The prayer for the dead is to be found in all the canons of the Mass, and the propitiatory character of the Mass as the sacrifice of Christ that may be offered for the living and the dead, including a particular dead person, is part of the Catholic faith.

22. The affirmations that the eucharist is 'the Lord's real gift of himself to his Church' (*Eucharistic Doctrine*, para. 8) and that the bread and wine 'become' the body and blood of Christ (*Eucharistic Doctrine: Elucidation*, para. 6) can certainly be interpreted in conformity with Catholic faith. They are insufficient, however, to remove all ambiguity regarding the mode of the real presence which is due to a substantial change in the elements. The Catholic Church holds that Christ in the eucharist makes himself present sacramentally and substantially when under the species of bread and wine these earthly realities are changed into the reality of his body and blood, soul and divinity.

23. On the question of the reservation of the eucharist, the statement that there are those who 'find any kind of adoration of Christ in the reserved sacrament unacceptable' (*Eucharistic Doctrine: Elucidation*, para. 9), created concern from the Roman Catholic point of view. This section of *Eucharistic Doctrine: Elucidations*, seeks to allay any such doubts, but one remains with the conviction that this is an area in which real consensus between Anglicans and Roman Catholics is lacking.

24. Similarly, in respect of the ordained ministry, *The Final Report* would be helped if the following were made clearer:

that only a validly ordained priest can be the minister who, in the person of Christ, brings into being the sacrament of the eucharist. He not only recites the narrative of the institution of the Last Supper, pronouncing the words of consecration and imploring the Father to send the Holy Spirit to effect through them the transformation of the gifts, but in so doing offers sacramentally the redemptive sacrifice of Christ;

that it was Christ himself who instituted the sacrament of orders as the rite which confers the priesthood of the New Covenant. This would complete the significant statement made in *Ministry and Ordination*, para. 13, that in the eucharist the ordained minister 'is seen to stand in sacramental relation to what Christ himself did in offering his own sacrifice'. This clarification would seem all the more important in view of the fact that the ARCIC document does not refer to the *character* of priestly ordination which implies a configuration to the priesthood of Christ. The character of priestly ordination is central to the Catholic understanding of the distinction between the ministerial priesthood and the common priesthood of the baptized. It is moreover important for the recognition of holy orders as a sacrament instituted by Christ, and not therefore a simple ecclesiastical institution.

25. The Commission itself has, in *Ministry and Ordination: Elucidation*, para. 5, referred to the developments within the Anglican Communion after the setting up of ARCIC I, in connection with the ordination of women. *The Final Report* states that the members of the Commission believe 'that the principles upon which its doctrinal agreement rests are not affected by such ordinations; for it was concerned with the origin and nature of the ordained ministry and not with the question who can or who cannot be ordained'. The view of the Catholic Church in this matter has been expressed in an exchange of correspondence with the archbishop of Canterbury, in which it is made clear that the question of the subject of ordination is linked with the nature of the sacrament of holy orders. Differences in this connection must therefore affect the agreement reached on *Ministry and Ordination*.

26. The question of apostolic succession is not dealt with directly in *The Final Report* of ARCIC I, but it is referred to in *Ministry and Ordination*, para. 16, and in *Ministry and Ordination: Elucidation*, para 4. The essential features of 'what is meant in our two traditions by ordination in the apostolic succession' are set down in *Ministry and Ordination*, para. 16, and the statement is made that 'because they [the ordaining bishops] are entrusted with the oversight of other Churches, this participation in his ordination signifies that this new bishop and his Church are within the communion of Churches. Moreover, because they are representatives of their Churches in fidelity to the teaching and mission of the apostles and are members of the episcopal college, their participation also ensures the historical continuity of this Church with the apostolic Church and of its bishop with the original apostolic ministry'.

27. These statements stand in need of further clarification from the Catholic perspective. The Catholic Church recognizes in the apostolic succession both an unbroken line of episcopal ordination from Christ through the apostles down through the centuries to the bishops of today and an uninterrupted continuity in Christian doctrine from Christ to those today who teach in union with the College of Bishops and its head, the Successor of Peter. As *Lumen Gentium* 20 affirms, the unbroken lines of episcopal succession and apostolic teaching stand in causal relationship to each other: 'Among those various ministries which, as tradition witnesses, were exercised in the Church from the earliest times, the

chief place belongs to the office of those who, appointed to the episcopate in a sequence running back to the beginning, are the ones who pass on the apostolic seed. Thus, as St. Irenaeus testifies, through those who were appointed bishops by the apostles, and through their successors down to our own time, the apostolic tradition is manifested and preserved throughout the world'. This question, then, lies at the very heart of the ecumenical discussion and touches vitally all the themes dealt with by ARCIC I: the reality of the eucharist, the sacramentality of the ministerial priesthood, the nature of the Roman primacy.

28. A final word seems necessary in relation to the attitude of *The Final Report* to the interpretation of Scripture insofar as the role of tradition is concerned. It is true that this subject was not treated specifically by the Commission, yet there are statements made which cannot be allowed to pass without comment in this reply. As is well known, the Catholic doctrine affirms that the historical-critical method is not sufficient for the interpretation of Scripture. Such interpretation cannot be separated from the living Tradition of the Church which receives the message of Scripture. *The Final Report* seems to ignore this when dealing with the interpretation of the Petrine texts of the New Testament, for it states that they 'do not offer sufficient basis' on which to establish the primacy of the Bishop of Rome. In the same way, *The Final Report* introduces with reference to the infallible judgements of the Bishop of Rome the need for such decision to be 'manifestly a legitimate interpretation of biblical faith and in line with orthodox tradition' (*Authority II*, para. 29).

29. Certainly, there is need, then, for further study concerning Scripture, Tradition, and the magisterium and their interrelationship since, according to Catholic teaching, Christ has given to his Church full authority to continue, with the uninterrupted and efficacious assistance of the Holy Spirit, 'to preserve this word of God faithfully, explain it and make it more widely known' (*Dei Verbum*, 9-10).

CONCLUSION

30. The above observations are not intended in any way to diminish appreciation for the important work done by ARCIC I, but rather to illustrate areas within the matters dealt with by *The Final Report* about which further clarification or study is required before it can be said that the statements made in the Final Report correspond fully to Catholic doctrine on the eucharist and on ordained ministry.

31. The quite remarkable progress that has been made in respect of authority in the Church indicates just how essential this question is for the future of Roman Catholic-Anglican dialogue.

32. The value of any consensus reached in regard to other matters will to a large extent depend on the authority of the body which eventually endorses them.

33. The objection may be made that this reply does not sufficiently follow the ecumenical method, by which agreement is sought step by step, rather than in full agreement at the first attempt. It must, however, be remembered that the Roman Catholic Church was

asked to give a clear answer to the question: are the agreements contained in this *Report* consonant with the faith of the Catholic Church? What was asked for was not a simple evaluation of an ecumenical study, but an official response as to the identity of the various statements with the faith of the Church.

34. It is sincerely hoped that this will contribute to the continued dialogue between Anglicans and Catholics in the spirit of the Common Declaration made between Pope John Paul II and Archbishop Robert Runcie during the visit of the latter to Rome in 1989. There it is stated: 'We here solemnly recommit ourselves and those we represent to the restoration of visible unity and full ecclesial communion in the confidence that to seek anything less would be to betray Our Lord's intention for the unity of his people'.

10. REPLY TO THE VATICAN RESPONSE TO THE FINAL REPORT OF THE ANGLICAN ROMAN CATHOLIC INTERNATIONAL COMMISSION

Anglican–Roman Catholic Dialogue Canada, 1993

I. INTRODUCTION

1.   In the continuing hope of that unity of the Church for which Christ prayed, the Anglican-Roman Catholic Dialogue of Canada receives the response of the Vatican to *The Final Report* of the Anglican Roman Catholic International Commission.

2.   We welcome the *Vatican Response* for what it is: a step on the journey toward the full, visible unity of the Roman Catholic and the Anglican Communions. We share the commitment 'to the restoration of visible unity and full ecclesial communion'[1] renewed by Pope John Paul II and Archbishop Robert Runcie in their 1989 meeting in Rome, and renewed once again in the visit of Archbishop George Leonard Carey to Pope John Paul II in 1992, who agreed on the 'urgent necessity of the theological dialogue, whose aim is to ensure agreement in the content of faith, although there may be diversity in its expression'.[2] Together with them and with the whole of our sister communions, we are fellow pilgrims on the road toward unity. Together with them we say: 'No pilgrim knows in advance all the steps along the path'.[3] But on this path, we find, with the *Vatican Response*, that *The Final Report* stands as a 'significant milestone',[4] not a roadblock.

3.   We are encouraged at the many areas of agreement that the *Vatican Response* notes, especially in the areas of eucharist, ministry, and the primacy of the Bishop of Rome. We are sobered and even puzzled in other places: where we thought agreement had been reached, the *Vatican Response* finds need for further clarifications or even seems to overlook the amount of genuine agreement already in the ARCIC text, especially on reception and on the relation of Scripture and Tradition. Finally, we are spurred to a deeper level of dialogue at points where the *Vatican Response* has shown us that further work is necessary before a substantial agreement can truly be reached, such as the exercise of authority by the papacy.

4.   In our reply, we want to probe just a few areas in order to contribute to the ongoing discussion to overcome our divisions. We do so in response to the hope expressed that the *Vatican Response* 'will serve as an impetus to further study in the same fraternal spirit that has characterized this dialogue in the past'.[5]

II. GENERAL CONCERNS

A. A Significant Milestone

5.   In the *Vatican Response*, the work of *The Final Report* is recognized as a 'significant milestone', not only in relations between our two communions but 'in the ecumenical movement as a whole'.[6] Recognizing 'notable progress' in many areas of former disagreement, the *Vatican Response* emphasizes that such progress is an occasion for rejoicing and consolation.[7] It lists a significant number of agreements on the eucharist, ministry, and authority. Even on some areas where agreement is not found, the *Vatican Response* sees 'certain signs of convergence that do indeed open the way to further progress in the future'.[8] It offers its reflection in the hope that its 'reply will contribute to the continued dialogue'.[9]

B. Requests for Clarification

6.   While areas of agreement are recognized and appreciated by the *Vatican Response*, at the same time further clarification is requested, even in these same areas. We asked ourselves as we read: what kind of clarification is requested?

7.   While the 1982 *Observations* of the Congregation for the Doctrine of the Faith more frequently cited 'ambiguities', this *Vatican Response* more often calls for 'clarifications'. This shows the progress of the discussion. But what kind of clarification would be suitable? A large number of Roman Catholic episcopal conferences, including the Canadian Conference of Catholic Bishops, have responded to *The Final Report*. We had thought that, as they interpreted *The Final Report* in their responses, these bishops' conferences had actually provided some of the clarification now sought by the *Vatican Response*. Furthermore, the published episcopal responses concluded *The Final Report* had achieved a more substantial agreement than is acknowledged in the *Vatican Response*, and these episcopal responses did not ask for many clarifications. What part did these episcopal conference responses play in the preparation of the *Vatican Response*? We would ask a similar question about the part played by the *Emmaus Report*,[10] a response of the provinces of the Anglican Communion to *The Final Report* presented in preparation for the 1988 Lambeth Conference. It would not be difficult to amplify further the kinds of insights in these responses with the clarifications they can provide, using historical, liturgical, exegetical, and theological reflections. If the nature of the clarifications sought by the Vatican could be specified, it would assist the work of ecumenical dialogue commissions and theologians requested to work on these matters.

C. Teaching and Practice

8.   But perhaps the *Vatican Response* seeks another kind of clarification. Does the Vatican fear that the teaching in *The Final Report* is not always expressed in Anglican practice? This is a fear that some Anglicans also express: that assurances in *The Final Report* about Roman

Catholic teaching are not consonant with certain practices in the Roman Catholic communion. If this is the kind of clarification sought by the Vatican, perhaps it is time to heed again the last words of *The Final Report*: 'We suggest that some difficulties will not be wholly resolved until a practical initiative has been taken and our two Churches have lived together more visibly in the one *koinonia*'.[11] Could such a practical initiative be taken in a new step on our journey so that our two communions could seek clarifications through a deeper practice of faith together as we prepare for fuller communion? This might be the best way to find the clarifications sought by the *Response*. In Canada, our two communions collaborate closely in areas such as pastoral care, seminary education, and social ministries. In addition, many Anglicans and Roman Catholics intermarry, with each spouse remaining faithful and active within their own communion. These many Canadian experiences of life together help to give us concrete knowledge of the practice as well as the theory of our ecumenical partners. They also help each communion see weakness in its own practice of the common faith.

D. Doctrinal Statements and the Faith of the Church

9.   Another area that puzzled us was the search undertaken by the *Response* to judge 'as to the identity of the various statements with the faith of the Church'.[12] The original mandate of Pope Paul VI and Archbishop Michael Ramsey in establishing the Commission asked its work to be 'founded on the Gospels and on the ancient common traditions'.[13] In its preface, ARCIC claims to have followed this method. 'From the beginning we were determined, in accordance with our mandate, and in the spirit of Philippians 3:13, "forgetting what lies behind and straining forward to what lies ahead", to discover each other's faith as it is today and to appeal to history only for enlightenment, not as a way of perpetuating past controversy', it claims.[14] It sought 'The avoidance of the emotive language of past polemics and . . . the restatement of doctrine which new times and conditions are, as we both recognize, regularly calling for. . .'.[15]

10. And yet many of the criticisms made by the Vatican, especially on questions related to authority, come from a comparison of *The Final Report* with traditions particular to the language and conceptual framework of Roman Catholic theology since the sixteenth century divisions. Do such criticisms constitute an exhortation to ecumenical workers to study more carefully the distinctive traditions of each communion since our division, in addition to the Gospels and the ancient common traditions that we share? If such additional sources are to be studied more carefully, still 'for enlightenment, not as a way of perpetuating past controversy',[16] we urge also the study of 'the new context'[17] in which Vatican II and theology since then have set all of the topics studied. As ARCIC comments, 'we are not dealing with positions destined to remain static'.[18] Can deeper study of the richness of each of our distinctive traditions since the sixteenth century be harvested for 'straining forward to what lies ahead',[19] rather than for perpetuating controversy?

11. If dialogue partners study the period of their separated traditions in order to overcome division, they may also find a way to distinguish between the substantial agreement necessary for communion in faith and the plurality of theological opinions and expressions that always characterize the one Church. We share with the *Vatican Response* the conviction that ambiguity of expression must be overcome. But we recognize that the same faith can be expressed in a variety of ways without undermining the bond of faith. How can Churches distinguish between ambiguity and the pluralism of expression that is part of the catholicity of the one Church of Christ? We suggest more attention be paid to establishing criteria by which to judge the distinction between these two.

12. In addition, words can express our faith with accuracy and depth, and practice can reflect the understanding these words express. But no words or practice can exhaust the mystery revealed to us in Jesus Christ, and Christians should not expect the words or practice of any one ecumenical partner to achieve an exhaustive clarity that is unavailable to the Church on earth.

E. The Urgency of Unity for Evangelization

13. Our Churches feel keenly the urgency of the mandate of Christ for the unity of his Church 'so that the world may believe. . .' (Jn 17:21). In Canada, the division of our two communions directly undermines the task of evangelization. Christians in Canada face many challenges from the secular sphere and many responsibilities in interreligious relationships. In many areas of Canada, there are insufficient numbers of ordained and lay ministers from one or both of our communions to serve congregations. The commission to evangelize in Christ's name impels us to find ways in which we can live our faith more deeply together and draw on the pluralism of expressions to proclaim the one faith of the Church.

III. EUCHARISTIC DOCTRINE
A. An Area of Notable Progress

14. We find the official response of the Roman Catholic Church on the *Eucharistic Doctrine* section of *The Final Report* generally positive. The *Vatican Response* acknowledges that 'it is in respect of *Eucharistic Doctrine* that the members of the Commission were able to achieve the most notable progress toward a consensus'.[20] The issues identified in the *Vatican Response* are not so much differences or disagreements as they are requests for clarification. The *Vatican Response* states:

It is clear, as already affirmed, that on questions of eucharist and the ordained ministry, greater progress has been made. There are, however certain statements and formulations in respect of these doctrines that would need greater clarification from the Catholic point of view.

With regard to the eucharist, the faith of the Catholic Church would be even more clearly reflected in *The Final Report* if the following points were to be explicitly affirmed. . . .[21]

Like the earlier 1982 'Observations on the Final Report of ARCIC' of the Sacred Congregation for the Doctrine of the Faith, the *Vatican Response* deals with eucharistic doctrine under three headings: eucharistic sacrifice, the presence of Christ, and reservation of the sacrament.

B. Eucharistic Sacrifice

i. The Role of the Church and Anamnesis

15. On the issue of eucharistic sacrifice, the authors of the *Vatican Response* request two affirmations which would more clearly reflect the Catholic faith. First—that in the eucharist, the

> Church, doing what Christ commanded his apostles to do at the Last Supper, make present the sacrifice of Calvary. This would complete, without contradicting it, the statement made in *The Final Report*, affirming that the eucharist does not repeat the sacrifice of Christ, nor add to it. . . . [22]

16. The request for an affirmation that the 'Church . . . makes present the sacrifice of Christ' comes as a surprise. Do not both Churches already affirm that it is Christ through the Holy Spirit in the Church, who 'makes present the sacrifice of Calvary'? Since both Churches agree with this, neither would have difficulty in affirming the Church's role in making present the sacrifice of Calvary.

17. The concern of making 'present the sacrifice of Calvary' seems to have been met in ARCIC's use of the term *anamnesis*. *The Final Report* states:

> The notion of *memorial* as understood in the Passover celebration at the time of Christ—i.e., the making effective in the present of an event in the past—has opened the way to a clearer understanding of the relationship between Christ's sacrifice and the eucharist. The eucharistic memorial is no mere calling to mind of a past event or of its significance, but the Church's effectual proclamation of God's mighty acts.[23]

18. It is significant that the *Vatican Response* did not take issue with ARCIC's use of the term *anamnesis*. We recall that nine years earlier, the Sacred Congregation for the Doctrine of the Faith expressed concerns about the adequacy of the term in its 'Observations'. Though cognizant of ARCIC's use of the term *anamnesis* in understanding the eucharistic sacrifice, the *Observations* expressed concern about its sufficiency:

. . . ARCIC has explained the reason for its use of the term *anamnesis* and has recognised as legitimate the specification of *anamnesis* as sacrifice, in reference to the tradition of the Church and her liturgy. Nevertheless, insofar as this has been the object of controversy in the past, one cannot be satisfied with an explanation open to a reading which does not include an essential aspect of the mystery.[24]

Since no such concerns are raised in the *Vatican Response*, we assume that its authors are now satisfied with the use of the word *anamnesis* as an explication of the mystery of the eucharistic sacrifice. If this is correct, it indicates a significant movement towards agreement.

ii. Propitiation and the Dead

19. Associated with the concept of *anamnesis* is the propitiatory nature of the eucharist. It is on this point that the *Vatican Response* requests a second affirmation:

> The sacrifice of Christ is made present with all its effects, thus affirming the propitiatory nature of the eucharistic sacrifice, which can be applied also to the deceased. For Catholics 'the whole Church' must include the dead. The prayer for the dead is to be found in all the canons of the Mass, and the propitiatory character of the Mass as the sacrifice of Christ that may be offered for the living and the dead, including a particular dead person, is part of the Catholic faith.[25]

20. The *Vatican Response* does not request propitiatory language, but rather an assertion confirming the propitiatory nature of the eucharist. This is a more positive attitude than that taken by the authors of *Observations* who virtually claim that the propitiatory nature of the eucharist is absent in *The Final Report*. The *Observations* stated that:

> . . .The propitiatory value that Catholic dogma attributes to the eucharist . . . is not mentioned by ARCIC. . . .[26]

21. *The Final Report* states that through the eucharist 'the atoning work of Christ on the cross is proclaimed and made effective'.[27]

22. The understanding of the eucharist as a propitiatory sacrifice has, and continues to have, a place in Anglican sacramental theology, though it is affirmed in different terms. Anglican members of the Canadian ARC dialogue recall the words of John Bramhall (1594-1663), the seventeenth-century archbishop of Armagh:

> We acknowledge an Eucharistical Sacrifice of praise and Thanksgiving; a commemorative Sacrifice or a memorial of the Sacrifice of the Cross; a representative Sacrifice, or a

representation of the Passion of Christ before the eyes of His Heavenly Father; an imperative Sacrifice, or an impetration of the fruit and benefit of his Passion by way of real prayer; and, lastly, an applicative Sacrifice, or an application of His Merits unto our souls. Let him that dare go one step further than we do; and say that it is a suppletory Sacrifice, to supply the defects of the Sacrifice of the Cross. Or else let them hold their peace and speak no more against us in this point of sacrifice for ever.[28]

This classical seventeenth-century statement continues to be cited by Anglicans.

23. By requesting an explicit affirmation of the propitiatory value of the eucharistic sacrifice for the *dead*, does the *Vatican Response* implicitly suggest that ARCIC has adequately dealt with the propitiatory nature of the eucharist for the *living*? We recall the assessment of the Canadian ARC dialogue on this question in its evaluation of *The Final Report*:

> Roman Catholic members have been satisfied that concerns they might once have described in propitiatory language have been adequately presented in other ways. The use of *anamnesis* is effective in showing how 'the atoning work of Christ on the cross is proclaimed and made effective' (ED 5) and the Church continues to 'entreat the benefit of his passion on behalf of the whole Church, participates in these benefits and enters into the movement of his self-offering' (*Eucharistic Doctrine*, 5).[29]

Surely when *The Final Report* speaks of the 'whole Church' it is synonymous with the 'communion of saints', which includes the living as well as the dead.[30]

24. The propitiatory nature of the eucharistic sacrifice 'applied' to the dead is a new issue raised in the *Vatican Response*—it is dealt with neither in *The Final Report* itself nor in *Observations*. Perhaps the intent of the *Vatican Response* on the point of the application for the deceased of the propitiatory sacrifice is to draw attention to a perception about the place prayer for the departed plays in Anglicanism. Since this question is not addressed in *The Final Report*, it may be of value to address it here.

25. The *Vatican Response* states that prayers for the dead 'are to be found in all the canons of the Mass'. Anglicanism is not opposed to intercessions, including petitions for the departed, in the eucharistic prayer. For instance, eucharistic prayer no. 6 in Canada's *The Book of Alternative Services* provides an opportunity for intercessions, including petitions for the departed.[31] Intercessory petitions, however, are not a typical feature of Anglican eucharistic prayers; prayers of intercession in Anglican eucharistic rites are normally found in the general intercession ('prayers of the people'). The invariable intercession in the Canadian *The Book of Common Prayer* contains a petition for the departed.[32] The prayers of the people in *The Book of Alternative Services* are to include petitions for the departed,[33] and models are provided in the litanies.[34] While intercessions, including petitions for the de-

parted, are not narrowly confined to the eucharistic prayer in Anglican liturgies, they are constitutive of the eucharistic rite as a whole.

Roman Catholic members of the Canadian ARC dialogue recall that in fact not all eucharistic prayers in the Roman rite contain prayers for the departed. The first ICEL editions of eucharistic prayers for Masses with Children and Masses of Reconciliation omit prayers for the departed in the canon. For example, both eucharistic prayer no. 3 of the Mass with Children and eucharistic prayer no. 2 for the Mass of Reconciliation lack such petitions.[35]

26. Within Anglicanism there is some hesitation about praying for the dead. Many evangelical Anglicans, in particular, are apprehensive about intercession for the departed. Perhaps the authors of the *Vatican Response* are cognizant of this tension within the Anglican Communion.

27. We recognize, however, that since the Reformation prayer for the dead has been a continuous element of Anglican liturgical formularies, in particular *The Book of Common Prayer*. We note the following collect from the Burial Office of the Prayer Book of 1552:

> Almightie God, with whom doe lyue the spirites of them that departe hence in the lord, and in whom the soules of them that be elected, after they be deliuered from the burden of the fleshe, be in ioye and felicitie: We geue thee hearty thankes, for that it hath pleased thee to deliuer thys N. Our brother out of the myseryes of this sinneful world: beseeching thee, that it may please thee of they gracious goodnesse, shortely to accomplyssh the nounbre of thyne electe, and to hasten thy kingdome, that we with this our brother, and al other departed in the true faith of thy holy name, maye haue our perfect consummacion and blisse, both in body and soule, in thy eternal and euerlasting glory. Amen.[36]

Anglican burial liturgies since 1552 have retained this collect; many supplementary prayers for the departed have been added to the Burial Office. For instance, the Burial Office in *The Book of Common Prayer (Canada)* ends with the ancient petition common to both our traditions. 'Rest eternal grant unto *him*, O Lord, and let light perpetual shine upon *him*'.[37]

28. The *Vatican Response* requests the affirmation that the 'sacrifice of Christ is made present with all its effects, thus affirming the propitiatory nature of the eucharistic sacrifice, which can be applied also to the deceased. For Catholics "the whole Church" must include the dead'. We find the language of 'application' curious, since the liturgical texts of neither of our traditions employ such terminology. We recognise that in the context of the eucharistic liturgy in general, and in the eucharistic prayer in particular, both our traditions pray for 'the whole Church' to include the living as well as the departed. When our Churches pray liturgically for particular individual Christians, living or dead, such petition is always understood to be in the context of the Church.

C. Christ's Presence in the Eucharist

29. The *Vatican Response* acknowledges the affirmations in *Eucharistic Doctrine* of the real presence of Christ in the eucharist. For example, they note: 'the bread and wine "become" the body and blood of Christ'. Moreover, the *Response* maintains that these affirmations

> . . . can certainly be interpreted in conformity with Catholic faith. They are insufficient, however, to remove all ambiguity regarding the mode of the real presence which is due to a substantial change in the elements. The Catholic Church holds that Christ in the eucharist makes himself present sacramentally and substantially when under the species of bread and wine these earthly realities are changed into the reality of his body and blood, soul and divinity.[38]

The *Vatican Response* is wary about the adequacy of the affirmations in *Eucharistic Doctrine* to *remove all ambiguity* pertaining to the mode of Christ's presence. Yet in spite of the negative tone of this judgement, it is a more positive evaluation of the *Eucharistic Doctrine* section of *The Final Report* than that in the *Observations*.

30. Like the *Vatican Response*, the *Observations* cite instances in *Eucharistic Doctrine* where affirmations of the presence of Christ are consistent with Roman Catholic teaching. However, *Observations* list several instances where expressions of the real presence can be perceived with the understanding that after the eucharistic prayer the bread and wine 'remain as such in their ontological substance even while becoming the sacramental mediation of the body of blood of Christ'.[39] These affirmations, the Sacred Congregation for the Doctrine of the Faith says, 'do not seem to indicate adequately what the Church understands by "transubstantiation"'.[40] Yet the *Vatican Response* cites no such instances in *The Final Report* where affirmations of the presence of Christ are judged inadequate.

31. The shift in language from 'inadequacy' to 'ambiguity' reveals a more positive appreciation of *Eucharistic Doctrine* on the part of the authors of the *Vatican Response*. Presumably the texts once cited by *Observations* as 'inadequate' can now be understood to be merely 'ambiguous'. Moreover, the *Response* affirms that all of the ARCIC statements on the eucharistic presence of Christ 'can certainly be interpreted in conformity with Catholic faith'.

32. While the *Vatican Response* speaks of Christ's presence in terms of 'substantiality' and 'substantial change', unlike *The Final Report* it does not actually use the term 'transubstantiation'. We would find it helpful to know whether the authors of the *Vatican Response* agree with the understanding of transubstantiation offered in *The Final Report*:

> The word *transubstantiation* is commonly used in the Roman Catholic Church to indicate that God acting in the eucharist effects a change in the inner reality of the elements. The term should be seen as affirming the *fact* of Christ's presence and of the

mysterious and radical change which takes place. In contemporary Roman Catholic theology it is not understood as explaining *how* the change takes place.[41]

33. It seems to us that like the *Observations*, the *Vatican Response* is anxious about the *mode* of Christ's presence, no doubt out of concern that his presence in the sacrament be clearly stated. But we think that affirmations of his presence are made unequivocally in *The Final Report*. We wonder why the authors of the *Vatican Response* seem to expect the members of ARCIC to say more about *how* Christ is present than the Fathers of the Council of Trent were able to say.[42] It is the reality of Christ's presence which is the primary matter of faith, not the precise mode of that presence.

D. Reservation of the Eucharist

34. Again, like the *Observations*, the *Vatican Response* expresses concern on the issue of the reservation of the eucharistic elements:

On the question of the reservation of the eucharist, the statement that there are those who 'find any kind of adoration of Christ in the reserved sacrament unacceptable', create concern from the Roman Catholic point of view. This section of *Eucharistic Doctrine: Elucidations* seeks to allay any such doubts, but one remains with the conviction that this is an area in which real consensus between Anglicans and Roman Catholics is lacking.[43]

35. In spite of the *Elucidations* on *Eucharistic Doctrine*, the *Vatican Response* is left with a 'conviction' that there is a lack of consensus on this point. In the context in which the word 'conviction' appears, it is clear that here the word has more to do with 'opinion' and 'supposition' than with 'judgement'. This is in marked contrast to the section on 'Reservation and Adoration of the Eucharist' in *Observations*. The authors of *Observations* have interpreted Elucidation no. 9 on reservation as admitting not only a difference in practice, but also in 'theological judgements' relating to it.[44] The *Vatican Response* does not mention 'theological judgements' on the issue; rather, a concern is expressed and a supposition is voiced.

36. Moreover, the *Observations* contrasted the Tridentine statement on the adoration of the blessed sacrament to the 'Black Rubric' of earlier editions of the *Book of Common Prayer*. In the *Vatican Response* there is no reference to either Trent or the 'Black Rubric' on the matter. Is this a tacit recognition of the reality of Anglican attitudes towards the reserved sacrament?[45]

While the sacrament is reserved in our Churches for distribution to the sick, each of our communions contains a range of different forms of eucharistic piety related to the reserved sacrament. In Canada, evangelical Anglicans and Eastern rite Catholic parishes do not regularly practice eucharistic devotion that focuses on the reserved sacrament, while some Anglo-Catholic and Western rite Roman Catholic parishes have sometimes made such devotional practices a valued part of their parish worship.[46]

E. A Convergence

37. The *Vatican Response* is clear that until ARCIC is able to endorse or incorporate the requested clarifications, it will be difficult for the Roman Catholic Church to speak of 'substantial agreement' between our two communions on eucharistic doctrine.

38. Nevertheless, the *Vatican Response*, at least with respect to eucharistic doctrine, already recognises and affirms a remarkable convergence. Rather than register objections, the *Response* merely invites 'more explicit clarifications' which would reflect more clearly the faith of the Roman Catholic Church. While calling for greater clarifications, the *Vatican Response* positively affirms that the faith of the Catholic Church is reflected in the agreed statement on eucharistic doctrine.

39. The General Evaluation at the beginning of the *Vatican Response* states that the Explanatory Note, the lengthier section of the *Response*, is intended to give a 'detailed summary of the areas where differences or ambiguities remain which seriously hinder the restoration of full communion in faith and in the sacramental life'.[47] Where clarifications are not requested in the Explanatory Note, we must assume that there exists an implicit endorsement of *The Final Report's* treatment of eucharistic doctrine; in particular we note the use of the term *anamnesis* as a way of understanding the sacrificial and propitiatory nature of the eucharist. Considering the treatment of eucharistic doctrine in *The Final Report* as a whole, the Canadian ARC dialogue finds no reason to consider our Churches divided on this great sacrament so intimately linked with the unity of the Church.

IV. MINISTRY AND ORDINATION
A. 'Significant Consensus'

40. It is encouraging to read in the *Vatican Response* the areas of ministry and ordination in which 'significant consensus' has been achieved by ARCIC I in *The Final Report*. The *Vatican Response* details these areas as: the clear distinction between the priesthood of all the baptised and that of the ordained; the recognition that the ordained priesthood belongs 'to another realm of the gifts of the Spirit'[48]; the sacramental nature of ordination; the necessity of ordained ministry to the nature of the Church, and the sacramental nature of the Church as a whole. The *Response* also positively affirms that 'it is only the ordained minister who presides at the eucharist'.[49] It should be noted however that *Ministry and Ordination* actually says, 'Hence it is right that he who has oversight in the Church and is the focus of its unity *should* preside at the celebration of the eucharist'.[50]

The nuance represented by the actual text, while certainly indicating the expectation that only the priest presides may be the reason for some concern as expressed later in the *Response*.

The *Vatican Response* then proceeds to detail the areas where 'complete agreement' or even 'convergence' has eluded the Commission.

B. Ordination and Sacraments

41. The *Vatican Response* calls for a clearer articulation that 'only a validly ordained priest can be the minister who, in the person of Christ, brings into being the sacrament of the eucharist'.[51] Throughout *The Final Report's* Ministry and Ordination sections, the responsibility for the sacraments is assigned to the ordained minister. The precise actions of the minister noted in the *Response* are not detailed in the *Ministry and Ordination* statement but are noted in the *Elucidations* section following,

> The Statement (para. 13) explains that the ordained ministry is called priestly principally because it has *a particular sacramental relationship with Christ as High Priest*. At the eucharist Christ's people do what he commanded in memory of himself and Christ unites them sacramentally with himself in his self-offering. But in this action it is only the ordained minister who presides at the eucharist, in which, in the name of Christ and on behalf of his Church, he recites the narrative of the institution of the Last Supper, and invokes the Holy Spirit upon the gifts.[52]

The *Elucidation* is clear that there is a special relationship between the priest and Christ in the celebration of the eucharist.

42. Some confusion may be evident in the use of the word 'ministers' in *The Final Report* inasmuch as deacons are included in those who share in the oversight of the Church. However, *The Final Report*, after detailing the responsibilities of the presbyter, including presiding at the eucharist and pronouncing absolution, also states, 'Deacons, although *not so empowered* are associated with bishops and presbyters in the ministry of word and sacrament and assist in oversight'.[53] A look at the practice of both communions would assist here in allaying fears, as neither Church allows any other than presbyters and bishops to preside at the eucharist. The preface to the Ordinal of the *Book of Common Prayer* of the Anglican Church of Canada affirms that the offices of deacon, priest, and bishop

> . . . were evermore had in such revered estimation, that no man might presume to execute any of them except he were called, tried, examined and known to have such qualities as are requisite for the same; and also by public prayer, with Imposition of Hands, were approved and admitted thereunto by lawful authority . . . according to

the form hereafter following or has had formally Episcopal Consecration or Ordination.[54]

The 'form hereafter' designates the bishop as the only lawful authority.

43. However, the concern may also lie in the desire for a clear articulation that the priest 'brings into being the sacrament of the eucharist' and thus 'offers sacramentally the redemptive sacrifice of Christ'. These actions are certainly implied in *The Final Report* when it states,

> Because the eucharist is the memorial of the sacrifice of Christ, the action of the presiding minister in reciting again the words of Christ at the last supper and distributing to the assembly the holy gifts is seen to stand *in a sacramental relation* to what Christ himself did in offering his own sacrifice.[55]

Further clarity about the exact nature of the concern for the authors of the *Response* would be helpful.

C. The Institution of Orders

44. A second area of concern for the *Vatican Response* is the origin of orders, asking for a clear statement 'that it was Christ himself who instituted the sacrament of orders'[56] and pointing specifically to the absence of any reference to the character of priestly ordination. We would want to affirm the wider context of priestly ministry which, in both our Communions, points to the unity of word and sacrament, with the priest as presider at both.[57] As noted above, and affirmed by the *Response*, the priest stands 'in sacramental relation to what Christ himself did in offering his own sacrifice'. Later in the same section of the *Report* this is reiterated:

> There is in the eucharist a memorial (*anamnesis*) of the totality of God's reconciling action in Christ, who *through his minister* presides at the Lord's Supper and gives himself sacramentally.[58]

Though the word 'character' is not used in *The Final Report* the reality of the indelible character of ordination is noted:

> In this sacramental act (ordination), the gift of God is bestowed upon the ministers, . . . and the Spirit seals those whom he has chosen and consecrated . . . so the gift and calling of God to the ministers are irrevocable. For this reason, ordination is unrepeatable in both our Churches.[59]

45. This should be reassuring to the authors of the *Response*, as it does affirm the distinction between the ministerial priesthood and the common priesthood of the baptised and is consistent with the positive affirmations made earlier by the *Response*. We wonder what additional clarifications are needed in the link between the priesthood of Christ and that of the ordained ministry.

46. The link between Christ and the institution of the sacrament of orders is implied in *The Final Report* when it states:

> [j]ust as the original apostles did not choose themselves but were chosen and commissioned by Jesus, so those who are ordained are called by Christ in the Church and through the Church.[60]

The desire to see a clearly stated link between Christ and the institution of orders echoes, by implication, the concern noted later in the *Response* regarding the historical-critical method. In the comments of this dialogue on the *Observations* by the Sacred Congregation for the Doctrine of the Faith the Roman Catholic sub-committee notes:

> [p]resent day Roman Catholic sacramental theology sees the institution of the sacraments in a different light than was possible at Trent. Institution of a sacrament by Christ does not necessarily imply a direct and explicit act in the course of the earthly life of Jesus by which he singled out certain words and actions and gave a mandate to his apostles to repeat these words and actions as a sacrament.[61]

Also, the response of the Canadian Conference of Catholic Bishops to *The Final Report* notes,

> That the threefold pattern of ministry emerged only gradually, . . . presents no more difficulty for the Catholic faith than does the similarly gradual formation of the New Testament canon itself.[62]

47. *The Final Report* is clear, 'we believe that the provision of a ministry of this kind is part of God's design for his people'.[63] In addition, the *Report* speaks of ordination as an expression of the continuing apostolicity and catholicity of the whole Church carrying on the commissioning of the apostles by Jesus Christ to those he calls in and through the Church. 'Not only is their vocation from Christ but their qualification for exercising such a ministry is the gift of the Spirit. . . '.[64] Given the newer formulations of the nature of the dominical institution accepted in current Roman Catholic theology, which are in accord with *The Final Report* formulation, we wonder what language or formulation would be acceptable to the authors of the *Response*?

D. The Ordination of Women

48. Certainly the greatest difficulty lying between our two Communions in regard to ministry and ordination concerns the ordination of women. The *Vatican Response* notes the important differences in our communions concerning the subject of ordination and its link with the nature of the sacrament of orders. This may underlie the concern in the previous section noting the relation of the priesthood and its 'configuration with the priesthood of Christ'.

49. The thorough discussion of the eucharist in *The Final Report* emphasizes the uniqueness of Christ's sacrifice and the work of the Holy Spirit in uniting people with Christ and his self-giving.

> Because the eucharist is the memorial of the sacrifice of Christ, the action of the presiding minister in reciting again the words of Christ at the last supper and distributing to the assembly the holy gifts is seen to stand in a sacramental relation to what Christ himself did in offering his own sacrifice.[65]

If the identification of the presider with Christ is the primary concern in the discussion of the ordination of women, we must ask, to what extent is the male gender of the presider a necessary condition for that sacramental relationship? Or to what degree does the institution of orders by Christ require the identity of present-day subjects with the original 'ordinands'?

50. The *Vatican Response* notes, '[d]ifferences in this connection must therefore affect agreement reached on ministry and ordination'.[66] The experience of the Anglican-Roman Catholic Dialogue in Canada on this issue has shown that our agreement has not been undermined in this area while we continue our dialogue. Areas of further dialogue and study are indicated for the future including the interpretation of scripture and the place of tradition and culture. In the discussion by ARC-Canada of the experience of women's ministries it has been proposed that 'the issue of women's ordination be approached as a disputed question about the enculturation of the Gospel'[67] as a way forward in our ongoing dialogue.

E. Apostolic Succession

51. The last area of concern noted by the *Response* is that of apostolic succession, an area of critical importance, as seen in its statement:

> This question, then, lies at the very heart of the ecumenical discussion and touches virtually all the themes dealt with by ARCIC I: the reality of the eucharist, the sacramentality of the ministerial priesthood, the nature of the Roman primacy.[68]

It is however difficult to determine the exact nature of the concern. As noted in *The Final Report* [*Elucidation*]:

> We both maintain that *episcope* must be exercised by ministers ordained in the apostolic succession. Both our communions have retained and remain faithful to the threefold ministry centered on the episcopacy as the form in which this *episcope* is to be exercised.[69]

There is nothing in *The Final Report* that contradicts *Lumen Gentium* (Vatican Council II's Dogmatic Constitution on the Church), no. 20. Our Churches seek to heal our division, and as the *Final Report* anticipates, full communion with the bishop of Rome will be a sign of its realization.

52. *The Final Report* and *Lumen Gentium* 20 each speaks of both the apostolic line of bishops in fidelity to the apostolic tradition and of the historical continuity with the same. The *Response* speaks of a 'causal' relationship between unbroken lines of episcopal succession and 'apostolic teaching'. For example, is the concern a reflection of a deeper worry in recognizing the apostolic teaching in a particular communion while unable to recognize an 'unbroken' line of succession? Or in being unable to recognize apostolic teaching because of a broken line of succession? If the latter, this would be a cause for deep concern in ecumenical discussion.

53. We are grateful for the positive appreciation by the *Response* of a number of areas in *Ministry and Ordination*, particularly in reference to the priesthood. However, some of the requests for clarification by the *Response* remain unclear in themselves and we would look for a more sharply articulated indication of the concerns expressed. Further work certainly remains, particularly concerning the ordination of women, and we look forward to ongoing dialogue in these areas.

V. AUTHORITY IN THE CHURCH
A. Remarkable Progress

54. The *Vatican Response* judges that 'quite remarkable progress . . . has been made in respect of authority in the Church',[70] and it singles out *Authority in the Church II*, 24-27 as offering 'a very positive presentation' of 'the magisterial authority of the Church'.[71] '[D]espite considerable convergence', however, 'full agreement on the nature and the significance of the Roman primacy has not been reached'.[72]

55. The *Response* begins its assessment of ARCIC's statement on authority by pointing out that the *Final Report* 'makes no claim to substantial agreement' on the question of authority. 'The most that has been achieved is a certain convergence, which is but a first step along the path that seeks consensus as a prelude to unity'.[73] It is true that *The Final Report* does not claim full agreement on authority, but the *Response* overlooks the very clear

claim by ARCIC that *Authority in the Church I*, 1-23 'amounts to a consensus on authority in the Church and, in particular, on the basic principles of primacy. This consensus is of fundamental importance'.[74]

B. Papal Infallibility and Reception

56. As an example of areas essential to Catholic doctrine on which complete agreement or even convergence is still lacking, the *Response* cites, as did the 1982 *Observations*, a statement by Anglican members of ARCIC:

In spite of our agreement over the need of a universal primacy in a united Church, Anglicans do not accept the guaranteed possession of such a gift of divine assistance in judgement necessarily attached to the office of the bishop of Rome by virtue of which his formal decisions can be known to be wholly assured before their reception by the faithful.[75]

The *Response* seems to assume that what Anglicans are opposing here is what Roman Catholics actually believe. Some Roman Catholics may hold the view that Anglicans reject, but Roman Catholic teaching does not oblige Catholics to make such an interpretation.[76] As ARC-Canada put it in 1985:

Do Roman Catholics really differ from Anglicans here? If Roman Catholics were proposed a definition for assent that did not seem to have explicit or implicit grounding in the Bible and seemed foreign to the faith they had been taught, would they not also have not just the right but the duty to make serious enquires before considering the definition?[77]

57. The *Response* judges that the crucial section, *Authority in the Church II*, 24-27, is a 'very positive presentation', and it welcomes the 'clear statement' that reception of a defined truth by the People of God 'does not create truth nor legitimize the decision'.[78] It would seem, however, says the *Response*, that *The Final Report*:

sees the 'assent of the faithful' as required for the recognition that a doctrinal decision of the pope or of an ecumenical council is immune from error (*Authority in the Church II*, 27 and 31). For the Catholic Church, the certain knowledge of any defined truth is not guaranteed by the reception of the faithful that such is in conformity with Scripture and tradition, but by the authoritative definition itself on the part of the authentic teachers.[79]

It seems to us that in the latter sentence the *Response* is opposing something that *The Final Report* is not affirming, the idea that reception by the faithful 'guarantees . . . the certain knowledge of defined truth'. *The Final Report* does not see reception as a 'guarantee', but as 'the ultimate *indication* that the Church's authoritative decision . . . has been truly preserved from error by the Holy Spirit'.[80]

58. We are disappointed that the carefully nuanced expression of *The Final Report's* view of reception found in *Authority in the Church II*, 25 and the accompanying *Elucidation* is not directly addressed by the *Response*. The *Response's* own formulation, that 'the certain knowledge of any defined truth is . . . guaranteed . . . by the authoritative definition itself on the part of the authentic teachers', seems, on the other hand, to leave no place for the *consensio ecclesiarum* that is a 'rule of faith even for papal definitions',[81] for the *assensus ecclesiae* which can never be lacking in doctrinal definitions, or for the *consensus totius communitatis* that is expressed in such definitions.[82]

59. As ARCIC notes, Vatican I lays down 'very rigorous conditions' for the exercise of papal infallibility.[83] For Roman Catholics, the judgement that the conditions have been fulfilled is decisive for the reception of a definition. We thus reaffirm what ARC-Canada stated in its Reception Statement of *The Final Report* in 1985: 'The assent of the faithful is not necessary for the gift of divine assistance to be operative but for it to be recognized'.[84]

C. Marian Dogmas

60. The *Response's* view that ARCIC 'has not been able to record any real consensus on the Marian dogmas' overlooks the fact that ARCIC did not undertake to study the dogmas themselves, but looked at them more as an illustration of the exercise of papal teaching authority. We are pleased to note how much Anglicans and Roman Catholics have in common with regard to Mary, as is clear from the *Response's* own citation of *Authority in the Church*: 'Catholics and Anglicans can agree in much that the dogmas of the Immaculate Conception and Assumption are designed to affirm'.[85] We think it is also noteworthy that both Anglicans and Roman Catholics observe festivals honouring Mary and recognize her place in the communion of saints, as well as in finding in Mary 'a model of holiness, obedience and faith. . .'.[86]

61. ARCIC is well aware that many Anglicans still have problems with the Marian definitions. Part of the reason for this, as the *Response* points out, is that more study needs to be done on the Petrine ministry itself. We are pleased that ARCIC II is continuing to work on these matters. We join with the suggestion of the Canadian Conference of Catholic Bishops that, in view of the important role the liturgy has played in enabling Catholics to develop a deep love for the Mother of God, attention to the richness of our different liturgical traditions might help Anglicans and Roman Catholics to move forward on a matter where full consensus does not yet exist.[87]

D. The Petrine Ministry

62. The incomplete accord on the Marian dogmas, says the *Response*, 'illustrates the need for much further study to be done in respect of the Petrine ministry in the Church'.[88] The *Response* finds examples which it believes 'illustrate the reservations that still exist on the part of the Anglican community' concerning the Petrine ministry. One example is that '[m]uch Anglican objection has been directed against the manner of the exercise and particular claims of the Roman primacy rather than against universal primacy as such'.[89] Devout and faithful Roman Catholics throughout the centuries, including canonized saints, have had and continue to have reservations about certain examples of the exercise of the Roman primacy that are judged to be harmful to the well-being of the Christian people. Roman Catholics likewise do not want to make exaggerated or otherwise misleading claims concerning the Roman primacy. While they are grateful for the primatial ministry of the Bishop of Rome, Roman Catholics know that it, too, is summoned by Christ to the continual reformation of which the Church always has need.[90]

63. Another example mentioned by the *Response* seems to us to be stating a simple question of fact, namely, that less than cordial relations between our two communions in the past 'have not encouraged reflection by Anglicans on the positive significance of the Roman primacy. . . .'.[91] Moreover, far from illustrating 'reservations that still exist' on the part of Anglicans, the quotation actually refers to *affirmations* by Anglican theologians that 'in changed circumstances, it might be possible for the Churches of the Anglican Communion to recognise the development of the Roman primacy as . . . an effect of the guidance of the Holy Spirit in the Church'.[92]

E. The Scope of Doctrinal Definitions

64. The *Response* repeats an objection against *Authority in the Church* about the scope of doctrinal definitions by councils that was already contained in the *Observations* of 1982. The objection seems to attribute to ARCIC a reductive understanding of the scope of doctrinal definitions—that is, that they are 'concerned with "fundamental doctrines"' or 'central truths of salvation'. In apparent opposition to this view, the *Response* notes:

> The Catholic Church believes that the councils or the pope, even acting alone, are able to teach, if necessary in a definitive way, within the range of all truth revealed by God.[93]

Setting aside the question of the pope 'acting alone',[94] ARC-Canada does not see any real opposition here. ARCIC nowhere excludes what the *Response* affirms in the sentence just cited. In fact, the text of ARCIC, in places other than the one cited by the *Response*, clearly supports the *Response's* affirmations.[95] *Authority in the Church* recognizes not only the need 'for a universal primate who, presiding over the *koinonia*, can speak with authority in the name of the Church' but also states that the purpose of this primatial ministry is:

to recall and emphasize some important truth; to expound the faith more lucidly; to expose error; to draw out implications not sufficiently recognized; and to show how Christian truth applies to contemporary issues.[96]

F. Status of a Church Not in Full Communion with the See of Rome

65. We agree with the *Response* that, according to Vatican II, 'a Church outside of communion with the Roman Pontiff lacks more than just the visible manifestation of unity with the Church of Christ which subsists in the Roman Catholic Church'.[97] ARCIC itself recognizes that the universal primate is not only the sign of the visible communion of the Churches, but also 'an instrument through which unity in diversity is realized'.[98] For ARCIC, then, as well as for Vatican II, a church not in full communion with the universal primate would lack not only a visible sign of universal Christian communion, but also a God-given means by which that communion is to be maintained.[99]

G. The Foundation of the Universal Primacy by Jesus

66. In its strongest negation of anything *The Final Report* has to say on the question of authority, the *Response* states:

[I]t is not possible . . . to accept the interpretation given in *Authority in the Church II*, concerning the *jus divinum* of the First Vatican Council, namely that it 'need not be taken to imply the universal primacy as a permanent institution was directly founded by Jesus during his life on earth' (no. 11). The Catholic Church sees rather in the primacy of the successors of Peter something positively intended by God and deriving from the will and institution of Jesus Christ.[100]

But this is not opposed to what *The Final Report* affirms. For *The Final Report*, the primacy is part of God's design for the universal communion.[101] The sentence from *Authority in the Church II* that caused difficulty for the *Response* does not deny that it is from Jesus that the Petrine ministry derives. The ARCIC statement can be understood to mean that the special commission given to Peter was made only after the resurrection, a view supported by New Testament scholarship.[102]

H. The Interpretation of Scripture in Relation to Tradition

67. In its final substantive critique concerning authority, the *Response* suggests that ARCIC 'seems to ignore' the Catholic affirmation:

that the historical-critical method is not sufficient for the interpretation of Scripture. Such interpretation cannot be separated from the living tradition of the Church which receives the message of Scripture. *The Final Report* seems to ignore this when dealing with the interpretation of the Petrine text of the New Testament, for it states that they 'do not offer sufficient basis' on which to establish the primacy of the Bishop of Rome.[103]

We find this objection puzzling inasmuch as *The Final Report* acknowledges the insufficiency of the historical-critical method by saying that the New Testament texts by themselves, isolated from the later interpretation by the Church, are not sufficient to establish the primacy of the Bishop of Rome. One of the reasons Anglican members of ARCIC were able to accept the Roman primacy was their belief in the providential guidance of the Church by the Holy Spirit, which is another way of speaking about the living Tradition of the Church.[104] For *Authority in the Church*, just as the *homoousion* of Nicaea is not found explicitly in the New Testament, but is a genuine development of it,[105] so, too, the development of the Petrine ministry of the Roman See is not grounded solely on history or solely upon explicit New Testament testimony, but also on 'the providential action of the Holy Spirit'.[106] We thus find in *The Final Report* a consensus rather than a disagreement on this important issue.

68. A second instance where the *Response* thinks *The Final Report* is deficient in its understanding of the interpretation of Scripture is *The Final Report's* statement that proposed definitions of faith need to be 'manifestly a legitimate interpretation of biblical faith and in line with the orthodox tradition'.[107] The *Response* does not make clear what is objectionable about the quoted phrase. Perhaps the problem lies with the term 'manifestly'. Definitions are surely unnecessary where there is no controversy about the meaning of a particular biblical teaching. To this extent the Scripture is not manifestly clear. For Roman Catholics as well as for Anglicans, however, doctrinal definitions must be grounded in the teaching of Scripture; to that extent there must be some clear, if only implicit, biblical basis for the definition. For both Churches, as well, a doctrinal definition would be problematical if it were not 'in line with orthodox tradition'.

I. Further Study Needed

69. In view of ARCIC's own recognition that more study is required before full agreement is reached on the question of *Authority in the Church*, we are not surprised that the *Response* also calls for further study of some points. We are encouraged by the *Response's* appreciation of the fact that 'quite remarkable progress' and 'considerable convergence' have already been achieved on the question of authority. We think that some of the objections raised by the *Response* are based on a misreading of *Authority in the Church*, while others seem to result from a disregard for the range of legitimate theological opinion that exists within the Roman Catholic Church. We are confident that there is a deeper and broader area of agreement than the *Response* has recognized.

VI. CONCLUSION

70. In this reply, we have spoken of how encouraged we are by some parts of the *Vatican Response*. We have also spoken of how sobered or puzzled other parts have made us. We look forward to our continuing cooperation with ARCIC and to continuing dialogue with the Congregation for the Doctrine of the Faith and the Pontifical Council for Promoting Christian Unity as well as the provinces of the Anglican Communion coordinated through the Anglican Consultative Council.

71. At their 1989 meeting, Archbishop Runcie and Pope John Paul II urged those who long for the unity of the Church 'not to abandon either their hope or work for unity'.[108] We pledge ourselves with willing hearts to collaborate in the work of further study in areas where it is necessary to achieve the goal of full communion. For our hope in the dialogue between our two communions we rely on the help of Jesus Christ whose prayer 'that all might be one . . . so that the world may believe. . .' (Jn 17:21) cannot fail.

NOTES

1   John Paul II and Robert Runcie, 'Common Declaration' (2 October 1989), *Origins* 19 (1989–90), p. 316.

2   'A Meeting of the Pope and Canterbury's Archbishop [John Paul II and George Leonard Carey] 25 May 1992', *Origins* 22 (1992–93), p. 51.

3   John Paul II and Robert Runcie, 'Common Declaration', p. 317.

4   *Vatican Response to 'The Final Report' of the Anglican Roman Catholic International Commission* [as 'Vatican Responds to ARCIC I *Final Report*'], *Origins* 21 (1991–92), 441–448. All page references to the *Vatican Response* are to this version; this first citation is to p. 441.

5   *Vatican Response*, p. 443.

6   *Vatican Response*, p. 441.

7   *Vatican Response*, p. 443.

8   *Vatican Response*, p. 443.

9   *Vatican Response*, p. 447.

10 Anglican Ecumenical Consultation, ed., *The Emmaus Report* (London: Church House, 1987).

11 Anglican Roman Catholic International Commission, *The Final Report*, 'Authority in the Church II' (London: SPCK and Catholic Truth Society, 1982), no. 33, p. 98; henceforth *The Final Report*.

12 *Vatican Response*, p. 447.

13 Paul VI and Michael Ramsey, 'Common Declaration by Pope Paul VI and the Archbishop of Canterbury' (24 March 1966), reprinted in *The Final Report*, p. 118.

14 *The Final Report*, 'Preface', pp. 1–2.

15 *The Final Report*, 'Preface', p. 2.

16 *The Final Report*, 'Preface', pp. 1–2.

17 *The Final Report*, Ministry and Ordination, no. 17, p. 38.

18 *The Final Report*, Authority in the Church II, no. 33, p. 98.

19   *The Final Report*, 'Preface', p. 1.

20   *Vatican Response*, p. 443.

21   *Vatican Response*, p. 445.

22   *Vatican Response*, p. 445.

23   *The Final Report*, Eucharistic Doctrine, no. 5, p. 14.

24   Sacred Congregation for the Doctrine of the Faith, *Observations on the ARCIC Final Report* [*Origins* 11(1981-82), 752-756], p. 753; henceforth *Observations*.

25   *Vatican Response*, p. 445.

26   *Observations*, p. 754.

27   *The Final Report*, Eucharistic Doctrine, no. 5, p. 14.

28   John Bramhall, from *A Replication to the Bishop of Chalcedon's Survey of the Vindication of the Church of England from the Criminous Schism* IX 6, in P. E. More and F. L. Cross, editors, *Anglicanism* (London: SPCK, 1951), p. 496.

29   'Anglican-Roman Catholic Dialogue of Canada's Response to ARCIC's *The Final Report*' (July, 1985), pp. 4-5.

30   We recall a petition from the Prayer of Consecration in the Canadian Prayer Book eucharistic rite: 'And we entirely desire thy fatherly goodness mercifully to accept this our sacrifice of praise and Thanksgiving, most humbly beseeching thee to grant, that by the merits and death of thy Son Jesus Christ, and through faith in his blood, we and all *thy whole Church* may obtain remission of our sins, and all other benefits of his passion' [*The Book of Common Prayer* (Canada) (Toronto: Anglican Book Centre, 1962), p. 83 (emphasis ours)].

31   'Remember all who have died in the peace of Christ, and those whose faith is known to you alone; bring them into the place of eternal joy and light'. Eucharistic Prayer, no. 6, *The Book of Alternative Services* (BAS) (Toronto: Anglican Book Centre, 1985), p. 210; henceforth *BAS*.

32   *The Book of Common Prayer (Canada)* (Toronto: Anglican Book Centre, 1962), p. 76: 'We remember before thee, O Lord, all thy servants departed this life in thy faith and fear; and we bless thy holy Name for all who in life and death have glorified thee; beseeching thee to give us grace that rejoicing in their fellowship, we may follow their good examples, and *with them be partakers of thy heavenly kingdom*' (emphasis added).

33   *BAS*, pp. 53, 70, 190, *et passim*.

34   For example, litany no. 1, *BAS*, p. 111: 'For all who have died (especially . . .), let us pray to the Lord', litany no. 18, *BAS*, p. 127: 'We pray for those who have died in the peace of Christ, and for those whose faith is known to you alone, that they may have a place in your eternal kingdom'.

35   *Masses with Children, Masses of Reconciliation* (Ottawa: Canadian Catholic Conference, 1975), pp. 98-102; 109-113.

36   'The Ordre for The Buriall of The Dead', The Book of Common Prayer 1552, in *The First and Second Prayer Books of Edward VI* (London: Everyman, 1952), p. 427.

37   The Book of Common Prayer (Canada) (Toronto: Anglican Book Centre, 1962), p. 601.

38   *Vatican Response*, p. 445.

39 *Observations*, p. 754.

40 *Observations*, p. 754.

41 *The Final Report*, Eucharistic Doctrine, no. 6, note 2, p. 14.

42 For Trent, Christ is at the right hand of the Father according to his natural mode of existence (*iuxta modum exsistendi naturalem*), and he is sacramentally present to us in his substance in a way we can scarcely express in words (*ea existendi ratione, quam etsi verbis exprimere vix possumus*)' [Denzinger Schönmetzer, 1636].

43 *Vatican Response*, p. 445.

44 *Observations*, p. 754. Cf. *The Final Report*, Eucharistic Doctrine, *Elucidation* 9: 'That there can be a divergence in matters of practice and in *theological judgements* [emphasis ours] relating to them, without destroying a common eucharistic faith, illustrates what we mean by substantial agreement' (p. 24).

45 The 'Black Rubric' is a rubric found in the 1552 *The Book of Common Prayer* [hereafter *BCP*], which denied 'any real and essential presence of Christ's natural flesh and blood' in the eucharistic elements. It was inserted at the last moment, without Parliamentary authority. It lasted as long as the *BCP* of 1552: one year. Elizabeth I had it removed from the 1559 *BCP*. The 1662 *BCP* inserted a greatly modified version at the end of the Communion Office which merely denied the 'Corporal Presence of Christ's natural Flesh and Blood'. In an amended form of the 1662 rubric, the Canadian *BCP* of 1959/62 adds: 'The Body of Christ is given, taken, and eaten, in the Supper, only after an heavenly and spiritual manner' (*BCP*, p. 92). Cf. the tenet of the catechism which teaches that the outward sign of the Lord's Supper is bread and wine, and the inward part, or thing signified, is the Body and Blood of Christ (*BCP*, p. 551). The 'Black Rubric' is not included in modern Anglican liturgical rites.

46 'Anglican-Roman Catholic Dialogue of Canada's Response to ARCIC's *The Final Report*' (July 1985), p. 6.

47 *Vatican Response*, 'General Evaluation', p. 443.

48 *Vatican Response*, p. 443.

49 *Vatican Response*, p. 443.

50 *The Final Report*, Ministry and Ordination, no. 12, p. 35 (emphasis added).

51 *Vatican Response*, 445.

52 *The Final Report*, Ministry and Ordination, *Elucidation* no. 2, p. 41 (emphasis added).

53 *The Final Report*, Ministry and Ordination, no. 9, p. 34 (emphasis added).

54 *The Book of Common Prayer (Canada)* (Toronto: Anglican Book Centre: 1962), p. 637.

55 *The Final Report*, Ministry and Ordination, no. 13, p. 35 (emphasis added).

56 *Vatican Response*, p. 445.

57 Vatican Council II describes the ministry of the presbyter as originating in the gospel message and deriving its power and force from the sacrifice of Christ; hence, the priestly ministry finds expression in the ministry of word and sacrament (Decree on the Ministry and Life of Priests, *Presbyterorum Ordinis*, nos. 2-5). Cf. 'The part of the ministers in the celebration of the sacra-

ments is one with their responsibility for ministry of the word' (*The Final Report*: *Ministry and Ordination*, no. 11, p. 35).

58 *The Final Report*, *Ministry and Ordination*, no. 13, pp. 35-36 (emphasis added).

59 *The Final Report*, *Ministry and Ordination*, no. 15, p. 37.

60 *The Final Report*, *Ministry and Ordination*, no. 14, p. 36.

61 Canadian Anglican-Roman Catholic Dialogue, 'Remarks on the Congregation for the Doctrine of the Faith's 'Observations on the Final Report of ARCIC' (April 1983) *One in Christ* 20 (1984), pp. 278-279. There are good grounds for holding that the Council of Trent itself did not teach that Jesus explicitly mandated the seven sacraments. When Trent says, for example, that the anointing of the sick was 'instituted' by Christ truly and properly as a sacrament of the New Testament, this is understood as follows: it was 'insinuated' in Mk [6:13], and 'commended and promulgated' to the faithful through the Apostle and brother of the Lord, James [Jas 5:14-15] (Denzinger Schönmetzer, 1695). The medieval understanding of 'institution by Christ' 'includes the development of sacramental life in the Church after Easter, no difference of principle being seen between Christ's institution and the action of the Holy Spirit in the Church. This way of expressing the matter is behind can. 1 of the Council of Trent's *Decree on the Sacraments* (Denzinger Schönmetzer, 1601)'—Karl Lehmann and Wolfhart Pannenberg, eds., *The Condemnations of the Reformation Era: Do They Still Divide?* (Minneapolis: Fortress Press, 1990), p. 73.

62 Canadian Conference of Catholic Bishops, 'Response of the Canadian Catholic Bishops to *The Final Report* of ARCIC I', *Ecumenism/OEcumenisme* (December 1987), p. 13.

63 *The Final Report*, *Ministry and Ordination*, no. 6, p. 32.

64 *The Final Report*, *Ministry and Ordination*, no. 14, p. 35.

65 *The Final Report*, *Ministry and Ordination*, no. 13, p. 35.

66 *Vatican Response*, p. 446.

67 Canadian Anglican-Roman Catholic Dialogue, 'Reflection on the Experience of Women's Ministries', *Origins* 21:38 (February 27, 1992), p. 616. [See chapter 14 of this volume.]

68 *Vatican Response*, p. 446.

69 *The Final Report*, *Ministry and Ordination*, *Elucidation*, no. 4, p. 43.

70 *Vatican Response*, p. 446.

71 *Vatican Response*, p. 444.

72 *Vatican Response*, p. 445.

73 *Vatican Response*, p. 443.

74 *The Final Report*, *Authority in the Church I*, no. 24, p. 64.

75 *Vatican Response*, p. 444, citing *Authority in the Church II*, no. 31, pp. 96-97.

76 Roman Catholic theologians today know that even the *ex sese* clause of Vatican I's definition of papal infallibility did not exclude all forms of reception. Vatican Council II makes this clear when it says in the *relatio* to *Lumen Gentium*, 25: 'The definitions of popes, the Body of Bishops, or of Councils which are preserved from error by the assistance of the Holy Spirit 'are irreformable of themselves and do not require the approbation of the people . . . but carry with them and express

the consensus of the whole community', *Schema Constitutionis DE ECCLESIA* (Rome: Typis Polyglottis Vaticanis, 1964, p. 98, N [e]).

77   Reception of *The Final Report* of the Anglican Roman Catholic International Commission by the Anglican-Roman Catholic Dialogue of Canada (Toronto, 1985), para. 75.

78   *Vatican Response*, p. 444, citing *Authority in the Church I, Elucidation*, no. 3, pp. 71-72.

79   *Vatican Response*, p. 444. We note that the text in *Origins* uses 'tradition', whereas the text released in Rome (4 December 1991) has 'Tradition'.

80   *The Final Report, Authority in the Church II*, no. 25, p. 92 (emphasis added).

81   According to Bishop V. Gasser's official exposition of the meaning of the proposed dogma on papal infallibility at Vatican I: J. D. Mansi, *Sacrorum Conciliorum Nova et Amplissima Collectio*, ed. L. Petit and J. B. Martin, tome 52 (Paris, 1926) cols. 1213 ff.

82   For the Vatican Council II reference to the latter two phrases, see note 58 (above).

83   Cf. *The Final Report, Authority in the Church I*, no. 24c (p. 65), and *Authority in the Church II*, no. 29 (pp. 94-95).

84   Cf. note 78 (above), para. 56.

85   Cf. *Vatican Response*, p. 444 and *The Final Report, Authority in the Church II*, no. 30 (pp. 95-96). The Anglican members of ARC-Canada had already expressed their disappointment that the 1982 *Observations* were 'perhaps unfair in failing to acknowledge the positive affirmations about Marian dogma which are present in' *The Final Report* in *One in Christ* 20 (1984), 268.

86   *The Final Report, Authority in the Church II*, no. 30, p. 96.

87   'Response of the Canadian Conference of Catholic Bishops to the ARCIC I *Final Report* of ARCIC I' (1982), *Ecumenism/OEcumenisme* (1987) p. 19.

88   *Vatican Response*, p. 444.

89   *The Final Report, Authority in the Church I, Elucidation*, no. 8, p. 77.

90   Vatican Council II Decree on Ecumenism, *Unitatis Redintegratio*, no. 6.

91   *The Final Report, Authority in the Church II*, no. 13, p. 87.

92   *Vatican Response*, p. 444, citing *The Final Report, Authority in the Church II*, no. 13.

93   *Vatican Response*, p. 444, citing *The Final Report, Authority in the Church I, Elucidation*, no. 3 (p. 71).

94   The danger of using such expressions was pointed out to Pope Paul VI by the Theological Commission using Vatican Council II; cf. Karl Rahner in Herbert Vorgrimler, ed., *Commentary on the Documents of Vatican II* (New York: Herder and Herder, 1967), p. 202.

95   Cf. *The Final Report, Authority in the Church I*, nos. 9, 14-15, 18-19; *Authority in the Church II*, nos. 24, 26, and especially 27. See also the separate responses to the similar objection by the 1982 'Observations by the Anglican and Roman Catholic members of ARC-Canada' in *One in Christ* 20 (1984), 269 and 283-284.

96   *The Final Report, Authority in the Church II*, nos. 26-27, p. 93.

97   *Vatican Response*, pp. 444-445, citing *The Final Report, Authority in the Church II*, no. 12, pp. 86-87.

98   *The Final Report, Authority in the Church II*, no. 11, p. 86.

99 In the first sentence of the paragraph of the *Response*, p. 7 [*Origins*, p. 444], which we are discussing the authors of the *Response* have inadvertently omitted the word 'full' when speaking about the incorporation of a Christian community 'into Catholic communion through union with the See of Rome'. For *Unitatis Redintegratio*, nos. 3-4, including the *Expensio Modorum*, it is clear that Christians, their Churches, and their ecclesial communities are already in a real, though perhaps imperfect communion with the Catholic Church as a result of their faith and baptism.

100 *Vatican Response*, p. 445.

101 *The Final Report, Authority in the Church I*, no. 24 (p. 65) and *Authority in the Church II*, no. 15 (p. 88).

102 For the question of the New Testament grounding of the Petrine ministry in the context of *The Final Report* see *One in Christ* 20 (1984), 279-280 and ARC-Canada's statement of reception of the *Final Report* (1985), nos. 52-58. For the specific question of Peter's role during the earthly ministry of Jesus and his later role in the post-resurrection New Testament witness, see Raymond E. Brown, Karl P. Donfried, and John Reumann, eds. *Peter in the New Testament: A Collaborative Assessment by Protestant and Roman Catholic Scholars* (Minneapolis: Augsburg/New York: Paulist Press, 193), pp. 157-168.

103 *Vatican Response*, p. 446. We already dealt with this difficulty in the statements mentioned in note 103 above.

104 *The Final Report, Authority in the Church II*, nos. 7-8 (p. 84).

105 *The Final Report, Authority in the Church I, Elucidation*, no. 2 (p. 70).

106 *The Final Report, Authority in the Church II*, no. 8 (p. 84) and *Authority in the Church I, Elucidation*, no. 8 (p. 76).

107 *Vatican Response*, p. 446, with reference to *The Final Report, Authority in the Church II*, no. 29 (p. 95).

108 John Paul II and Robert Runcie, 'Common Declaration', *Origins* 19 (1989-1990), 317.

11. HOW CAN WE RECOGNIZE 'SUBSTANTIAL AGREEMENT'?

Anglican–Roman Catholic Consultation–USA, 1993

INTRODUCTION

1.   With the issuance of the Anglican Roman Catholic International Commission's *Final Report* in 1982, a new context was established for Anglican-Roman Catholic dialogue, a context shaped in large measure by the invitation for response and reception that accompanied *The Final Report*. Now that responses have been given by both Churches, the context has changed again. We of the Anglican-Roman Catholic Consultation-USA understand this context to be one of continuing study and reception, which we look forward to with hope that further clarifications of the issues addressed by this dialogue at every level will deepen the unity that we already share and bring us closer to that full unity that the Lord intends for his people.

2.   In this country, our two Churches have been in productive dialogue since 1965. During that time, ARC-USA has issued eight major documents and four texts that were reactions to three agreed statements of ARCIC.[1] It is from this experience that we face the new context. While looking forward in hope, we also recognize among ourselves a range of assessments concerning the import and implications of the two Churches' responses to *The Final Report*. Nevertheless, we find ourselves both encouraged and challenged by this new context, and we hope to stir up in the members of our Churches the same sense of encouragement and challenge.

3.   Therefore, in this document we will indicate a number of points in the responses that we find both significant and of concern, and we will set forth our own understanding of the path forward in this new context.

STATUS OF THE RESPONSES

4.   On March 24, 1966, Pope Paul VI and Archbishop of Canterbury Michael Ramsey met in Rome and signed a common agreement declaring their intention 'to inaugurate between the Roman Catholic Church and the Anglican Communion a serious dialogue which, founded on the Gospels and on the ancient common traditions, may lead to that unity in truth for which Christ prayed'.[2] Following the 1968 Malta Report of the joint preparatory commission, the Anglican Roman Catholic International Commission (ARCIC I) met for the first time in 1970. In 1982, ARCIC I issued its Final Report, which includes three agreed statements, two elucidations, a further statement on authority in the Church and an introduction to the Church as *koinonia*.

5.   In issuing the Final Report, ARCIC I hoped to help 'begin a process of extensive prayer, reflection, and study that will represent a marked advance toward the goal of organic union between the Roman Catholic Church and the Anglican Communion'.[3]

6.   Even as ARCIC I began its work on salvation and the nature of the Church, the Anglican Communion and Roman Catholic Church each began its own process of study and response to *The Final Report* of ARCIC I.

7.   In the Anglican Communion, in preparation for the Lambeth Conference of 1988, the Anglican Consultative Council[4] asked each province to consider 'whether the agreed statements on eucharistic doctrine, ministry and ordination, and authority in the Church (I and II), together with elucidations, are consonant in substance with the faith of Anglicans and whether *The Final Report* offers a sufficient basis for taking the next concrete step toward the reconciliation of our Churches grounded in agreement in faith'.[5] The formal synodical responses of 19 out of 29 provinces were summarized and discussed in the *Emmaus Report* issued in 1987. The Lambeth Conference, meeting the next year, responded to *The Final Report* by a resolution in which the conference 'recognizes the agreed statements of ARCIC I on eucharistic doctrine, ministry and ordination, and their elucidations, as consonant in substance with the faith of Anglicans and believes that this agreement offers a sufficient basis for the direction and agenda of the continuing dialogue on authority'.[6]

8.   We note here that the authority of the Lambeth response for Anglicans is not entirely clear. This point arises out of a statement printed in the 1988 Lambeth Conference proceeding (p. 9, no.1). This statement, which is similar to statements found in Lambeth proceedings since 1888, says that 'resolutions passed by a Lambeth conference do not have legislative authority in any province until they have been approved by the provincial synod of the province'. At the same time, however, the *Emmaus Report* emphasizes that 'though there can be no question of a legislative or juridical decision, there are moments when the Lambeth conferences have discerned, articulated, and formed the common mind of the Anglican Communion on important matters of faith and morals. . . . In the end the bishops have a special responsibility for guarding and promoting the apostolic faith, a responsibility which is theirs by ordination and office'.[7] The Lambeth Conference of 1988 did recognize 'the agreed statements of ARCIC I on eucharistic doctrine, ministry and ordination, and their elucidations, as consonant in substance with the faith of Anglicans and believes that this agreement offers a sufficient basis for taking the next step forward toward the reconciliation of our Churches grounded in agreement in faith'.[8]

9.   The December 1991 document from the Vatican is the official response of the Roman Catholic Church to *The Final Report*. It is described as 'the fruit of close collaboration between the Congregation for the Doctrine of the Faith and the Pontifical Council for Promoting Christian Unity'.[9] Since the apostolic constitution of 1988, *Pastor Bonus*, the

Congregation for the Doctrine of the Faith has had final responsibility in matters of faith and doctrine.

10. When *The Final Report* was issued in 1982, Cardinal Willebrands, then president of the Secretariat for Promoting Christian Unity, also asked Roman Catholic episcopal conferences to evaluate *The Final Report*. He asked for careful study and considered judgement, and requested that the replies of the conferences address the question of 'whether it [*The Final Report*] is consonant in substance with the faith of the Catholic Church concerning matters discussed'.[10]

11. Since a number of these evaluations were never published and none is cited in the Vatican response, it is hard to determine how much influence these evaluations had on the December 1991 text. The Vatican response, however, would still be the official position of the Roman Catholic Church concerning the *Final Report*,[11] even in the unlikely case that the conference evaluations were not used at all.

12. Where the Lambeth response found 'consonance in substance on the eucharist and ministry and ordination', the Vatican response judged 'that it is not yet possible to state that substantial agreement has been reached on all the questions studied' by ARCIC I, although the Vatican response considers *The Final Report* a 'significant milestone not only in relations between the Catholic Church and the Anglican Communion but in the ecumenical movement as a whole'.[12]

13. ARCIC I itself claimed only 'a high degree of agreement' on authority. With this, both the Lambeth response and the Vatican response seem to concur. Lambeth found ARCIC I's *Authority in the Church I* and *II*, together with the elucidation, 'a firm basis for the direction and continuing dialogue on authority',[13] while the Vatican said that 'the most that has been achieved is a certain convergence, which is but a first step along the path that seeks consensus as a prelude to unity'.[14]

14. The Vatican response does not close off discussion of the issues in *The Final Report*. On the contrary, it encourages further study and clarification (cf. para. 30). Its authors hope that the response itself will contribute to the dialogue that is leading to 'the restoration of visible unity and full ecclesial communion' (para. 34).

15. Accordingly, *The Final Report* constitutes both resource and agenda in the Anglican-Roman Catholic relationship. Together with the responses to it, *The Final Report* clarifies certain questions and poses certain challenges that seem to mark where the next steps must be taken in our journey together.

THE SEARCH FOR A COMMON LANGUAGE

16. ARCIC I's method was to engage in serious dialogue on 'persisting historical differences' in order to contribute to the 'growing together' of the two Churches.[15] Therefore, ARCIC I was 'concerned not to evade the difficulties, but rather to avoid the controversial language in which they have often been discussed. We have taken seriously the issues that

have divided us and have sought solutions by re-examining our common inheritance, particularly the Scriptures'.[16] This method was approvingly summarized by John Paul II in his address to the Commission:

> Your method has been to go behind the habit of thought and expression born and nourished in enmity and controversy to scrutinize together the great common treasure, to clothe it in a language at once traditional and expressive of the insights of an age which no longer glories in strife but seeks to come together in listening to the quiet voice of the Spirit.[17]

17. The Vatican response, however, does not allude to ARCIC I's method. It perceives ambiguities in the language of *The Final Report*. Thus, it calls for certain clarifications to ensure that 'affirmations are understood in a way that conforms to Catholic doctrine [of the eucharist]' (para. 6). Likewise, it calls for clarification of statements on ordained ministry in *The Final Report*. The Vatican response seems to urge that clarification be given through the use of language that is closer to and even identical with traditional Roman Catholic theological formulations. (For example, the response identifies a number of points it would like to have 'explicitly affirmed'. One of these is 'the propitiatory character of the Mass as the sacrifice of Christ'. The *Response* also asks that clarification be given on a number of matters and cites 'the fact that the ARCIC document does not refer to the character of priestly ordination, which implies a configuration to the priesthood of Christ'.[18])

18. If an agreed statement does not employ the traditional language of one or both Churches, does it thereby fail to express adequately the faith of those Churches? Some commentators have pointed to the obstacle to ecumenical progress created by one Church's demanding adherence to its own formulation. It seems to us that the Vatican response calls us to more painstaking study of the criteria by which each Church should evaluate the language of agreed statements.

THE ISSUE OF SUBSTANTIAL AGREEMENT

19. The use of phrases such as *substantial agreement, substantial identity* and *consonant in substance* in *The Final Report* and in the Vatican Response to it has been widely criticized as ambiguous. *Substantial* and *in substance* can mean either 'in very large part' or 'fundamental, basic'. In addition, the term *substantial* carries overtones from various historical theological controversies and from its use in scholastic theology.

20. The resolution that makes up the brief Lambeth response to ARCIC I 'recognizes the agreed statements of ARCIC I on eucharistic doctrine, ministry and ordination, and their elucidations, as consonant in substance with the faith of Anglicans'.[19] In formulating this reply, the Lambeth response seems to have taken *consonance in substance* in a broader sense as meaning something like 'compatibility'. Thus, while the overall evaluation of the

Lambeth Conference was positive, it also reported 'continuing anxieties' regarding eucharistic sacrifice and presence as well as on 'Ministry and Ordination', requests 'for a clarification of "priesthood"'. As E. J. Yarnold has remarked: 'The point seems to be that a statement is consonant with Anglican faith if it can be said to fall within the legitimate range of Anglican comprehensiveness, though individual Anglicans would be under no obligation to subscribe to it themselves'.[20]

21. The Vatican response, on the other hand, seems to have taken *consonance in substance* as meaning full and complete identity: 'What was asked for was not a simple evaluation of an ecumenical study, but an official response as to the identity of the various statements with the faith of the Church' (para. 33). From this perspective, the Vatican response must be understood, then, as claiming that ARCIC I failed to reach agreement on basic issues.

22. The main criterion for judgement used by the Churches—consonance in substance with the faith—was identically stated. But, as we have noted here, the meaning of this phrase varies between the two Churches. We suggest, then, that beyond the ambiguity in the term *substantial* there exists a much larger issue which lies in the assumption that everyone knows what substantial (in the sense of 'fundamental') agreement would look like and how it might be expressed.

THE ISSUE OF DOCTRINAL LANGUAGE

23. The intrinsic problem is the complex question of doctrinal language. How does one express the faith of the Church? This is, of course, a question with a long history of controversy.

24. What is meant by 'the faith of the Church'? For members of the Anglican and Roman Catholic communities, the tendency may be to assume, without very much hesitation, that the faith of the Church is identical with the official pronouncements of the community, however these pronouncements may be framed. But the fact is that the faith of the women and men who make up our communities is never simply the same as the words of our doctrinal formulas, liturgical forms, and catechetical statements. In Roman Catholic theology, a distinction has long been made between the *fide implicita* of the members of the Church and magisterial doctrinal statements. What must always be kept in mind is that the saving faith of the Church is the concrete faith of the people of God, which the official formulations of the faith are intended to support.

25. Yet two further questions arise: First, how does one know what the faith of any person or any group is, save through that faith's expression in word and deed? Second, by what processes and on what grounds have the words of councils, popes, bishops, and theologians come to be accepted as more authoritative than the word of any other believer or group of believers?

26. The first of these questions cannot be answered by appealing to the words of doctrine, for at least as many differences exist in the devotional styles and practices of

various believers as in their verbal expressions of faith. The *lex orandi* does not circumvent the question of adequacy of expression that confronts the *lex credendi*.

27. The second question is not simply another way of raising the issue of magisterial authority. The problem to which it points is that the words of official doctrinal and liturgical formulas, as well as the faith statements of any individual or community, all fall short of the mysteries that they seek to express. At best, when Christians seek to articulate the faith of the Church, we deal with degrees of inadequacy.

28. Certainly in our communities we live and pray together in the assumption that there is an agreement which, despite the differences in the ways we express our faith both in word and in practices, is substantial. But how do we know that? We pray the creed together Sunday after Sunday, and as we recite the words of the creed, we assume that the persons surrounding us intend substantially the same as we do. But on what grounds do we make this assumption?

29. The Vatican *Response*'s use of the language of official Roman Catholic formulas to test whether agreement has been reached on the substance of faith seems at odds with the practice employed in other ecumenical conversations. For example, few would argue against the statement that the doctrines of the Trinity and the Incarnation are the central articles of the Christian creed and that those articles have received normative expression in the formulas of the first four ecumenical councils.

30. Nevertheless, the Roman Catholic Church has been willing to join in a common declaration of faith which deliberately avoids conciliar language that has proven controversial. One such declaration was deemed sufficient to permit some sacramental sharing between the Roman Catholic and the Syrian Orthodox Churches. In their 1984 declaration, Pope John Paul II and Patriarch Zakka I appeal to the Council of Nicæa and then affirm:

> The confusion and schisms that occurred between their Churches in the later centuries, [the pope and the patriarch] realize today in no way affect or touch the substance of their faith, since these arose only because of differences in terminology and culture and in the various formulas adopted by different theological schools to express the same matter.[21]

Here the substance of faith is distinguished from culturally determined terminology and formulas of theological schools, including terminology and formulas worked out and adopted by one of the first four ecumenical councils.

31. From this example, it is apparent that the Roman Catholic Church has found it possible to affirm 'substantial agreement' without agreement on specific doctrinal formulas, even when those formulas are as hallowed as the Chalcedonian formula. This common declaration does not indicate how the 'substance' of faith is to be discerned when even the formula of Chalcedon is judged a matter of 'terminology and culture'.

32. This question raises the issue of doctrinal language. If, indeed, thought is dependent upon language and experience is dependent upon thought, then it is highly problematic to claim that one can distinguish the substance of faith from the culturally determined language of its expression.[22] How does one discern the substance beneath the words save through the words? It is a mistake to assume that when one speaks of the mysteries of faith, one can refer beyond the various attempts to speak about those mysteries to the mysteries themselves as if they are simply 'there' and available for inspection.

33. One way of dealing with this puzzle of doctrinal language is to accept orthopraxies as the test of orthodoxy; that is, to recognize that doctrines are expressions of the communal life of the Church and that shared life may make differing doctrinal formulas intelligible and reveal them to be compatible and even identical in intent. But such an interpretation means that attempts to share life must precede or at least accompany attempts to compare doctrinal statements. It might even suggest that shared sacramental life must precede or at least accompany attempts to compare doctrines on sacraments.

34. In any case, the very different understanding of 'substantial agreement' in the Lambeth and Vatican responses to *The Final Report* raises important questions on the understanding of doctrine and the hermeneutics of doctrinal language at work in the dialogues. These questions lie beneath any assumptions that the substance of faith is readily available for consultation as the criterion of doctrinal language. These questions must be addressed in the future by our two Churches.

THE CHALLENGE OF RECEPTION IN THE NEW CONTEXT

35. We understand that the importance of the process of reception was not fully realized in 1966 when Archbishop Ramsey and Pope Paul VI established the Anglican–Roman Catholic dialogue. How were the Commission's agreements to be fully accepted or rejected by each Church? As has been noted above, the Anglican Communion has produced a response of its bishops gathered at the Lambeth Conference of 1988, but while the bishops have 'a special responsibility for guarding and promoting the apostolic faith, their response is not a legislative or juridical decision'.[23] The dependence of the Roman Catholic Church's response on prior consultations of bishops' conference remains unclear. We ask whether texts such as *The Final Report* require new procedures of reception that more adequately reflect our affirmation of the real but imperfect communion in which we already live.

36. The sparse documentation style of the Vatican and Lambeth responses has also complicated the process of receiving them. While the Vatican response is longer and more detailed, neither response contains adequate reference to the materials upon which the responses build. With further documentation, the bases for the judgements expressed would be easier to discern. To this extent, the contribution of the responses to the dialogue could be made more effective than it currently is. We hope that future responses from our two

Churches will provide the material needed to facilitate understanding, appreciation, and acceptance of their judgements.

37. ARCIC I said:

We are convinced that if there are any remaining points of disagreement they can be resolved on the principles here established. We acknowledge a variety of theological approaches within both our communions. But we have seen it as our task to find a way of advancing together beyond the doctrinal disagreements of the past.[24]

We take this to indicate that ARCIC I claims 'substantial agreement' in the sense that, whatever differences may remain on the issues explored in *The Final Report*, they would not today provoke division between our two Churches. Hence, they cannot warrant our continuing division.

38. Thus, we take our two Churches' different judgements on whether 'substantial agreement' has been reached as both encouragement and challenge: encouragement, in that both responses rejoice in the notable progress that has been achieved; challenge, in that we are confronted with our willingness to stay divided over matters that would not initiate a division. This reality places in front of us our need for continuous repentance of our willingness to be divided and continuous conversion toward the unity Christ offers us with one another, which is a mirror of his own unity with the Father.

NOTES

1 George Tavard, 'The Work of ARCUSA: A Reflection Postfactum', *One in Christ* 29:3, pp. 247-259.

2 The common declaration by Pope Paul VI and the archbishop of Canterbury, March 24, 1966, is *Called to Full Unity: Documents on Anglican-Roman Catholic Relations 1966-1983*, ed. Joseph W. Witmer and J. Robert Wright (Washington, D.C.: United States Catholic Conference, 1986), p. 3.

3 Herbert J. Ryan, 'Foreword to the American Edition', Anglican Roman Catholic International Commission, *The Final Report* (Cincinnati/Washington, D.C.: Forward Movement Press/United States Catholic Conference, 1982), p. vi.

4 The Anglican Consultative Council was created after the 1968 Lambeth Conference to provide communion-wide continuity of consultation and guidance on policy; it has neither legislative nor jurisdictional powers.

5 *The Emmaus Report: A Report of the Anglican Ecumenical Consultation* (Cincinnati: Forward Movement, 1987), p. 44.

6 Resolution 8, The Lambeth Conference 1988, published in *The Truth Shall Make You Free*, pp. 210-212.

7 *The Emmaus Report*, p. 73; cf. Lambeth Conference 1978, Resolution 13.

8 Lambeth 1988, Resolution 8.

9 'Vatican Response to ARCIC *Final Report*' in *Origins* 21:28 (Dec. 19, 1991), p. 443.

10 National Conference of Catholic Bishops, 'Evaluation of the ARCIC Final Report', published in *Origins* 14:25 (1984), p. 409.

11 Report of the Catholic Theological Society of America Committee on the Profession of Faith and the Oath of Fidelity, April 15, 1990, pp. 51-52.

12 *Origins* 21:28, p. 441.

13 See note 6.

14 *Origins* 21:28, p. 443.

15 *The Final Report*, p. 1.

16 *The Final Report*, p. 5.

17 *One in Christ*, pp. 16, 341.

18 'Vatican Response to ARCIC *Final Report*' in *Origins* 21:28, p. 445.

19 See note 5.

20 *The Tablet*, Dec. 7, 1991, p. 1525.

21 'Toward a Fully Unanimous Gospel Witness', common declaration by Pope John Paul II and Patriarch Zakka I of Antioch, June 23, 1984. *Catholic International* 2:14 (July 15-31,1991), pp. 662-663.

22 This problem is foreshadowed in John XXIII's opening speech to the Second Vatican Council: 'The substance of the ancient doctrine of the deposit of faith is one thing, and the way in which it is represented is another'. Quoted in Francis A. Sullivan, 'The Vatican Response to ARCIC I', *Bulletin/Centro Pro Unione*, 39.

23 *The Emmaus Report*, p. 73.

24 *The Final Report*, p. 16.

12. REQUESTED CLARIFICATIONS ON EUCHARIST AND MINISTRY

Anglican Roman Catholic International Commission, 1993

In this paper we seek to answer the queries raised in the 1991 Response of the Holy See to *The Final Report* of ARCIC (1982) concerning the eucharist and the ordained ministry. We are encouraged by what is said in the *Response* that this may 'serve as an impetus to further the study'.

The Commission was inspired by two official statements of the Roman Catholic Church. The first came from the address by Pope John XXIII at the opening of the Second Vatican Council, when he said: 'The substance of the ancient doctrine of the deposit of faith is one thing, and the way in which it is presented is another'.[1] The second statement is paragraph 17 of *Unitatis Redintegratio* which, in speaking of East and West, includes the words, '. . . sometimes one tradition has come nearer than the other to an apt appreciation of certain aspects of a revealed mystery, or has experienced them in a clearer manner. As a result, these various theological formulations are often to be considered as complementary rather than conflicting'. This concept has been endorsed by the *Catechism of the Catholic Church* (1992), which affirms that when the Church 'puts down her roots in a variety of cultural, social and human terrains, she takes on different external expressions and appearances in each part of the world. The rich variety of ecclesiastical disciplines, liturgical rites and theological and spiritual heritage proper to the local churches, in harmony among themselves, shows with greater clarity the catholicity of the undivided Church'. In our study of eucharist and ministry we discovered beneath a diversity of expressions and practice a profound underlying harmony. This harmony is not broken when an element of the truth is more strongly affirmed in one tradition than in another, in which nevertheless it is not denied. Such is especially the case with eucharistic adoration, as we shall later show.

EUCHARIST

The *Response* to *The Final Report*, whilst approving the main thrust of the statement on *Eucharistic Doctrine*, asks for clarification concerning the following points:

(a) the essential link of the eucharistic memorial with the *once-for-all* sacrifice of Calvary which it makes sacramentally present;

(b) 'the propitiatory nature of the eucharist sacrifice, 'which can be applied also to the deceased'. The *Response* stressed the fact that 'for Catholics the whole Church must include the dead'. It appears to want reassurance that the Anglican Communion shares the same view;

(c) certitude that Christ is present sacramentally and substantially when 'under the species of bread and wine these earthly realities are changed into the reality of his body and blood, soul and divinity';

(d) the adoration of Christ in the reserved sacrament.

The *Response* of the Holy See states that the Catholic Church rejoices because the members of the Commission were able to affirm together 'that the eucharist is a sacrifice in the sacramental sense, provided that it is clear that this is not a repetition of the historical sacrifice'. In the mind of the Commission the making present, effective, and accessible of the unique historic sacrifice of Christ does not entail a repetition of it. In the light of this the Commission affirms that the belief that the eucharist is truly a sacrifice, but in a sacramental way, is part of the eucharistic faith of both our Communions. As has been stated in the *Elucidation* on *Eucharistic Doctrine*, para. 5: 'The Commission believes that the traditional understanding of sacramental reality, in which the once-for-all event of salvation becomes effective in the present through the action of the Holy Spirit, is well expressed by the word *anamnesis*. We accept this use of the word which seems to do full justice to the semitic background. Furthermore it enables us to affirm a strong conviction of sacramental realism and to reject mere symbolism'.

When we speak of the death of Christ on Calvary as a sacrifice, we are using a term to help explain the nature of Christ's self-offering, a term which is not exhaustive of the significance of that self-offering. However, it has become normative for the Christian tradition because of its intimate relation with the unique propitiatory character of the death of Christ. This theme of propitiatory sacrifice is clearly emphasised in the classical eucharistic liturgies of the Churches of the Anglican Communion (e.g., the English *Book of Common Prayer*, 1662), where the words immediately preceding the *Sursum Corda* have always included 1 Jn 2:1, 2, 'If anyone sin, we have an advocate with the Father, Jesus Christ the righteous, and he is the propitiation for our sins'. So the Prayer of Consecration begins:

Almighty God, our heavenly Father, who of thy tender mercy didst give thine only Son Jesus Christ to suffer death upon the Cross for our redemption; who made there (by his one oblation of himself once offered) a full, perfect, and sufficient sacrifice, oblation, and satisfaction, for the sins of the whole world; and did institute, and in his holy Gospel command us to continue, a perpetual memory of that his precious death, until his coming again. . . .

Similarly, the propitiatory dimension of the eucharist is explicit in *The Final Report* when it says that through the eucharist 'the atoning work of Christ on the cross is proclaimed and made effective' and the Church continues to 'entreat the benefits of his passion on behalf of the whole Church'. This is precisely what is affirmed at the heart of the eucharistic action in both classical and contemporary Anglican liturgies (e.g., *Book of Common Prayer*, 1662):

> O Lord and heavenly Father, we thy humble servants entirely desire thy fatherly goodness mercifully to accept this our sacrifice of praise and thanksgiving, most humbly beseeching thee to grant, that by the merits and death of thy Son Jesus Christ, and through faith in his blood, we and *all thy whole Church* may obtain remission of our sins, and all other benefits of his passion.[2]

'All thy whole Church' must be understood in the light of the article in the Nicene Creed which precedes it, 'I believe in the one holy catholic and apostolic Church . . . in the resurrection of the dead and the life of the world to come'. For this reason commemoration of the faithful departed has continued to be part of the intercessions in Anglican eucharistic liturgies past and present (compare also the liturgical provision for a eucharist at a funeral and in the Commemoration of the Faithful Departed in the *Alternative Service Book*, 1980, of the Church of England, pp. 328 ff and 936 f).

The Holy See's *Response* gladly recognises our agreement with regard to the real presence of Christ: 'Before the eucharistic prayer, to the question "What is that?" The believer answers: "It is bread". After the eucharistic prayer, to the same question he answers: "It is truly the body of Christ, the Bread of Life"'. It also acknowledges that, 'The affirmations that the eucharist is "The Lord's real gift of himself to his Church" (*Eucharistic Doctrine*, para. 8), and that bread and wine "become" the body and blood of Christ (*Eucharistic Doctrine: Elucidation*, para. 6) can certainly be interpreted in conformity with Catholic faith'. It only asks for some clarification to remove any ambiguity regarding the mode of the real presence. The *Response* speaks of the earthly realities of bread and wine being changed into 'the reality of his body and blood, soul and divinity'. In its preparatory work the Commission examined with care the definition of the Council of Trent (DS 1642, 1652), repeated in the *Catechism of the Catholic Church* (1992) (no. 1376). Though the Council of Trent states that the soul and divinity of Christ are present with his body and blood in the eucharist, it does not speak of the conversion of the earthly realities of bread and wine into the soul and divinity of Christ (DS 1651). The presence of the soul is by natural *concomitantia* and the divinity by virtue of the hypostatic union. The *Response* speaks of a 'substantial' presence of Christ, maintaining that this is the result of a substantial change in the elements. By its footnote on transubstantiation the Commission made clear that it was in no way dismissing the belief that 'God, acting in the eucharist, effects a change in the inner reality of the elements' and that a mysterious and radical change takes place. Paul VI in *Mysterium Fidei* (AAS 57, 1965) did not deny the legitimacy of fresh ways of expressing this change even by using new words, provided that they kept and reflected what transubstantiation was intended to express. This has been our method of approach. In several places *The Final Report* indicates its belief in the presence of the living Christ truly and really in the elements. Even if the word 'transubstantiation' only occurs in a footnote, *The Final Report* wished to express what the Council of Trent, as evident from its discussions, clearly intended by the use of the term.

Reservation of the Blessed Sacrament is practiced in both our Churches for communion of the sick, the dying, and the absent. The fear expressed in the *Response* that a real consensus between Anglicans and Roman Catholics is lacking concerning the adoration of Christ's sacramental presence requires careful analysis. Differences in practice do not necessarily imply differences in doctrine, as can be seen in the case of East and West. The difficulty is not with reservation of the sacrament but with the devotions associated with it which have grown up in the Western Church since the twelfth century outside the liturgical celebration of the eucharist. To this day these devotions are not practiced in the Eastern Churches, just as they had not been during the Church's first thousand years. Nevertheless, the belief concerning Christ's presence has been and remains the same in East and West. Obviously the distinction between faith and practice is especially pertinent here. We recognised the fact that some Anglicans find difficulty with these devotional practices because it is feared that they obscure the true goal of the sacrament. However, the strong affirmation that 'the Christ whom we adore in the eucharist is Christ glorifying his Father' (*Eucharistic Doctrine: Elucidation*, para. 8) clearly shows that in the opinion of the authors of the document there need be no denial of Christ's presence even for those who are reluctant to endorse the devotional practices associated with the adoration of Christ's sacramental presence. Provision for the reservation of the sacrament is found within the Anglican Church according to pastoral circumstances. In the Church of England, for example, this is regulated by the faculty jurisdiction of the diocesan bishop.

The 1662 *Book of Common Prayer* authoritatively expresses the historic Anglican teaching that the consecrated elements are to be treated with reverence. After communion the rubric instructs the minister to 'return to the Lord's Table, and reverently place upon it what remaineth of the consecrated Elements, covering the same with a fair linen cloth'. A further rubric states that 'the Priest . . . shall, immediately after the Blessing, reverently eat and drink the same'. Such reverence remains the Anglican attitude (cf. the collect provided for the Thanksgiving for the Institution of Holy Communion, *Alternative Service Book 1980*, p. 920):

Almighty and heavenly Father, we thank you that in this wonderful sacrament you have given us the memorial of the passion of your Son Jesus Christ. Grant us so to reverence the sacred mysteries of his body and blood, that we may know within ourselves and show forth in our lives the fruits of his redemption; who is alive and reigns with you and the Holy Spirit, one God, now and for ever.

MINISTRY AND ORDINATION

The Holy See's *Response* acknowledged that 'significant consensus' has been achieved with regard to *Ministry and Ordination*. Encouraged by this we seek to give the requested clarifications.

Concerning the ordained ministry the *Response* asks ARCIC to make clearer the following affirmations:

(a) only a validly ordained priest, acting 'in the person of Christ', can be the minister offering 'sacramentally the redemptive sacrifice of Christ' in the eucharist;

(b) the institution of the sacrament of orders, which confers the priesthood of the New Covenant, comes from Christ. Orders are not 'a simple ecclesiastical institution';

(c) the 'character of priestly ordination implies a configuration to the priesthood of Christ';

(d) the apostolic succession in which the unbroken lines of episcopal succession and apostolic teaching stand in causal relationship to each other.

Crucial to the ARCIC agreement is the recognition that the ordained ministry is an essential element of the Church and that it is only the episcopally ordained priest who presides at the eucharist (*Ministry and Ordination: Elucidation*, para. 2). In several instances *The Final Report* states that the celebration of the eucharist is the sacramental memorial of the once-for-all self-offering of Christ on the cross to his Father (as described above). In the celebration of the eucharistic memorial, the self-offering of Christ is made present. The community, gathered around the ordained minister who presides in Christ's name at the celebration, enters into communion with this self-offering. In reciting the narrative of the institution, in praying the Father to send the Holy Spirit to effect the transformation of the gifts and through them of the faithful, in distributing these holy gifts to the assembly, the presiding minister stands in a special sacramental relation to what Christ himself did at the Last Supper, pointing to his redemptive sacrifice on the cross. Together with the assembly, but exercising his own specific ecclesial function, the one who presides is thus the minister of the sacramental self-offering of Christ.

The *Response* seeks the amplification and completion of that part of *The Final Report* which we have just clarified by affirming that Christ himself instituted the sacrament of orders. Concerning ordained ministers *The Final Report* states, 'Not only is their vocation from Christ but their qualification for exercising such a ministry is the gift of the Spirit' (*Ministry and Ordination*, para. 14), received in and through the Church. In this way they carry on the commission given to the apostles by Jesus in person. After the resurrection the Holy Spirit conferred upon the apostolic group what was necessary for the accomplishment of their commission. They in turn were led by the Lord to choose collaborators and successors who, through the laying on of hands, were endowed with the same gift of God for ministry in the Church.

Thus the sacramental ministry is something positively intended by God and derives from the will and institution of Jesus Christ. This does not necessarily imply a direct and explicit action by Jesus in the course of his earthly life. A distinction needs to be drawn between what Jesus is recorded as saying and doing, and his implicit intentions which may not have received explicit formulation till after the resurrection, either in words of the risen Lord himself or through his Holy Spirit instructing the primitive community: 'All this I have spoken while still with you. But the Counsellor, the Holy Spirit, whom the Father will send in my name, will teach you all things and will remind you of everything I have said to you' (Jn 14:25, 26).

The Final Report had no intention of excluding the notion of sacramental 'character', which is found in official Anglican documents (e.g., the Canon Law of the Church of England, c. 1.2). The Commission believed it to be more constructive to retain the idea without the use of a term which has sometimes been misconstrued. *The Final Report* emphasizes the Spirit's seal and the irrecovability of the gifts and calling of God of ministers. This is the meaning of 'character' as described by Augustine, assumed in the Council of Trent (DS 1767, 1774) and taught in the *Catechism of the Catholic Church* (1992) (no. 1582). Thus *The Final Report* states:

> In this sacramental act, the gift of God is bestowed upon the ministers, with the promise of divine grace for their work and for their sanctification; the ministry of Christ is presented to them as a model for their own; and the Spirit seals those whom he has chosen and consecrated. Just as Christ has united the Church inseparably with himself, and as God calls all the faithful to lifelong discipleship, so the gifts and calling of God to the ministers are irrevocable. For this reason, ordination is unrepeatable in both our Churches (*Ministry and Ordination*, para. 15).

Anglicans and Roman Catholics agree that the communion of the Churches in the apostolic tradition involves not only all the existing Churches of today but also those of the past, extending back to the first apostolic community. This communion is rooted in the apostolic faith and mission, but it involves far more than this. The sacramentality of the Church requires a sacramental continuity, expressed especially in the eucharist, celebrated in communion with the bishop: 'The communion of the Churches in mission, faith, and holiness, through time and space, is thus symbolized and maintained in the bishop' (*Ministry and Ordination*, para. 16).

The prime function of the episcopal ministry is to safeguard the continuity of the local churches with the apostolic Church in its faith, teaching, and mission. Thus each episcopal ordination is part of a successive line which links the bishops of today with the apostolic ministry. We believe that this is precisely what *Lumen Gentium* wanted to express:

> Among those various ministries which, as tradition witnesses, were exercised in the Church from the earliest times, the chief place belongs to the office (*munus*) of those who, appointed to the episcopate in a sequence running back to the beginning, are the ones who pass on the apostolic seed. Thus, as St. Irenaeus testifies, through those who were appointed bishops by the apostles, and through their successors down to our own time, the apostolic tradition is manifested and preserved throughout the world (*Lumen Gentium*, 20).[3]

The Commission stated that its concern was the origin and nature of the ordained ministry, not the question of who can or cannot be ordained (*Ministry and Ordination: Elucidation*, para. 5). However, the *Response* maintains that the ordination of women affects *The Final Report's* claim to have reached substantial agreement on *Ministry and Ordination*. We are confronted with an issue that involves far more than the question of ministry as such. It raises profound questions of ecclesiology and authority in relation to tradition. This subject is part of the mandate entrusted to ARCIC II.

LETTER BY CARDINAL E. CASSIDY (PRESIDENT OF THE PONTIFICAL COUNCIL FOR THE UNITY OF CHRISTIANS) TO THE CO-CHAIRMEN OF ARCIC II (1994)

✠ Mark Santer,
Bishop of Birmingham

✠ Cormac Murphy-O'Connor,
Bishop of Arundel and Brighton

On 4 September 1993, you sent me a document containing 'Clarification of certain aspects of the Agreed Statements on eucharist and ministry' which had been submitted to and approved by the ARCIC II meeting taking place in Venice at that time.

This document has been examined by the appropriate dicasteries of the Holy See and I am now in a position to assure you that the said clarifications have indeed thrown new light on the questions concerning eucharist and ministry in *The Final Report* of ARCIC I for which further study had been requested.

The Pontifical Council for Promoting Christian Unity is therefore most grateful to the members of ARCIC II, and to those from ARCIC I who prepared these clarifications. The agreement reached on eucharist and ministry by ARCIC I is thus greatly strengthened and no further study would seem to be required at this stage.

There is one observation that I should like to bring to your notice in this connection. It concerns the question of *Reservation of the Blessed Sacrament*, and in particular the comparison which is made on page [117] of the 'Clarifications' between the practice of the Orthodox Churches (and the Catholic Churches of Eastern Rite) and that of the Anglican Communion. Orthodox and Eastern-rite Catholics have a very clear and uniform practice concerning the reservation of the Blessed Sacrament. While there are differences in respect to devotions connected with the reserved sacrament, adoration of the reserved sacrament is normal for Orthodox and Greek-Catholics. The 'Clarifications' do not seem to make clear that this can be said unreservedly and uniformly for Anglicans. In fact the 'Clarifications' state that 'provisions for the reservation of the sacrament is found within the Anglican Church *"according to pastoral circumstances"'* and that 'in the Church of England, for example, this is regulated by the faculty jurisdiction of the diocesan bishop'. It seems important to stress that the *Response* of the Holy See to *The Final Report* was concerned not with the question of devotions associated with Christ's presence in the reserved sacrament, but with the implications of diverse Anglican practice regarding reservation itself and attitudes towards the reserved sacrament.

The remarkable consensus reached up to now on the themes dealt with by ARCIC I will only be able to be seen in its full light and importance as the work of ARCIC II proceeds. This would appear to be particularly the case in respect of the study of the questions still open in relation to the third part of *The Final Report* of ARCIC I, dealing with *Authority in the Church*. It would seem urgent, then, that this question be taken up as soon as possible by ARCIC II.

With the expression of my deep esteem and kind personal greetings,

Yours sincerely in the Lord,
EDWARD CARDINAL CASSIDY

NOTES

1   This quotation is from Pope John XXIII's Italian text. However, the official Latin text in translation reads, 'For the deposit of faith, or the truths which are contained in our venerable doctrine, are one thing, and the way in which they are expressed is another, with, however, the same sense and meaning'.

2   A nuanced example of propitiatory language in association with the eucharist is found in the writings of the seventeenth-century Anglican divine, Jeremy Taylor: 'It follows then that the celebration of this sacrifice be, in its proportion, an instrument of applying the proper sacrifice to

all the purposes for which it was first designed. It is ministerially, and by application, an instrument propitiatory: it is eucharistical, it is an homage and an act of adoration: and it is impetratory, and obtains for us and for the whole Church, all the benefits of the sacrifice, which is now celebrated and applied; that is, as this rite is the remembrance and ministerial celebration of Christ's sacrifice, so it is destined to do honour to God . . . to beg pardon, blessings, and supply of all our needs' (*Discourse* XIX, 4).

3   Inter varia illa ministeria quae inde a primis temporibus in ecclesia exercentur, teste traditione, praecipuum locum tenet munus illorum qui, in episcopatum constituti, per successionem ab initio decurrentem, apostolici seminis traduces habent: Ita, ut testatur S. Irenaeus, per eos qui ab apostolis instituti sunt episcopi et successores eorum usque ad nos, traditio apostolica in toto mundo manifestatur et custoditur.

13. FIVE AFFIRMATIONS ON THE EUCHARIST AS SACRIFICE

Anglican–Roman Catholic Dialogue in the United States, 1994

At the forty-first meeting of the Anglican-Roman Catholic Dialogue of the United States of America (ARC/USA), on January 6, 1994, having in mind the significant agreement on the eucharist represented by *The Final Report* of the Anglican Roman Catholic International Commission and responding to the request in the *Vatican Response to the ARCIC I Final Report* for clarification, we wish as the official representatives of our two Churches in the United States to make together the following affirmations:

1. We affirm that in the eucharist the Church, doing what Christ commanded his apostles to do at the Last Supper, makes present the sacrifice of Calvary. We understand this to mean that when the Church is gathered in worship, it is empowered by the Holy Spirit to make Christ present and to receive all the benefits of his sacrifice.

2. We affirm that God has given the eucharist to the Church as a means through which all the atoning work of Christ on the cross is proclaimed and made present with all its effects in the life of the Church. His work includes 'that perfect redemption, propitiation, and satisfaction, for all the sins of the whole world' (Cf. Art. 31 BCP [USA], p. 874). Thus the propitiatory effect of Christ's one sacrifice applies in the eucharistic celebration to both the living and the dead, including a particular dead person.

3. We affirm that Christ in the eucharist makes himself present sacramentally and truly when under the species of bread and wine these earthly realities are changed into the reality of his body and blood. In English the terms *substance*, *substantial*, and *substantially* have such physical and material overtones that we, adhering to *The Final Report*, have substituted the word *truly* for the word *substantially* in the clarification requested by the Vatican *Response*. However, we affirm the reality of the change by consecration as being independent of the subjective disposition of the worshipers.

4. Both our Churches affirm that after the eucharistic celebration the body and blood of Christ may be reserved for the communion of the sick, 'or of others who for weighty cause could not be present at the celebration' (BCP, pp. 408-409). Although the American *Book of Common Prayer* directs that any consecrated bread and wind not reserved for this purpose should be consumed at the end of the service, American Episcopalians recognize that many of their own Church members practice the adoration of Christ in the reserved sacrament. We acknowledge this practice as an extension of the worship of Jesus Christ present at the eucharistic celebration.

5. We affirm that only a validly ordained priest can be the minister who, in the person of Christ, brings into being the sacrament of the eucharist and offers sacramentally the redemptive sacrifice of Christ which God offers us.

As the Vatican *Response* had already recorded the notable progress toward consensus represented by *The Final Report* in respect of eucharistic doctrine, in the light of these five affirmations ARC/USA records its conclusions that the eucharistic as sacrifice is not an issue that divides our two Churches.

14. ANGLICAN ORDERS: A REPORT ON THE EVOLVING CONTEXT OF THEIR EVALUATION IN THE ROMAN CATHOLIC CHURCH

Anglican–Roman Catholic Dialogue in the United States, 1990

INTRODUCTION

The Anglican–Roman Catholic Consultation in the United States has since 1986 addressed the question of the evaluation by the Holy See of Anglican orders. In 1985 Jan Cardinal Willebrands, using a phrase taken from the ARCIC *Final Report*, had recognized that 'a new context' is now affecting the discussion of Anglican orders within the Roman Catholic Church because of the development of the thinking in the two Communions regarding the nature of the eucharist and ordained ministry. It has been the purpose of ARC-USA to discuss and to outline the positive dimensions of the 'new context'.

We wish to underline at the outset the limits of this study. We have focused our attention on factors that seem most to encourage the reconciliation of our two Communions. Other observers may point to additional features of Anglican/Roman Catholic relationships in the last century, such as an interpretation of *Apostolicæ Curæ* as an infallible pronouncement of the Holy See, the encyclical *Mortalium Animos* of 1928, or the reluctance of some Anglicans to move toward belief in the eucharist celebration as a sacrifice.

And there are recent developments which have been omitted from consideration in this statement, such as the ordination of women to the priesthood and episcopate within the Anglican Communion. No realistic observer can exclude these events for 'the new context'. Yet we have acted on the suggestion of Cardinal Willebrands in his 1985 letter that it is the negative judgement of Pope Leo XIII in *Apostolicæ Curæ* (1896) against the validity of Anglican ordinations that is still 'the most fundamental' issue that hinders the mutual recognition of ministries between the Roman Catholic Church and the Anglican Communion. Here we stress only the manner in which the themes addressed in *Apostolicæ Curæ* have been a point of departure for dialogue and debate between our two Communions for almost a century, and we record the progress made on these issues.

1. OVERVIEW

The question of the validity of orders conferred according to the *Anglican Ordinal* has come up occasionally in Roman Catholic theology since the period of the Reformation. In 1550 the Archbishop of Canterbury, Thomas Cranmer, issued a new ritual of ordination, that was destined to replace the medieval rituals hitherto in use in England, of which the rite of Sarum (Salisbury) was the most widespread. When Cardinal Reginald Pole, under Queen Mary, tried to restore the old religion in England, he received instructions from Popes Julius III and Paul IV regarding the mode of reconciliation of schismatic priests and bishops. Nonetheless, the exact meaning and scope of these instructions, as well as the actual decisions of Reginald Pole, have been a matter of scholarly debate.

In the late nineteenth century, Pope Leo XIII, acceding to urgent pleading from some unofficial groups of Anglicans and from a few Roman Catholics, commissioned a team of scholars to examine the problem. This resulted in the pope's apostolic letter, *Apostolicæ Curæ* (1896), in which Leo XIII concluded that the orders conferred with the use of the *Anglican Ordinal* were not valid according to the standards of the Roman Catholic Church.

And yet the aspiration for Christian unity between Anglicans and Roman Catholics did not come to an end in 1896. Almost immediately, this aspiration found expression in private talks, mutual friendships, and scholarly exchanges which bore witness to a slow and gradual convergence. This quiet convergence was nurtured by theological renewal and it was reinforced in both Communions by somewhat similar liturgical reforms derived from a wider knowledge of early Christian worship. Gradually there was official recognition of an evolution toward a new context quite different from the one of 1896. On the Anglican side the Lambeth Conferences of 1908, 1920, 1930, 1968, and 1988 gave official voice to this movement, and on the Roman Catholic side the Second Vatican Council (1962-1965) was the most important event that signaled a new context.

Following Vatican Council II, developing ecumenical relations between the Anglican Communion and the Roman Catholic Church have called attention again to the question of Anglican orders. The conditions of our times have become quite different from what they were in 1896. Theology and style of leadership have evolved in the two Churches. It is now not uncommon to think that the position of the problem of Anglican orders is no longer what it was under Pope Leo. A fresh examination of the data has shed new light on the subject.

2. HOW THE QUESTION WAS RAISED AT THE END OF VATICAN COUNCIL II

The question of Anglican orders was brought to the attention of Pope Paul VI on November 20, 1965, before the Secretariat for Christian Unity, that was still occupied by the work of Vatican Council II, and busy with the composition of the Ecumenical Directory and the preparation of international bilateral dialogues, was able to face the problem. This was in a private audience with the bishop of Huron, Ontario, George Luxton, of the Anglican Church of Canada.

According to the bishop, the pope invited him 'to add to our personal conversation'. This was done in a long letter to Paul VI that the bishop released to the public in English and Latin in February 1966. The letter begins with a summary of the papal audience. In their meeting the bishop of Huron gave information on projects of reunion between Anglicans and other Christians in Nigeria, Ghana, East Africa, Sri Lanka, North India, Pakistan, and Canada. The pope asked if these would be 'new' Churches. The bishop answered that there would be continuity of ministry in 'the historic episcopate'. As the bishop of Huron reminds Pope Paul in his letter, 'you mentioned the Bull of Leo XIII as a definitive statement of your Church on Anglican Orders, and noted that it was given after a careful study of historical events and related documents'.

One may note the word, 'definitive'. What is the implication of this term in the context of a private conversation? It comes naturally to the mind of a Roman Catholic referring to a solemn statement made by a pope. It seems to fit naturally in a reference made by Paul VI to a decision taken by his predecessor Leo XIII. But the use of the term does not amount to a doctrinal declaration that the decision in question, while it was definitive in the mind of Leo XIII, must always remain definitive.

The bishop of Huron then 'expressed the hope that these same events and documents, when studied in the new climate of our inter-Church relationships, might possibly allow other interpretations than those that were apparent at the close of the nineteenth century. It was then that you expressed yourself as willing to receive from me and to consider any related material that I might be able to send'.

The bishop also included three requests in his letter: (1) that a review of Anglican orders be made, (2) that Pius V's sentence of excommunication on Queen Elizabeth be revoked, on the model of the recent decision concerning the excommunication of the patriarch of Constantinople, and (3) that, as a long-range project, there be envisaged an eventual 'intermingling of the Orders of the Roman Catholic Church with our own Orders and with the Orders of other Communions which are in full intercommunion with us'.

The first request deserves to be quoted at length:

That you ask one of your Commissions to review the matter of Anglican Ordinal with the Early Ordinals, with the Roman one described by Hippolytus . . . ; the Eastern Rite of St. Serapion . . . ; the later Byzantine Rite, the Gregorian and the Gelasian Sacramentaries, as well as the Spanish Mozarabic rite. *In all these the matter and form are very close to that of the English Reformation Ordinal.* Also the Commission might review the *whole* of the English Ordinal through phases of development for a further testing of its intention to continue (as the Preface declares) 'The Orders of Ministers'. . . . etc.

When this new study, which I am requesting, is set in our present climate of theological dialogue, we believe that your Commission would arrive at different conclusions. Our conviction in this matter is strengthened by the fact that in recent years new interpretations of the doctrine of Eucharistic Sacrifice have been proposed by distinguished scholars in the Roman Catholic Church [reference to Eugene Masure, Maurice de la Taille, and Abbot Anscar Vonier]. Since the heart of the argument in *Apostolicæ Curæ* turns on the understanding of Eucharist Sacrifice by the English Reformers, these new interpretations of your theologians seem to call for a reconsideration of the earlier verdict of seventy years ago.

At the end of his letter, the bishop of Huron recalls that in their conversation Paul VI 'noted that the intermingling of Anglican Orders with theirs [those of the Old Catholics of Europe] is relevant to any modern review of Anglican Orders'. Further, the bishop remembers that 'the possibility' of 'the participation' of Roman Catholic bishops 'as co-consecrators' in Anglican ordinations 'came to your mind at the close of my November audience with you, and that you mentioned having heard it under discussion'.[1]

3. *APOSTOLICAE CURAE* (1896)

Pope Leo's letter of 1896 is at the heart of this 1966 exchange because it laid out the doctrinal basis for the official Roman Catholic rejection of the validity of Anglican ordained ministry. The ultimate judgement of Pope Leo XIII is that Anglican orders are 'absolutely null and utterly void'. Leo XIII asserts that the Roman See has always treated Anglican orders as null and void whenever the question has arisen in practice and that this policy of non-recognition could be traced back without break to the period of the Marian restoration of the Roman Catholic Church in England, 1553-1558. *Apostolicæ Curæ* interprets the instructions sent by Popes Julius III and Paul IV to the Roman legate in England, Cardinal Pole, as stating explicitly that those ordained in the Church of England must be absolutely re-ordained to become Roman Catholic priests.[2]

Apostolicæ Curæ presents a theological defense of this tradition of Vatican rejection of the validity of Anglican orders. It is based on the argument that the Church of England ordinal was defective in 'intention' and 'form'. By 'defect of intention' Leo XIII meant that by the omission of any reference to the eucharist as a sacrifice and to a sacrificing priesthood in the ordination ritual of the 1552 *Book of Common Prayer*, the Church of England intended to introduce a radically new rite into England, one markedly different from those approved by the Roman Catholic Church. By 'defect of form' Leo XIII meant that the words of the Anglican ordination prayer, 'Receive the Holy Ghost', did not signify definitely the order of the Catholic priesthood with its power to consecrate and offer the body and blood of Christ in the eucharistic sacrifice.

This is the position of *Apostolicæ Curæ* in 1896: the exclusion of the concept of sacrifice from eucharistic worship in 1552 signified that the Church of England did not intend to ordain bishops and priests in the way that such ordinations had taken place before the Reformation, in the Catholic Church in England. The exclusion of a sacrificing priesthood nullified any Anglican intention to do what the Catholic Church does at an ordination.

One key element in the new context for the evaluation of Anglican orders today is that in 1978 the Vatican archives were opened through the year 1903. This has brought to light documents that show that the decisions of *Apostolicæ Curæ* were arrived at through a more complex process than we had previously imagined. The process, it must be admitted, is not so important as the conclusion. However, it is helpful to observe the process. The documents now available to scholars definitely confirm the existence of two distinct groups among the eight members of an apostolic commission appointed by Leo XIII in January 1896 to reexamine the validity of Anglican orders. Leo's commission was divided, and four members of the commission believed that a 'historic continuity' with the medieval Church in England could be traced in modern Anglicanism. In 1896 Vatican opinion on the invalidity of Anglican orders was not as solidly negative as we once imagined, prior to 1978. It would not be to our purpose to comment on the opinions of the four members who were in favor of invalidity because these arguments found their way into *Apostolicæ Curæ*. Almost unknown today are the positions of the papal commissioners who concluded positively in favor of the orders.[3]

For example, one member of the papal commission, Louis Duchesne, believed that the practice of regarding Anglican orders as null and void did not derive from 'an ecclesiastical sentence' given in full knowledge of all the facts in the case. For a second commission member, Pietro Gasparri, the material succession of Anglican orders was intact. A third member, Emilio De Augustinis, held that the ordination rite of the 1552 Book of Common Prayer safeguarded the substance of the sacrament of order, and that the formula *Accipe Spiritum Sanctum*, contained in the 1552 book, was a valid form of Catholic ordination. A fourth member, T. B. Scannell, believed approvingly that 'true Roman caution' had prevented the papacy from making a definitive negative judgement on Anglican orders in the sixteenth century.[4]

Today we can study these conclusions for ourselves: (1) Rome in the sixteenth century did not state categorically and explicitly that all orders conferred with the *Anglican Ordinal* of 1552 were null and void; and Anglican orders were not consistently rejected by the Roman See during the Marian Restoration in England of 1553 to 1558. (2) The vague nature of the instructions sent to Reginald Pole, the Roman Catholic legate in England during that period, suggests that re-ordination was not the only means of reconciliation of ministries in the sixteenth century. This conclusion is amplified by the fact that Pole himself was not a priest until March 1556. In any case, whatever conclusions we may reach today about the sixteenth century, we do have much more information about the background of the papal decision of 1896. This has made enough historical facts available to us to justify new investigation and appraisal.[5]

Why did Leo XIII reject the historical arguments of four members of his commission? The recently opened documents in the Vatican inform us that Pope Leo XIII apparently decided that the issue of reconciliation with the Church of England was not a matter of historical continuity alone. More importantly, to the pope, validity was a matter of sacramentology and of ecclesiology. The new documents suggest this interpretation of *Apostolicæ Curæ*: Greater weight must be given to theological and institutional unity between Rome and Canterbury than to the proof of historical and sacramental continuity.

Leo XIII thus decided that historical proof of a continuation of sacramental validity with the Church of England was not the central question between Anglicanism and Roman Catholicism. History is not the question. Theology is the question. For there to be sacramental validity within the Church of England from the perspective of Rome, Anglicans and Roman Catholics must be in one institutional community of faith, which implies agreements about the theology of sacraments and ministry, and some Anglican recognition of the papacy.[6]

From this standpoint, Leo XIII was not saying 'no' to Anglicanism. Today we can read letters in the Vatican archives in which Leo XIII and his Secretary of State, Cardinal Rampolla, wished to encourage further contacts and discussions with Anglicans after the promulgation of *Apostolicæ Curæ*. They urge Anglicans and Roman Catholics to move toward unity in faith before the issue of sacramental validity is resolved. In the light of new historical documents, *Apostolicæ Curæ* did not end a process of dialogue. It began a process of dialogue. The Vatican response was theological, not political. It set out clear theological conditions for validity. Could this not imply that given theological developments, there could be some *future* discernment of substantial agreement between Anglicans and Roman Catholics on sacraments and ministry which could sustain a positive judgement of *future* ordinations in the mind of Rome?

This does not mean that we doubt the intention of Leo XIII in 1896 'to settle definitively the grave question about Anglican ordination', as he later wrote to the Archbishop of Paris. But the documentation in the Vatican archives suggests that this decision on the precise technical point of Anglican orders was not meant to end contact between the two Communions.

After 1896 Cardinal Rampolla supported informal visits, meetings, correspondence, and prayer in order to 'maintain good relations with the Anglicans' and to encourage Anglicans to continue to persevere in 'positive sympathies toward the Roman Church'. In a similar manner, the chief Anglican protagonist of 1896, Lord Halifax, also believed that dialogue would continue. He wrote: 'We have failed for the moment . . . but God means to do the work himself . . . the matter is as certain as it ever was'.[7]

4. FROM *SAEPIUS OFFICIO* (1897) TO THE ANGLICAN/ROMAN CATHOLIC PREPARATORY COMMISSION (1967)

The next stages of this process of dialogue were *Sæpius Officio* and the Malines Conversations. Anglican prelates and the Vatican continued a private dialogue through correspondence, and then in March 1897 the Archbishops of Canterbury and York replied to *Apostolicæ Curæ* in the encyclical letter *Sæpius Officio*. The document derived considerable authority from the fact that it was addressed on behalf of the Anglican Communion to all the bishops of Christendom. Here the Anglican archbishops argued that the Anglican Church makes it clear that she intends to confer the office of priesthood instituted by Christ and all that it contains. Canterbury and York contended that the Church of England teaches the doctrine of the eucharistic sacrifice in terms at least as explicit as those of the canon of the Roman Mass: 'Further we truly teach the doctrine of Eucharistic sacrifice and do not believe it to be a "nude commemoration of the sacrifice of the Cross", an opinion which seems to be attributed to us . . . we think it sufficient in the Liturgy which we use in celebrating the holy eucharist . . . to signify the sacrifice which is offered at that point of the service in such terms as these'.

Finally, the archbishops pointed out that the words and acts required by the pope in 1896 are not found in the earliest Roman ordinals, so that if their omission renders an ordination invalid, the orders of the Church of Rome are on no surer footing than those of the Church of England.

The archbishops were making two essential responses to the arguments of Rome: (1) 'We plead and represent before the Father the sacrifice of the cross'. (2) 'The whole action . . . we are accustomed to call the Eucharistic sacrifice'. Their summary of the Anglican understanding of the eucharistic sacrifice deserves to be quoted in some detail: 'The matter is indeed one full of mystery and fitted to draw onwards the minds of men by strong feelings of love and piety to high and deep thoughts. But, inasmuch as it ought to be treated with the highest reverence and to be considered a bond of Christian charity rather than an occasion for subtle disputations, too precise definitions of the manner of the sacrifice of the eternal Priest and the sacrifice of the Church, which in some ways certainly are one, ought in our opinion to be avoided rather than pressed into prominence'.

The general tone of the letter is also important, because it assumes that the bishops of the Anglican Communion are engaged in an on-going debate with 'our venerable brother', the pope. It was even understood that the outcome of this debate might be positive. The archbishops wrote: 'God grant that, even from this controversy may grow fuller knowledge of the truth, greater patience, and a broader desire for peace in the Church of Christ. . . '. In the same hope of eventual resolution of these matters with Rome, the Lambeth Conference of 1908 proclaimed that there could be no fulfillment of the purpose of God in any scheme of reunion that 'does not ultimately include the great Latin Church of the West'.[8] And the dialogue continued in this sense: the Vatican responded to *Sæpius Officio*, re-stating its conclusions of the 1896 investigation in a French and Latin letter to the archbishops of Canterbury and York of June 1897 (letter number 38245 in the Vatican archives), and inviting a continuing study of the doctrinal issues between the two Churches.

The document *Sæpius Officio* argued that there is a continuity of Anglican belief in the eucharistic sacrifice, stretching from the sixteenth to the nineteenth century, and, since *Sæpius Officio* was formally endorsed by the Lambeth Conference in 1930, into the twentieth century. At the 1930 Lambeth Conference a delegation of Orthodox bishops asked what Anglicanism teaches on the eucharistic sacrifice. The answer given by the Lambeth committee in charge quoted the passage from *Sæpius Officio* mentioned here, and this passage was endorsed by the whole Lambeth Conference in its Resolution Thirty-three.

Further, the Malines Conversations, meetings of a group of Anglican and Roman Catholic theologians held in Belgium between 1921 and 1925 under the presidency of Cardinal D. J. Mercier, did stimulate movement for greater unity in sacramental theology and ecclesiology. It was informally agreed by Anglican and Roman Catholics at Malines that the pope should be given a primacy of honor, that the body and blood of Christ are indeed taken in the eucharist, that the sacrifice of the eucharist is a true sacrifice, but after a mystical manner, and the episcopacy is by divine law.

The impression has been left that the Malines Conversations 'ran into the sands and got nowhere'; and yet Pope Paul VI said in 1966 that these conversations were 'epoch-making'. Why was this so?

First, Malines may be seen as a new start continuing the debate that had begun at the time of *Apostolicæ Curæ*. Pius XI had no objection to what Cardinal Mercier was doing, and the pope was urged in this direction by his Secretary of State, Cardinal Gasparri. This was the same Pietro Gasparri who had been one of the papal commissioners in 1896; his judgement had been that Anglican orders were at the least doubtfully valid.

Second, two key figures at Malines, Lord Halifax and Fernand Portal, had also been key figures in 1896. Malines built on the talks, discussions, lectures, and private friendships that Halifax and Portal had kept alive for the twenty-five years since *Apostolicæ Curæ*. And there was a real advance from 1896: in 1896 Anglican orders had been considered by a commission that included only Roman Catholics. Malines was a mixed conference with theologians from both sides meeting on a basis of equality.

Finally, by 1925, the Anglican group at Malines expressed conclusions on the eucharistic sacrifice that moved a step closer to the position of Leo XIII in *Apostolicæ Curæ*. A memorial written on behalf of the Anglicans by Lord Halifax on May 21, 1925, defined the distinctive priesthood of the ordained ministry in such a way that there is a marked connection to the sacrificial character of the eucharistic. The priest is defined as one who offers up the sacrifice of the cross by prayers and a commemorating rite. The faith of Halifax in the eventual triumph of reunion was so strong that even when the Malines conversations came to an end with the death of Cardinal Mercier, Halifax then in his ninetieth year was said to have uttered: 'Now for a new departure'.[9]

5. THE PREPARATORY COMMISSION FOR DIALOGUE BETWEEN THE ANGLICAN COMMUNION AND THE ROMAN CATHOLIC CHURCH (1967)

Despite the attempts at Malines, and individual contacts between scholars and members of religious orders of the two Churches, polarization is the word that best describes the debate on Anglican orders down to the 1960s.

Apostolicæ Curæ produced an enormous amount of literature, Roman Catholic authors generally explaining and defending the papal decision, Anglicans affirming the effective transmission of valid orders in England through the turmoils of the Reformation.[10]

A significant shift in this polarization took place in the context of the Anglican/Roman Catholic Preparatory Commission that was established by Pope Paul VI and Archbishop Michael Ramsey. At the first meeting of this commission (Gazzada, January 1967), the documentation from the bishop of Huron was made available to the members. At the second meeting (Huntercombe Manor, August-September 1967), the Preparatory Commission invited two of its members, Canons Findlow and Purdy, to 'make a preliminary report on the question of the advisability and/or procedure to be followed in reconsideration of the problem of Orders'.

The Findlow-Purdy report was presented at the last meeting (Mosta, Malta, December 1967-January 1968). It was based in part on a brief memorandum that Canon Findlow had prepared 'with the Archbishop of Canterbury's knowledge'. The memorandum evoked the past (*Apostolicæ Curæ*, and the Bull of Paul VI, *Praeclara Carissimi*). It looked at the present (the contemporary approach to sacramentality, *Unitatis Redintegratio*, the Lambeth Appeal to all Christian People of 1920, the Church of England/Methodist Proposals). It discarded several suggestions: concentration on the Irish line of Archbishop De Domini, or increasing the Old Catholic participation in Anglican consecrations, or making retrospective applications of the Apostolic Constitution of Pius XII on the Matter and Form of Sacred Orders (1948) 'as a possible means of validating the invalid'. It recognized that 'the concept and understanding of the Church has developed, as it must, and is developing still'. Turning to the future, the memorandum noted that the time has 'not quite yet' come for 'a reopening of the old question of Anglican orders in the wider context of the whole Church on earth, its faith, its ministry and its sacraments'. It suggested that a special commission be given the task of outlining a *modus discutiendi* rather than *agendi*.

The Findlow-Purdy report also drew on considerations contained in two papers by Archbishop McAdoo and Bishop Christopher Butler. These papers, however, treated the question of orders only incidentally. The report included a rather lengthy survey of recent literature: J. J. Hughes's books on *Apostolicæ Curæ*, articles by Daniel O'Hanlon and Franz Josef van Beeck in favor of some recognition of all Protestant ministries, other articles by Harry McSorley and Gregory Baum.

The report concluded by outlining two possible courses of action. First, there could be a joint inquiry by a pair of scholars into *Apostolicæ Curæ*; this could take account of various criticisms that have been made of the decision of Leo XIII, and 'consider what aspects of the problem were ignored. . .'. Second, another pair of scholars could investigate 'the possibility of, and formulae for, a commission or recognition (Lambeth 1920)'. In other words, it recommended that a search be initiated for an acceptable form of what is now called the reconciliation of ministries. 'This', the report concluded, 'is likely to produce quicker results'.

As it examined the Findlow-Purdy report, the Preparatory Commission had in hand a mimeographed essay by a Dominican, Fr. J. Smith. This is essentially an examination of the then recent volumes by Francis Clark (*Anglican Orders and Defect of Intention*, 1956) and J. J. Hughes (*Absolutely Null and Utterly Void*, 1969 and *Stewards of the Lord*, 1970). Smith's judgement is that J. J. Hughes has succeeded 'in his main endeavor to bring forth solid arguments to show the validity of Anglican orders'. Smith also provides a convenient summary of several suggestions made in modern Roman Catholic theology in favor of the recognition of Anglican orders.

There is 'an approach in terms of matter, form and intention', that is inspired by *Apostolicæ Curæ* but reaches opposite conclusions. In addition, Smith mentions 'an approach through the concept:

'- of reception *in voto* (Kung)',
'- of extraordinary ministers (van Beeck)',
'- of a wider understanding of apostolic succession and an application of the principle of *Ecclesia supplet* along the lines of the Orthodox "economy" (Villain, Tavard)'.

Toward the end of his essay, Smith explains these suggestions further, and he adds some others:

(1) After making 'a special study of the teaching of councils and popes about the legitimacy of ministers of the Eucharist from Innocent III to Vatican I, McSorley believes that it is within the Roman Catholic Church's power of the keys to declare valid and legitimate ministries she has formerly called invalid or illegitimate'.

(2) 'Killian McDonnell . . . favours an understanding of Reformation ministries as a set of charismatic ministries standing in a different way in the apostolic succession alongside episcopal orders, and believes that they should be acknowledged by the Roman Catholic Church on the principle of *Ecclesia supplet* and the working of the "economy"'.

(3) 'Father Coventry draws attention to two meanings of validity: recognition by the [Roman Catholic] Church, and "strength, authenticity, full value", and raises the question of the relationship between these two meanings; this leads him to the

view that orders should be "recognized as orders insofar as a Church is recognized as Church, and not vice versa"'.

Father Smith's own conclusion is the following:

It is evident how much the new argument, in all its versions, depends upon the renewal of theology taking place under the stimulus of Vatican II. . . . The co-inherence of church and sacrament is no longer to be understood in a way that makes church character ('ecclesiality') and the sacraments a possession of the Roman Catholic Church that must be jealously guarded and kept to herself alone.

6. THE MALTA REPORT (1968)

The recommendation of the Preparatory Commission was embodied in *The Malta Report*. This report is the first document issued from an official commission of the two Communions that illustrates the emergence of the new context for the evaluation of Anglican orders by the Roman Catholic Church.

After examining the documents at its disposal, the Preparatory Commission included a specific recommendation. Although this *Malta Report* does not discuss the substance of the question, it notes that the contemporary desire for 'intercommunion' points to the urgency of the matter. And it sets the question in the broad context of ecclesiology:

19. We are agreed that among the conditions required for intercommunion are true sharing in faith and the mutual recognition of ministry. The latter presents a particular difficulty in regard to Anglican Orders according to the traditional judgment of the Roman Catholic Church. We believe that the present *growing together of our two Communions* and the needs of the future require of us a very serious consideration of this question *in the light of modern theology*. The theology of the ministry forms *part of the theology of the Church* and must be considered as such. It is only when sufficient agreement has been reached as to the *nature of the priesthood* and the *meaning attached in this context to the word validity* that we could proceed, working always jointly, to the application of this doctrine to the Anglican ministry of today. We would wish to *reexamine historical events* and past documents only to the extent that they can throw light upon the facts of the present situation.[11]

The points underlined contain the outline of an approach to the matter of Anglican orders. The question should be reexamined, (1) in the light of modern theology; (2) and in the context of an ecclesiology of 'Communion'; (3) the process should include an agreement on the nature of the priesthood; (4) and on the meaning of sacramental validity; (5)

but it need not return to the debates concerning the events of the sixteenth century except if and when this may be necessary to throw light on the modern situation. The contemporary question deals with the advisability of taking a step forward toward the reconciliation of the Churches by recognizing Anglican orders today, whatever may have been the problems of the past.

7. THE WORK OF ARCIC I (1970 TO 1981): THE FORMULATION OF A 'SUBSTANTIAL AGREEMENT'

The recommendation of *The Malta Report* became part of the project of ARCIC I. How this first commission that had charge of the international dialogue between the two Communions acted on the recommendation of *The Malta Report* further illustrates the growth of the new context for the evaluation of Anglican orders.

Not all the work proposed by the Preparatory Commission was attempted. ARCIC I arrived at what it identified as a 'substantial agreement' on the sacrament of the eucharist (*Windsor Statement*, 1971, with the *Elucidations* of 1979), and on ministry and ordination (*Canterbury Statement*, 1973, with the *Elucidations* of 1979). It formulated the beginning of a substantial agreement on authority in the Church (*Venice Statement*, 1976, with the *Elucidations* of 1981, and the second *Windsor Statement*, 1981).

The agreed statement on authority in the Church included the principle of the primacy of the bishop of Rome in the college of bishops, but not all the range of authority that the Roman Catholic tradition has come to recognize in the primate. Four questions were left open in 1976:

(1) The meaning and relevance of the Petrine texts of the New Testament,
(2) The question of the divine right (*jus divinum*) that is attributed in the Roman Catholic Church to the Roman primacy, and that is seen in the agreed statement as resulting from the divine providence by which God guided the Church in its history,
(3) The nature and extent of this primatial jurisdiction of the bishop of Rome,
(4) The doctrine of papal infallibility as defined at Vatican I and as reformulated at Vatican II.

By 1981 and the publication of *The Final Report*, substantial agreement was reached on the first two points. Some progress was made on the last two. But the agreement registered was neither complete nor final.

Following the lead of *The Malta Report*, ARCIC I did not delve into such historical questions as Cranmer's sacramental theology, the ordination of Matthew Parker as archbishop of Canterbury, the meaning of the bulls of Julius III and Paul IV. It did not investigate what is meant by the validity of sacraments and specifically of the sacrament of orders.

8. ARCIC I AND THE *KOINONIA* ECCLESIOLOGY'

ARCIC I went beyond what was explicitly foreseen by the Preparatory Commission regarding ecclesiology, although *The Malta Report* contained a hint of it. The introduction to *The Final Report* was itself discussed, composed, and endorsed by ARCIC as an agreed statement. It drew attention to the ecclesiology that was at work in the documents of ARCIC, and that underlay its claim of having arrived at substantial agreements in matters of doctrine. This ecclesiology was focused on 'the concept of *koinonia* (communion)'. This concept draws on the close relationship that exists between eucharistic communion and the Church as the community that gathers for the eucharistic celebration. It identifies the Church precisely as the eucharistic community. Or, in the formula that was used by Pope John Paul II and Archbishop Runcie, in their common declaration of October 3, 1989, 'the Church is a sign and sacrament of the communion in Christ which God wills for the whole of creation'.

ARCIC I saw the notion of communion as the key to the images of the Church in the New Testament (no. 4). It embodies the principle of the believers' relationship to God and Christ in the Holy Spirit, and to one another in Christ (no. 5). It is related to the eucharist, to ministerial *episcope* and the primacy (no. 6), to the visibility of the Church (no. 7), to the spiritual life of community of Christians (no. 8), and to the unity that Christ wills for his Church (no. 9). It is therefore in the light of its eucharistic doctrine and practice that the continuation of orders in the Anglican Communion is to be assessed. The insight of ARCIC I on the Church as communion was in line with a previous study by (the future) Cardinal Jerome Hamer. It has been echoed in much recent writing.[12] In an address given at Great St. Mary's in Cambridge, on January 18, 1970, Cardinal Jan Willebrands described the Church of the future, in which Anglicans and Roman Catholics will be reconciled. To do so, he drew on an essay in which Dom Emmanuel Lanne had shown that the universal Church is not only a communion of communions, but a communion of diverse types of communions. In the universal communion, therefore, several *typoi* of the Church must be at home:

> When there is a long coherent tradition, commanding men's love and loyalty, creating and sustaining a harmonious and organic whole of complementary elements, each of which supports and strengthens the others, you have the reality of a *typos*.

> Such complementary elements are many. A characteristic theological method and approach . . . A spiritual and devotional tradition . . . A characteristic canonical discipline, the fruit also of experience and psychology. . . .

Through the combination of all these, a *typos* can be specified.[13]

This trend of thought leads evidently to the idea that contemporary Anglicanism, with its liturgies, its spirituality, its episcopal organization, and its customary mode of authority, qualifies as an ecclesial *typos*, which would have its proper place in the reconciled universal Church. If a *typos* of the Church is understood to be a eucharistic community, standing in apostolic succession, teaching the Catholic faith, and practicing its mode of worship and government within the oneness of the universal Church, then the Anglican Communion throughout the world would be such a *typos*.

9. THE NOTION OF 'SISTER CHURCHES'

The question of the transmission of apostolic succession by way of episcopal ordination is not a matter of sacramental theology only. Since it is in the Church that priests and bishops fulfill their tasks, the sacraments are to be seen on the background of ecclesiology. Precisely, Pope Paul VI raised the question of the ecclesial status of the Anglican Communion, as he envisaged the future reconciliation of the Anglican and the Roman Catholic Churches.

On October 25, 1970, at the canonization of the forty martyrs of England and Wales, victims of the Reformation, the pope included this passage in his homily:

> There will be no seeking to lessen the legitimate prestige and the worthy patrimony of piety and usage proper to the Anglican Church, when the Roman Catholic Church—this 'humble Servant of the servants of God'—is able to embrace her ever beloved Sister in the one authentic Communion of the family of Christ, a communion of origin and of faith, a communion of priesthood and of rule, a communion of the saints in the freedom of love of the Spirit of Jesus. Perhaps we shall have to go on waiting in prayer in order to deserve that blessed day. But already we are strengthened in this hope by the heavenly friendship of the forty martyrs of England and Wales who are canonized today.[14]

Pope Paul did not call the Anglican Communion a 'sister Church'. Yet by evoking a future embrace of it as the Roman Catholic Church's 'ever beloved Sister', he implicitly suggested that it has the making of a sister Church. In this case, ecclesial sisterhood is virtual. It needs to be elicited and actualized. In other words, Pope Paul proposed a model for the work that should lead to a reconciliation of the two Churches.

Precisely, the ecumenical climate is affected by images and symbols, no less than by clear formulations and attitudes. The warmth that is implied in the expressions used by Paul VI contributes to the new context for the evaluation of Anglican orders.

10. VATICAN II AND THE SACRAMENTALITY OF THE EPISCOPATE

The new context for the evaluation of Anglican orders results in part from the orientation given by Vatican Council II to sacramental theology. In the Western Middle Ages the scholastic understanding of episcopal ordination differed widely from that which was suggested in the early patristic writings of St. Ignatius of Antioch. For the scholastics, episcopal ordination is simply the solemn granting of wider responsibility and authority to a person who has already received the fullness of the sacrament of orders in sacerdotal ordination. Episcopacy as such was not thought to be a sacrament: the sacrament was the priesthood. In the sixteenth century, however, the reform of the English ordinal was made on the principle that the ordination of a bishop is as sacramental as that of a priest. Accordingly, the sacramentality of the episcopate has been the common teaching of Anglican theologians.

There was an additional discrepancy in the sixteenth century between the Roman Catholic and the Anglican understanding of ordination. When Pope Paul IV denied the value of the ordination of Matthew Parker (December 17, 1559), this was due to the fact that the *Anglican Ordinal* included an explicit denial of papal authority; for the pope understood that episcopal ordination, while it does not give sacramental grace, signifies the grant of episcopal jurisdiction by the bishop of Rome.

On these two counts, Vatican II returned to the patristic tradition. In the first place, the constitution *Lumen Gentium* adopted a view of episcopacy that had been increasingly accepted among Catholic theologians, though it had not yet been endorsed magisterially: being the highest form of the sacrament of orders, the episcopate is itself a sacrament. The conciliar text runs as follows:

> The holy synod teaches that the fullness of the sacrament of orders is conferred by episcopal consecration, that fullness, namely, which both in the liturgical tradition of the Church and in the language of the Fathers of the Church is called the high priesthood, the acme of the sacred ministry. . . . In fact, from the tradition, which is expressed especially in the liturgical rites and customs of both the Eastern and the Western Church, it is abundantly clear that by the imposition of hands and through the words of consecration, the grace of the Holy Spirit is given, and a sacred character is imprinted. (*Lumen Gentium*, 21)

In the second place, Vatican II taught that the sacramental ordination of bishops introduces them into the episcopal college. From the perspective of Vatican II hierarchical communion is also needed for incorporation into the episcopal college. The bishops' jurisdiction therefore pertains to them as 'vicars and legates of Christ', not as 'vicars of the Roman Pontiffs' (*Lumen Gentium*, 27).

These reforms of the Catholic theology of the episcopate contributed to the new context for the evaluation of Anglican orders. This is all the more striking as they were followed by a reform of the ritual of ordination.

11. THE REFORM OF THE SACRAMENT OF ORDERS BY PIUS XII (1947) AND PAUL VI (1972)

Already Pope Pius XII, in the apostolic constitution *Sacramentum Ordinis* (November 30, 1947) explicitly excluded the 'porrection' of instruments from the 'matter' of ordination. In this ceremony, of medieval origin, the ordinand touches a chalice that is presented by the ordaining bishop. This gesture, the pope declared, was not required 'by the will of Our Lord Jesus Christ for the substance and validity of the sacrament'. Furthermore, 'if it was at one time made necessary to [the sacrament's] value by the Church's will and statute, all know that the Church can change and abrogate its statutes'. The matter of the sacrament is simply the laying on of hands, that is of biblical origin. For the priesthood, it is 'the first laying on of hands, that is done in silence'; for episcopacy, it is 'the laying on of hands that is done by the "consecrator". As to the form, it is in both cases contained in the "preface"'.

The logical consequence was drawn by Pope Paul VI. Through a series of *motu proprio* documents, Pope Paul reformed the sacrament of orders. In *Sacrum Diaconatus Ordinem* (June 18, 1968), he re-established the permanent diaconate. In *Pontificalis Romani Recognitio* (June 18, 1968), the Latin rite for the ordination of bishops came closer to the oriental rite; in the ordination of priests he 'brought closer unity to the rite', doing away with the porrection of instruments. For the three sacred orders, Pope Paul specified which 'words of the consecratory prayer . . . belong to the essential nature [of the sacrament], so that they are required for the validity of the action'.[15] These are for the priesthood:

> *Da, quaesumus, omnipotens Pater, his famulis tuis Presbyterii dignitatem; innova in visceribus eorum Spiritum sanctitatis; acceptum a te, Deus, secundi meriti munus obtineant censuramque morum exemplo suae conversationis insinuent.*

> [Almighty Father, grant to these servants of yours the dignity of the priesthood. Renew within them the Spirit of holiness. As co-workers with the order of bishops may they be faithful to the ministry that they received from you, Lord God, and be to others a model of right conduct.]

For the episcopate, the words are:

> *Et nunc effunde super hunc electum eam virtutem, quae a te est, Spiritum principalem, quem dedisti dilecto Filio tuo Jesu Christo, quem Ipse donavit sanctis apostolis, qui constituerunt*

ecclesiam per singula loca ut sanctuartium tuum, in gloriam et laudem indeficientem nominis tui.

[So now pour out upon this chosen one that power which is from you, the governing Spirit whom you gave to your beloved Son Jesus Christ, the Spirit given by him to the holy apostles, who founded the Church in every place to be your temple for the unceasing glory and praise of your name.]

In *Ministeria Quædam* (August 15, 1972), Paul VI abolished the minor orders of porter and exorcist and the subdiaconate (keeping the ministries of lector and acolyte). In *Ad Pascendum* (same date), he established norms for the permanent diaconate and for admission of candidates to the priesthood.

The chief thrust of this reform was to simplify and clarify the ritual of ordination. Unlike the reform of the ordinal that was effected in the sixteenth century by Archbishop Cranmer, the reform of Paul VI was not tied to a shift in the theology of the Church or of the sacraments. Paul VI himself formulated his principle: to keep close to the patristic rites and to those of the Oriental Church. Yet by doing so, he also narrowed the gap between the *Anglican Ordinal* and the *Pontifical*. Thus the Roman reform of the ritual of ordination helped to shape the new context for the evaluation of Anglican orders.

12. THE LETTER OF CARDINAL WILLEBRANDS ON *APOSTOLICAE CURAE* (1985)

In the conclusion of the Canterbury Statement on Ministry, ARCIC I recognized the emergence of a new context:

17. We are fully aware of the issues raised by the judgment of the Roman Catholic Church on Anglican Orders. The development of the thinking in our two Communions regarding the nature of the Church and of the ordained ministry, as represented in our Statement, has, we consider, put these issues in a new context. Agreement on the nature of ministry is prior to the consideration of the mutual recognition of ministries. What we have to say represented the consensus of the Commission on essential matters where it considers that our doctrine admits no divergence. . . . Nevertheless, we consider our consensus, on questions where agreement is indispensable for unity, offers a positive contribution to the reconciliation of our Churches and of their ministries.

The nature of this new context was explored in a letter addressed by Cardinal Willebrands to the co-chairs of ARCIC II (July 13, 1985). The president of the Pontifical Council for Christian Unity recognized that a 'new context' is now affecting the discussion of Anglican orders. He approved the principle that a study of the question 'cannot be a purely historical one'. The cardinal summed up *Apostolicæ Curæ*. Leo XIII's decision rested on the belief that the *Anglican Ordinal* betrays a *nativa indoles ac spiritus*, a 'natural character and spirit', that was judged unacceptable by the pope. This *nativa indoles* was found in 'the deliberate omission of all references to some of the principal axes of Catholic teaching concerning the relationship of the eucharist to the sacrifice of Christ, and to the consequence of this for an understanding of the nature of the Christian priesthood'.

In the light of the liturgical renewal, the cardinal drew the conclusion that the doctrinal agreements of ARCIC I, once endorsed by the proper authorites of the Anglican Communion in a solemn 'profession of faith', could remove what Leo XIII perceived as the Anglican *nativa indoles*. This in turn could 'lead to a new evaluation of the sufficiency of these Anglican rites as far as concerns future ordinations'. Such a study could prescind 'at this stage from the question of the continuity in the apostolic succession of the ordaining bishop'.[16]

Thus the new context that is now in the making may make it possible to reach a decision for the future without passing judgement on the past.

13. THE RESPONSE OF THE LAMBETH CONFERENCE (1988)

One of the conditions of Cardinal Willebrands has now been met by the Anglicans at the 1988 Lambeth Conference, which officially recognized the agreed statements of ARCIC on *Eucharistic Doctrine, Ministry and Ordination* and their *Elucidations*, as 'consonant in substance with the faith of Anglicans'. These statements can now be used pastorally and academically as examples of the doctrinal teaching of the Anglican Communion, and they point to a convergence in theology of ministry and eucharist which brings to an end the era of polarization.

Lambeth voted that such an agreement on eucharist and ministry offers a sufficient basis for taking 'the next step forward' towards the reconciliation of ministries of the two Churches grounded in this agreement in faith. The willingness expressed in Lambeth Resolution Seven to explore even more seriously with Roman Catholics 'the concept of a universal primacy in conjunction with collegiality' is related to the need for a 'personal focus' of unity and affection and the realisation that such a universal primacy would symbolize and strengthen in new ways the fundamental unity of the human family.

In preparing for Lambeth 1988, the provinces of the Anglican Communion also gave a clear 'yes' to Lambeth on both the statement on *Eucharistic Doctrine* and the statement on *Ministry* of ARCIC I. No province rejected the statement in *The Final Report* that 'the Eucharist is a sacrifice in the sacramental sense', and many were extremely positive that *The Final Report* is 'a helpful clarification' that 'sufficiently expresses Anglican understanding'. The provinces also reacted in a positive manner to this statement of *The Final Report*: 'Because the Eucharist is the memorial of the sacrifice of Christ, the action of the presiding minister in reciting again the words of Christ at the last supper and distributing to the assembly the holy gifts is seen to stand in a sacramental relation to what Christ himself did in offering his own sacrifice'. The provinces saw such a statement as giving help 'to further the reconciliation of ministries and growth towards full communion'.

In the light of the debate since *Apostolicæ Curæ*, the Lambeth Conference resolutions on ARCIC I assume historic proportions. And further, not only the Lambeth Conference, but now also twenty-five of the twenty-seven provinces of the Anglican Communion have accepted the eucharistic doctrine and ministry sections of *The Final Report*. One may ask if the prevailing mind of the Anglican Communion is still as contrary to the Roman Catholic understanding of eucharist, priesthood, and ordination as Pope Leo XIII believed it was.[17]

14. SIGNIFICANT GESTURES

The relationships between the Anglican Communion and the Roman Catholic Church are now evolving in a context that is marked, not only by an ecumenical shift in doctrine and liturgy, but also by a growing number of ecumenical events that have allowed the archbishops of Canterbury and the bishops of Rome to know each other personally.

Archbishop Fisher was received by John XXIII on a private 'visit of courtesy' on December 2, 1960. Archbishop Ramsey paid an official visit to Paul VI in March 1966. On this occasion, the two bishops joined in leading a prayer service at St. Paul's-Outside-the-Walls. Pope Paul called this 'not yet a visit of perfect unity, but . . . a visit of friendship placing us on the way to unity'.[18] In an unusual symbolic gesture, he passed his own episcopal ring from his finger to that of the archbishop of Canterbury. Archbishop Coggan was received by Paul VI in April 1977, and they jointly presided at a liturgy of the word in the Sistine Chapel.

John Paul II paid an official visit to the cathedral of Canterbury, where he was received by Archbishop Runcie (May 1982). This visit was returned when Archbishop Runcie came to Rome in September-October 1989. On this occasion the two prelates worshiped together at the Church of St. Gregory, from which Gregory the Great had sent Augustine to England to preach the Gospel to the Anglo-Saxons.

It is apparent that such symbolic gestures can be diversely assessed. By themselves, they do not imply that the difficulties faced by Leo XIII are no longer operative. Yet their cumulative effect reinforces the impression that relations between the two Communions have entered a phase marked by serenity and cordiality. This is a feature of the new context for the evaluation of Anglican orders.

15. CONCLUSION

The purpose of the present survey has been to draw attention to the changing climate between the Anglican and the Roman Catholic Communions since the condemnation of Anglican orders by Leo XIII. There has been a growth in understanding and friendship between members of the two Churches. Vatican Council II marked a point of no return.

With the creation of the Pontifical Council for Christian Unity, the wish to substitute dialogue for polemic was given an institutional instrument. The movement of rapprochement has begun to bear fruit in the work of ARCIC I, ARCIC II, and a number of regional and national joint Commissions.

A new context for the resolution of pending problems between the Churches is thus in the making. This context is now posing new questions. Among them there is that of a possible re-evaluation of Anglican orders by the Roman Catholic magisterium. To what extent the new context allows for new approaches to the apostolic letter *Apostolicæ Curæ* and to its conclusion is a question that deserves discussion. To what extent this context has also been negatively affected by the ordination of women in the Anglican Communion is itself a point that should receive careful examination.

At the conclusion of the present report, ARC-USA invites theologians of their two Churches to assess anew the past and present climate of their relationships, as well as this report, and to suggest possible ways forward to preserve and promote the ecumenical impact of Vatican II and of the recent dialogues, even in the face of whatever serious difficulties still exist.

ARC-USA trusts that its own efforts will contribute to the clarification of at least some of the issues involved in the assessment of the new context in which the Churches now live.

Long Branch, New Jersey
May 8, 1990

NOTES

1 The bishop of Huron had his correspondence with Pope Paul printed and distributed widely: *A Local Item in the Roman Catholic-Anglican Dialogue . . . 1965-1966*, 7 pages.

2 The definitive Latin text of *Apostolicæ Curæ* is in Leonis XIII, *Acta*, vol. VI, Rome, 1897, pp. 258-275. In G. Rambaldi, 'A proposito della Bolla *Apostolicæ Curæ* di Leone XIII', *Gregorianum* (61, 4, 1980), pp. 677-743, Rambaldi provides the entire text of the first schema of an Italian draft by Cardinal Camillo Mazzella, the first Latin text and the final text. For an English edition see *Apostolicæ Curæ*, trans. by G. D. Smith (London: Catholic Truth Society, 1956) and *Anglican Orders* (English) (SPCK, 1957).

3 The foundation of any new look at *Apostolicæ Curæ* has to be the new material now open to us in the Vatican archives. This consists primarily of four dossiers:

1. Segreteria di Stato, Anno 1901, Rubrica 66, Fasc. 1, 2, 3;
2. Espitola ad Principe, 142;
3. Lettere Latrine, 1896;
4. Spoglia Rampolla, pacco 3.

These materials add new information to our understanding of the preparation and meaning of *Apostolicæ Curæ* in the following ways:

1. Here we find the previously unpublished positive *Vota* of Louis Duchesne and Emilio De Augustinis with negative hand-written comments in English, perhaps expressing the views of the negative papal commissioners. Spoglia Rampolla contains the manuscript of a positive evaluation by Baron Friedrich Von Hugel, 'Memoire, addresse par ordre à son Eminence la Cardinal Rampolla sur les Rapports entre les Catholiques Anglais et les Anglicans', dated December 1895.

2. Here we find the various drafts of *Apostolicæ Curæ* from the first scheme of a full Italian draft by Cardinal Camillo Mazzella, Prefect of the Papal Palace, through the definitive Latin text. The various drafts contain changes and notations in Leo XIII's hand, so that we can see how the pope shaped the final versions of the document and came to his own conclusions on the issue of Anglicans orders.

3. In addition, there are many letters of Cardinal Mariano Rampolla del Tindaro (1843-1913), the papal Secretary of State, who maintained an extensive correspondence with the Anglican hierarchy, and with Lord Halifax, the President of the English Church Union, W. E. Gladstone, the Prime Minister of Great Britain, Fernand Portal, the French priest who had worked closely with Lord Halifax, the scholars Louis Duchesne, Pietro Gasparri, Emilio DeAugustinis, Friedrich von Hugel, and Luigi Tosti, the abbot of Monte Cassion. Rampolla emerges as the Vatican figure who is the leading advocate of reconciliation with the Anglicans. There are also reports from the future Cardinal Raphael Merry del Val, an opponent of reconciliation with the Anglicans, building a case against the validity of Anglican orders, as well as letters from the English, Irish, and Scottish Roman Catholic hierarchy urging no recognition of validity.

4 Recent publications in Italian and French make the positions of all the papal commissioners available to us today.

1. Louis Duchesne, of the Institute Catholique in Paris—G. Rambaldi, 'La memoria di Mg. L. Duchesne sulle Ordinazioni Anglicane ed un suo esame critico contemporaneo', *Gregorianum* (62, 4, 1981), pp. 681-746. Here Rambaldi provides the entire French text of Duchesne's positive evaluation of Anglican orders, 'Memoire sur les ordinations Anglicanes', with a historical introduction which shows how Duchesne was involved by Leo XIII and Cardinal Rampolla in the project. More on Duchesne's position is contained in G. Rambaldi, 'Leone XIII e la memoria di L. Duchesne sulle Ordinazioni Anglicane', *Archivum Historice Pontificiae* (19, 1981), pp. 333-345.

2. Emilio De Augustin, Rector of the Gregorian University in Rome—G. Rambaldi, 'Il Voto del Padre Emilio De Augustinis sulle Ordinazioni Anglicane', *Archivum Historicum Societatis Jesu* (50, 1981), pp. 48-75. Here Rambaldi provides the entire Italian text of De Augustinis' positive evaluation of Anglican orders, 'Sulla Validita delle Ordinazioni Anglicane', with a historical introduction. More on De Augustinis' position in relation to the Constitution *Sacramentum Ordinis* of Pius XII and the 1985 letter of Cardinal Willebrands on *Apostolicæ*

Curæ can be found in G. Rambaldi, 'La Sostanza del Sacramento dell'Ordine e la validita delle ordinazioni anglican secondo E. De Augustinis, S.J.', *Gregorianum* (70, 1, 1989) pp. 47–91.

3. Pietro Gasparri of the Institut Catholique in Paris—Pietro Gasparri, *De la valeur des Ordinations Anglicanes* (Paris, 1895).

4. T. B. Scannell, an English Catholic priest in Kent. His position and that of his three colleagues are analyzed and contrasted with the negative opinion in G. Rambaldi, 'La bolla *Apostolicæ Curæ* di Leone XIII sulle Ordinazione Anglicane—II', *Gregorianum* (66, 1, 1985), pp. 53–88. The substance of Scannell's position can be found in the letters to *The Tablet*: Aug. 24, 1895; Oct. 18, 1895; Nov. 9, 1895.

5   For analysis in English of the new historical materials in the Vatican archives, see three articles of R. W. Franklin, 'The Historic Episcopate and the Roman Church: From Huntington's Quadrilateral to 1988', in *Quadrilateral at One Hundred*, ed. J. Robert Wright (London, Oxford, Cincinnati: Mowbray and Forward Movement, 1988), pp. 98–110; '*Apostolicæ Curæ*', *Ecumenical Trends* (15, 5, 1986), pp. 80–82; 'The Historical Foundations of *Apostolicæ Curæ*', *Ecumenical Trends* (16, 2, 1987), pp. 24–29. See George Tavard, *A Review of Anglican Orders: The Problem and the Solution*, Collegeville: The Liturgical Press, 1990.

6   G. Ramaldi reconstructs the stages of the pope's thinking from the response to the positive commissioners through the various drafts and schema of *Apostolicæ Curæ* in two articles, 'A proposito della Bolla *Apostolicæ Curæ* di Leone XIII', *Gregorianum* (61, 4, 1980), pp. 677–743; 'Relazione e voto del Raffaele Pierotti, O.P., Maestro del S. Palazzo Apostolico sulle Ordinazioni Anglicane', *Archivum Historicæ Pontificæ* (20, 1982), pp. 337–388.

7   The letter of Leo XIII to the archbishop is found in *Acta Sanctæ Sedis* (29, 1896-1897), p. 664. The importance of this sentence in any future evaluation of Anglican orders was underlined by James O'Connor in a paper on *Apostolicæ Curæ* presented to ARC-USA in July 1987. The larger context of the sentence is discussed by G. Rambaldi, 'Una Lettera del Cardinal Richard sulla Fine della "Revue Anglo-Romaine"', *Archivum Historiæ Pontificiæ* (18, 1980), pp. 403–410. The encouraging letters of Cardinal Rampolla quoted here are to Cardinal Domenico Ferrata, Pro-Nuncio in Paris, 24 September 1896 (33180 in Vatican archives) and to Abbot Luigi Tosti of Monte Cassiono, 9 October 1896 (33468 in Vatican archives). Other letters encouraging dialogue and contact were sent by Cardinal Rampolla to Lord Halifax on March 15, 1897 (36409) and to Frederick Temple, archbishop of Canterbury on June 21, 1897 (38245). The Vatican initiative toward Anglicanism in the 1890s and the complex understanding of reconciliation within the Curia are discussed by G. Rambaldi in two articles, 'Un Documento Inedito sull Origine della Lettera di Leone XIII "Ad Anglos"', *Archivum Historiæ Pontificiæ* (24, 1986), pp. 405–414; 'Verso l'Incontro tra Cattolici e Anglicani negli Anni 1894-1896', *Archivum Historiæ Pontificiæ* (25, 1987), pp. 365–410. The sentiments of Halifax are quoted in Roger Greenacre, *Lord Halifax* (London: Church Literature Association, 1983, p. 17). See also Regis Ladous: *L'Abbe Portal et la Campagne Anglo-Romaine*, 1890-1912 (Lyon: Université de Lyon, 1973).

8   *Sæpius Officio* (London: The Church Literature Association, 1977), pp. 13-16, 38-39. For a more complete analysis of *Sæpius Officio* see E. R. Hardy, 'Priesthood and Sacrifice in the English Church', *The Holy Cross Magazine* (July, 1943), pp. 1-10. Other important Anglican letters to Rome after *Apostolicæ Curæ* encouraging dialogue and found in the Vatican archives are W. E. Gladstone to Abott Luigi Tosti, September 23, 1896 (33468), Lord Halifax to Cardinal Rampolla, March 5, 1897 (36409) and March 20, 1897 (36681), Frederick Temple, Archbishop of Canterbury, to Leo XIII, April 4, 1897 (38245) and to Cardinal Rampolla April 1, 1897 (38245). *The Lambeth Conferences: 1867-1948* (London, 1948), p. 128.

9   Leo XIII, in the French and Latin response to *Sæpius Officio* (Letter 38245 in Vatican archives) argues that despite 'the preservation of Catholic traditions in England . . . the doctrine discussed in your brochure on ordination and on the priesthood as well as on the sacrifice of the mass show that your doctrine is not that of the Roman Catholic Church'. For new documentation on Malines, see John A. Dick, *The Malines Conversations Revisited* (Louvain: Louvain University Press, 1990). Paul VI is quoted by Owen Chadwick in *The Tablet* (17 February 1990), p. 216. Excerpts from the memorial of Halifax can be found in G. K. A. Bell, *Documents on Christian Unity: Second Series* (London, 1930), pp. 36-37. Halifax is quoted in Margot Mayne, 'Catholic Reunion: The Noble Cause', *Church Observer* (Spring, 1984), p. 14.

10   The most complete bibliography through 1968 is given in John Jay Hughes, *Absolutely Null and Utterly Void* (Washington and Cleveland: Corpus Books, 1968), pp. 309-342.

11   Alan C. Clark and Colin Davey, *Anglican/Roman Catholic Dialogue. The Work of the Preparatory Commission* (London: Oxford University Press, 1974), pp. 112-113; emphasis added. This is reprinted in Anglican Roman Catholic International Commission, *The Final Report* (London: CTS/ SPCK, 1982), pp. 114-115.

12   See Jerome Hamer, *The Church is a Communion* (New York: Sheed and Ward, 1964); Jean-Marie Tillard, *Eglise d'Eglises. L'ecclesiologie de communion* (Paris: Cerf, 1987).

13   *Secretariat for Christian Unity Information Bulletin* (11, III, 1970), p. 14.

14   Quoted in Robert Hale, *Canterbury and Rome. Sister Churches* (New York: Paulist Press, 1982), p. 16.

15   These texts are quoted from *La Documentation Catholique* (Paris, July 7, 1968, no. 1520, col. 1169), and the English translation is taken from *The Rites of the Catholic Church as Revised by Decree of the Second Vatican Ecumenical Council and Published by Authority of Pope Paul VI*, vol. 2 (New York: Pueblo Publishing Company, 1980), pp. 83 and 95.

16   *Origins* (1987), pp. 662-663. The phrase *nativa ordinalis indoles ac spiritus* appears first in *Apostolicæ Curæ* on p. 270 [736-737]. Not all recent letters from Rome on Anglican relations have had the positive tone of Cardinal Willebrands'. An important critique of *The Final Report* came from the Prefect of the Congregation of the Doctrine of the Faith, Cardinal Joseph Ratzinger, 'Observation on *The Final Report* of ARCIC', *Enchiridion Vaticanum*, vol. 8 (Bologna: Edizioni Dehoniane, 1984). For Cardinal Ratzinger, *The Final Report* 'does not yet constitute a substantial and explicit agreement on some essential elements of Catholic faith'. Similarly, the Committee on Doctrine of the

United States National Conference of Catholic Bishops, in its 'Evaluation of the ARCIC Final Report', *Origins* (14, 25, 1984), pp. 409-413, found that 'an unfinished agenda precludes our saying at present that this doctrinal agreement in faith includes all that is essential for full communion between the two Churches'. Some recent Roman Catholic publications have defended the conclusions of *Apostolicæ Curæ* on Anglican orders. See Christopher Monckton, *Anglican Orders: Null and Void?* (Canterbury: Family History Books, 1987); and Brian W. Harrison, 'The Vatican and Anglican Orders', *Homiletic and Pastoral Review* (89, 1, 1988), pp. 10-19.

17   The full texts of the Lambeth resolutions may be found in the *Ecumenical Bulletin* (November-December 1988), pp. 19-21; *The Final Report*, pp. 20, 35; see also on these points Emmanuel Sullivan, 'The 1988 Lambeth Conference and Ecumenism', *Ecumenical Trends* (17, 10, 1988), pp. 145-148; and Thomas Ryan, 'The 1988 Lambeth Conference', *America* (September 24, 1988), pp. 162-164.

18   *La Documentation Catholique* (April 17, 1966, n. 1469, col. 673, not 1). See also Edward Yarnold, *Anglican Orders—A Way Forward?* (London: Catholic Truth Society, 1977).

15. REFLECTION ON THE EXPERIENCE OF WOMEN'S MINISTRIES

Anglican–Roman Catholic Dialogue Canada, 1991

INTRODUCTION

Great mutual understanding has been achieved in ecumenical dialogue between the Anglican and the Roman Catholic Communions. This mutual understanding impelled Pope John Paul II and Archbishop Robert Runcie in their visit a year ago to say, 'We here solemnly recommit ourselves and those we represent to the restoration of visible unity and full ecclesial communion in the confidence that to seek anything less would be to betray our Lord's intention for the unity of his people'.[1] At the same time, they urged our two Communions not to be 'unrealistic about the difficulties facing our dialogue at the present time'. And they continued, 'The question and practice of the admission of women to the ministerial priesthood in some provinces of the Anglican Communion prevents reconciliation between us even where there is otherwise progress toward agreement in faith on the meaning of the eucharist and the ordained ministry'.[2]

Yet they urged those working for visible unity of our Communions 'not to abandon either their hope or work for unity' and noted, 'While we ourselves do not see a solution to this obstacle, we are confident that through our engagement with the matter our conversations will in fact help to deepen and enlarge our understanding'.[3]

It is in this spirit of realism and of hope that the Anglican-Roman Catholic Dialogue of Canada offers this reflection on the experience of the ministries of women in Canada. Our aim is to contribute toward overcoming all that prevents reconciliation between us. We have set ourselves a twofold task in this agreed statement: to survey the various ministries of women as they have evolved in our two Communions in Canada and to consider the present state of our Canadian theological reflection on the role of women in the Church. We intend this discussion to assist Anglicans and Roman Catholics who are carrying on ecumenical dialogue here in Canada and in other parts of the world. Since we are aware that in many respects our Canadian cultural context contributes distinctively both to the practice of women in ministry and to theological reflection on their role in the Church, we wish to pay special attention to that context. We do so with the expectation that reflection on our experience of women in ministries in Canada may help to show a way past our present disagreements and differences.

Canadian women have offered a wide range of Christian service in both our communions, and in general it has been experienced positively. An important dimension of their apostolate has naturally been 'in the ordinary circumstances of family and social life' and 'in each and in all of the secular professions and occupations'.[4] Here their contribution has inevitably changed as the place of women in the family and in the world has changed. Women have also long served in more specifically ecclesiastical contexts, for instance, as religious, Christian teachers, fund-raisers, administrators, providers of hospitality, theological scholars, liturgical leaders, and pastors. Here too in recent years there have been changes in the roles and expectations of women. Some have favored such changes, and some have not. There have also been pressures to resist the admission of women to additional contexts of leadership, including, for Roman Catholics, the priesthood and, for Canadian Anglicans, the episcopate.

In referring to the service offered by women, Anglicans are more likely to speak of the *ministries* of women, Roman Catholics of the *apostolate* of women. In this document we use both these terms, mindful that the word *ministerium* was not often used among Roman Catholics to include lay service before the *moto proprio* of Paul VI, *Ministeria Quædam*, in 1972. Sometimes we follow his usage and use *ministry* to refer to some forms of lay service. But in doing so we intend no collapse of the distinction between lay and ordained ministries. On the contrary, we presuppose here the common understanding of our two Churches: that the ministry of the ordained 'is not an extension of the common Christian priesthood, but belongs to another realm of the gifts of the Spirit'.[5]

1. CIRCUMSTANCES UNDERLYING THE STATUS AND FUNCTION OF WOMEN IN OUR COMMUNIONS IN CANADA

Underlying the changing ways in which women are ministering and seeking to minister in our communions in Canada are the geography of the land, the development of distinctly Canadian ecclesiastical institutions, the experience of women in other Christian contexts in Canada, the role of women in Canadian society, emerging understandings of ministry, the impact of Christian feminism, and the personnel needs of the Church.

1.1　Geography

Canada is one of the least densely populated countries in the world: The second largest nation in the world in physical size, we have a population (1981 census) of only about 24 million. (Of these, 11.2 million are Roman Catholics, half of them in the officially francophone province of Quebec, and 2.4 million are Anglicans.) About two-thirds of the population is concentrated within 100 miles of the United States, along a border over 3,000 miles long. In the vast territory outside our population clusters, the Church is called to serve many hundreds of sparsely populated and isolated towns and villages. In these places especially, clergy are frequently in short supply and gravely overworked, and lay people or religious may well be commissioned to share in their ministry.

1.2   Our National Identity

In addition to our original native peoples, Canada is a country of two founding nations, French and British, with a significant multicultural immigration since the end of the nineteenth century. It was settled by French pioneers in the seventeenth century, began to be governed by the British during the eighteenth, acquired an independent national parliamentary government in 1867 and 'repatriated' its constitution in 1982. Since the 1960s, Canadian nationalism—and, in Quebec, Quebec nationalism—have been significant political and cultural realities. The Church in Canada, too, has in many ways reflected this political and cultural change from colonialism to sovereign nationhood. In the days when French and British settlers regarded themselves essentially as colonists from Europe, the Canadian Church remained in Europe's shadow. For instance, the first Roman Catholic bishop in Quebec, François de Laval, consecrated in 1685, remained a vicar apostolic; and it was not until 1908 that parts of Canada began to be removed from the mission jurisdiction of the Congregation for the Propagation of the Faith. And Anglicans could not consecrate bishops without the royal mandate until 1867, had no national synod until 1893, and used the English Prayer Book until 1921. Since then, however, it has been increasingly appropriate to speak of 'Canadian Catholics' or 'Canadian Anglicans'. The Canadian Conference of Catholic bishops began meeting annually in 1944, one of the first national conferences of Roman Catholic bishops. The 'Church of England in Canada' became the 'Anglican Church of Canada' in 1958. Both our Communions have therefore been increasingly willing to adapt the patterns of Christian ministry to that context rather than simply repeating European traditions. One result is that the roles and expectations of women in ministry in the Canadian Church may differ somewhat from what one would find in the European Churches. On the other hand, since the Canadian Church itself reflects regional and multicultural diversity, there is also within it a diversity in the roles and expectations of women in ministry.

1.3   Social Activism

Both Communions in Canada have developed a tradition of Christian social activism. In the Roman Catholic Church 'Catholic social action' can be traced to Bishop Armand François Marie de Charbonnel of Toronto in the mid-nineteenth century, but the tradition grew dramatically after *Rerum Novarum* (1891). Catholic action groups emerged, especially in Quebec, for farmers, workers, and youth; Catholic trade unions, the Catholic Family Movement, credit unions, newspapers, academic programs of social analysis, the Antigonish movement of community organization, the urban apostolate connected with Madonna House in the small town of Combermere, Ontario, and similar organizations in the past century attest the social conscience of Canadian Catholicism.

The broad range of Catholic Action organizations prior to Vatican II, especially Young Christian Workers and Young Christian Students, provided a context of prayer, study, and

Christian formation for the lay apostolate to society. And for at least 40 years the agenda of Catholic activists has included concern with the oppression and mistreatment of women in the community. Among Anglicans, a vigorous Christian social activism in the late nineteenth century was institutionalized in the Council of Social Service in 1917. During World War II, in the Diocese of Montreal a movement began of socially conscious clergy and laity called the Anglican Fellowship for Social Action which challenged the labor exploitation of the Quebec government. By the 1970s, coalitions of the various Canadian Churches— United, Roman Catholic, Anglican, Lutheran, etc.—had organized to provide research and theological critique of major Canadian issues (northern development, native rights, the economy, poverty, immigration), and the role of Canadian Churches in advocating social justice is well known. Here, too, justice for women has been a part of the Church's witness, with numerous committees, task forces, and ministries devoted to it. There have been those in both Communions who have applied their critique of the status of women in Canadian society also to the Church.

1.4   Women's Christian Movements

Long before there were secular feminist movements, Christian women in Canada were organizing for social and religious purposes. In the nineteenth century churchwomen were organizing to welcome fugitive slaves from the United States, campaigning for alcoholic temperance and prohibition and for moral reform, advocating women's suffrage, and administering educational and social agencies such as the Young Women's Christian Association. There were some Christian movements in which women gave conspicuous leadership such as the Holiness Revival beginning in the 1850s and the Salvation Army. In all these areas churchwomen understood themselves as being constrained by the love of Christ. In our own century these examples multiplied still more, and some Christian groups began commissioning or ordaining women to various ministries; particularly notable is the ordination of a woman in 1936 in the United Church of Canada, then and now the country's largest Protestant denomination. These examples have helped some Canadian Anglicans and Roman Catholics envision and apply new possibilities for the ministry of women in their own communions, although it has also strengthened others in their resolve to resist these models.

1.5   The Experience of Women in Canadian Society

It may be that frontier experience tended to collapse roles based on gender distinctions and to erode European patterns of subordinate roles for women. Studies of the colonial days of New France indicate that women were accorded considerable social and religious authority and influence, far more than they enjoyed in the mother country. In the past century, women have been gradually admitted to previously all-male professions: Emily Stowe in 1880 was the first woman to be licensed to practice medicine in Canada; Clara

Brett Martin in 1897 was the first woman to be admitted to a law society; female suffrage in federal elections was granted in 1918; and women became eligible for the House of Commons in 1919 and for the Senate in 1929.

Since then industrialization has brought women increasingly into the economic mainstream of society. Most Canadian women between 18 and 65 now have jobs outside the home, and the proportion of women in the traditionally male professions and in upper levels of corporate management has risen dramatically in the past generation. The growing understanding that discrimination on the basis of gender is a violation of natural justice was entrenched in 1982 in the constitution of the country. Various federal and provincial enactments of human rights legislation outlaw discrimination on the basis of gender in a variety of areas.

All these developments have inevitably had consequences for the way in which Canadian Christians perceive the role of women in the Church, and many have contrasted the role of women in the Church and their role in the community. As the Anglican rector of St. James' Cathedral, Toronto, Canon Plumptre, was writing already in 1922, 'Young women by the score, who see that in the Church more than in any other sphere their sex is a discount, if not a discredit, are seeking other fields for their life's work'. Many identify certain policies of the Churches regarding women as discriminatory. Of these, some have left the Church altogether; some others have changed denominations; still others, while remaining loyal to their Communion, have joined groups seeking change; and many are simply quietly resentful. On the other hand, other Canadian Christians argue that there is no necessary analogy between what the secular world considers the proper status of women and what divine revelation establishes as the proper status of women.

1.6   Promotion of Lay Ministries and Lay Apostolates

Both our Communions have in our generation given new expression to the Gospel's proclamation that all the baptized belong to the priestly people redeemed by Jesus Christ, thus reaffirming the value of the ministry of women. Among Roman Catholics, the Vatican II decree *Lumen Gentium* (1964) associated 'the common priesthood of the faithful and the ministerial or hierarchical priesthood'; each 'in its own special way is a participation in the one priesthood of Christ'.[6] By baptism all the faithful, and not only men, are consecrated to participation in the liturgy, the prophetic office of Jesus Christ, and the mission of the Church. Since Vatican II the Roman Catholic Church has made distinct progress, and in some cases dramatic progress, toward declericalization. In the Anglican Communion, similarly, the bishops have reminded their people through the resolutions of the Lambeth Conference that 'the Christian ministry is committed to the whole people of God; and not, as is often believed, to the ordained ministry alone',[7] and have recommended 'that no major issue in the life of the Church should be decided without the full participation of the laity in discussion and in decision'.[8] It is proper to acknowledge, however, that the funding, accountability, and recognition of lay ministries in the Anglican Church have been poor. This may have been a factor contributing to the increase in female candidates for ordination within the Anglican Church of Canada.

The fresh recognition of the common priesthood of the faithful has been explicitly applied to women's Christian service. The decree *Apostolicam Actuositatem*, on the apostolate of the laity, stated, 'Since in our times women have an ever more active share in the whole life of society, it is very important that they participate more widely also in the various fields of the Church's apostolate'.[9] At the close of Vatican II the council fathers strongly affirmed woman's 'basic equality with man', her fuller realization of her vocation, and her increasing influence in the world. In 1984 the Canadian Conference of Catholic Bishops has devoted a plenary session to the role of women in the Church, and in 1985 it recommended that the Synod of Bishops be developed into a synodal process, with the participation at various levels of lay men and lay women, since they are 'responsible with us for the mission of Christ entrusted to the Church'. In the Anglican Church of Canada, the General Synod affirmed in 1965 that 'men and women are called to share a common concern for the life and mission of the Church and have a common responsibility to fulfill this mission'. It asked the Church to offer leadership in winning equal status for women, urged diocesan synods to permit women the right of election to all the lay offices of the Church, and recommended equal pay for work of equal value for male and female lay ministers.

1.7   Academic Scholarship

In both our secular and Christian academic institutions there has been an explosion of scholarship in the past generation on women's issues, women's history, and the role of women in Bible, doctrine, and tradition. Some, but not all, of this scholarship accepts the description *feminist*, in that it posits that historical documents created by those in power tend to neglect, downplay, or marginalize those who are not in power, women among them. While some radical feminists have concluded that sexism is so inextricably woven into the fabric of Christian Scripture and doctrine that they can no longer participate with integrity in the Church, more moderate writers in this area have concluded that the New Testament takes an essentially egalitarian view of men and women, that women in the primitive Church were generally admitted to roles of influence, and that women, however invisible in tradition, have taken real leadership in the Churches throughout their history.

1.8   Personnel Shifts and New Opportunities in the Church

A shortage of ordained men has sometimes opened new doors to women's ministries. In 1928, in the Anglican Diocese of Brandon, Bishop W. W. H. Thomas was unable to find any men to minister in the extremely remote Swan River Valley and appointed Marguerite Fowler to what would become St. Faith's Mission. The results were, he said, 'so remarkable' that he established an order of voluntary 'messengers'. The Bishop's Messengers were commissioned to take services, baptize in cases of emergency, and bury the dead. Archbishop Carrington, in *The Anglican Church in Canada*, wrote, 'They were put in charge of isolated settlements; they did the work that the men couldn't be got to do, one of them gently explained to me'.[10]

Roman Catholic religious orders of women in sparsely populated Canadian regions frequently would find themselves offering the majority of ministries in that area because few priests were available. Today the Anglican Church still has many small congregations that have no resident priest, although this is largely due to limited diocesan funding and the difficulty of deployment of priests in sparsely populated areas. And personnel needs in many parts of the Roman Catholic Church in Canada have recently become intense.

A published 1984 study of human resources for the Canadian Conference of Catholic Bishops suggested that the number of priests had dropped 9 percent between 1977 and 1983, and projected that the number under the age of 65 would drop a further 22 percent by 1993. This situation of shortage is intensified by the requirement of celibacy for Catholic priests and bishops of the Latin rite. Of 4,692 Roman Catholic parishes (excluding missions), 17 percent had no resident priest. A 1984 presentation to the Canadian Conference of Catholic Bishops based on submissions of English-speaking Canadian women claimed widespread concern that because of limitations placed by the Church upon women's opportunities to minister to others many 'might not experience . . . needed healing ministry'. The increase in women pastoral associates in parish settings may be seen as in part a result of a shortage of male clergy.

2. AREAS OF WOMEN'S APOSTOLATE IN OUR COMMUNIONS

In the past generation women in both our Communions have undertaken an increasing number of tasks of ministry and roles of Christian leadership, primarily in the secular world and family, but also, and increasingly, in more specifically ecclesiastical contexts.

2.1 Callings in the Secular World and in the Family

Both our Communions recognize that women with responsibility in families, in community activities, and in secular occupations are, like men, 'called there by God so that by exercising their proper function and being led by the spirit of the Gospel they can work for the sanctification of the world from within, in the manner of leaven'.[11] Most women (and most men) exercise by far the largest part of their apostolate and their Christian leadership in non-ecclesiastical areas and are satisfied that in doing so they are being entirely faithful to God's calling.

2.2 Religious Orders

Many Roman Catholic women, and some Anglican women, have committed themselves to community religious life, variously emphasizing common prayer, study, and ministries in ecclesiastical and secular settings. Many religious communities begin as groups of laywomen working together on a common Christian task and progress by degrees toward recognition as self-governing communities under Church-approved structures of oversight. Most in Canada are active rather than cloistered, and contribute to many areas of Christian service, including education, medicine, the care of orphans and the destitute, social work, housekeeping, and so on.

Roman Catholic religious orders for women have existed in Canada since 1639, when two cloistered orders arrived in Quebec, one founding a hospital and the other a school. Several women religious have been particularly honored in Canada, such as the Ursuline Marie de l'Incarnation (1599-1672), a theological and devotional writer. Anglophone religious orders in Canada date from 1847, when the Loretto Sisters in Toronto and the Sisters of Charity at Red River began educational work. In 1986 there were reportedly 34,895 women religious in a Roman Catholic population of 11 million (0.3 percent), down sharply from 1966, when there were recorded 51,770 women religious in a Catholic population of under 9 million (0.6 percent).

In Canada the 'institutional face' of the Roman Catholic Church, its vital infrastructure of services, has been provided in great part by the apostolic endeavors of women. The typical Catholic experience of 'official' Church, outside of the immediately sacramental, was frequently by way of a sister. These ministrations were very much at the heart of the living, worshiping Church and not some accidental appendage. The contributions of sisters to the liturgical worship of local parishes as teachers of prayer and through the development and direction of choirs is too obvious to require comment.

The less public benefaction afforded by the personal and communal prayer of such communities and the essential spiritual endowment of contemplative orders is not so immediately appreciated without reflection. In more recent years a number of religious communities have committed themselves to develop, staff, administer, and financially sustain prayer centers. At this point the role of woman as teacher of prayer assumed new dimensions through increased activity in spiritual counseling and retreat work, traditional church activities more commonly exercised by clergy prior to Vatican Council II.

The networking of women's religious communities was advanced considerably with the foundation of a national bilingual organization and office, the Canadian Religious Conference, in 1950. For some time now the president of the Canadian Religious Conference has sat as an observer in the regular meetings of the Canadian Catholic Conference of Bishops. The regional divisions of the Canadian Religious Conference have assisted individual religious communities with research and reporting facilities on church and social questions. As well, they have helped to develop stimulating educational and formation programs.

In the Anglican Communion, religious orders, which had been suppressed at the Reformation, began to be revived in the mid-nineteenth century, in the wake of the Anglo-

Catholic movement. The Sisterhood of St. John the Divine, founded in 1884 in Toronto with Hannah Grier Coome as first superior, and the Sisters of the Church, who began Canadian work in 1891, exist to this day, but there are only two other women's communities in the Anglican Church of Canada. Although the numbers of formally professed Anglican religious in Canada are very small, it may be argued that many Anglican women for whom religious orders have not been a practical option have nevertheless had comparable but less structured experiences of cooperative ministry, mutual accountability in Christ, and corporate prayer.

2.3   Deaconesses

The first Anglican deaconesses in Canada were 'set apart' by the bishop of Toronto with the laying on of hands in 1894; the deaconess movement was favored by Anglican evangelicals as an alternative to women's religious orders. Deaconesses functioned in many ways similarly to Roman Catholic sisters, with particular responsibility for Christian education and youth work, and the care of immigrants, the unemployed, and the socially marginalized. Deaconess training schools and community houses in Toronto and Saskatoon also served a role as church social service and Christian education centers.

2.4   Parish-Based Women's Organizations

Of all the church-related structures, these are the ones in which the largest number of laywomen have been active in both our Communions. Among Anglicans, the Woman's Auxiliary was founded in Ottawa in 1885 by Roberta Elizabeth Tilton, inspired by a U.S. Episcopal precedent. It quickly expanded to other dioceses and became a national organization in 1905. Until the early 1940s its focus was mission. It mobilized women parishioners to raise funds for missions, gather food and clothing for the needy, oversee the education of the children of missionaries, publicize the mission of the Church, maintain an ambitious publishing program, and recruit, train, pay, and pension women missionaries. It was relatively independent, and in its heyday was the strongest and most efficiently administered organization in Canadian Anglicanism. Through an amalgamation of parish organizations in 1968, the WA became the Anglican Church Women and broadened its understanding of mission. A typical parish ACW might sponsor study groups, social projects, fundraising drives, or hospitality at parish functions and other events. In recent years many ACW parish chapters have closed, reflecting partly the more complete integration of women into the formerly male-dominated structures of the Church, partly changing expectations of women, partly the professionalization of church work, and partly shifting demographics as most younger women work outside the home and have limited time for charitable activity. In 1974 the national structure of ACW was disbanded, and the Women's Unit of the Program Committee was formed to coordinate all women's groups and concerns for the Anglican Church of Canada.

The Catholic Women's League of Canada was formed nationally in 1920, with parish, diocesan, provincial, and national levels of organization. Since the 1950s it has also had chapters for business and professional women. It is 'committed to the upholding of Christian values and education in the modern world'. It has published a journal, called *The Canadian League*, since about 1926. It organizes fund-raising, hospitality and social projects, and, like the National Women's Unit of the Anglican Church, it has also taken a keen advocacy role on issues of peace and justice. In 1983 its membership was 130,000. Both the ACW and the CWL currently reflect tensions on issues relating to women like inclusive language and women's ministries.

2.5   Women in Administration

Anglican women who owned or rented pews were admitted to parish vestries as early as the 1870s as a result of decisions in the civil courts, but the eligibility of women for most administrative positions had to be won by diocesan canon, which did not widely happen until the 1920s or later. A recommendation of the Lambeth Conference in 1918 that women should be admitted to the lay councils of the Church on equal terms with men was not widely honored in Canada for several decades. Rural dioceses such as the Diocese of Caledonia in northern British Columbia might send a woman delegate to General Synod as early as 1924 (she was refused her seat), but in urban areas like Toronto and Montreal women were not admitted to diocesan synods until the 1950s or later. It was not until 1965 that General Synod passed a resolution in line with the Lambeth recommendation of 1920. General Synod and most diocesan synods now generally attempt to give women significant representation on committees, and it is no longer unusual for women to serve as warden or in other parish offices as diocesan program staff or in other appointments.

In the Roman Catholic Church in Canada women have been admitted to positions of administrative authority in diocesan or national structures in significant numbers only since Vatican II. A 1977 survey indicated that 27 percent of diocesan office directors across Canada were women and 60 percent of diocesan assistant directors. A number of women are functioning as chaplains and as judges in church courts. Under the new Code of Canon Law women are eligible to be appointed chancellors of dioceses, and some serve this role in Canada. The Canadian Conference of Catholic Bishops has recommended that women be included in formalized consultative processes leading up to each Synod of Bishops.

2.6   Pastoral Roles in Parishes

In both our Communions women have been appointed to pastoral roles in parish or school settings, particularly in outlying areas. Among Anglicans, in addition to the Bishop's Messengers in the dioceses of Brandon and Athabasca, there have been since the 1920s women lay readers to lead church services and women with license to administer the eucharistic elements. Women in these roles are now extremely common indeed. A particular kind of parish leadership has frequently fallen on clergy wives in Anglicanism, who often have acted as honorary ACW presidents, parish secretaries, intermediaries between priest and people, Bible study leaders, musicians, and pastoral counselors. However, the expectation that the clergy wife will be her husband's unpaid assistant appears to be dying.

Roman Catholic parishes have increasingly invited women to serve on pastoral teams and as pastoral associates in vacant parishes. A study for the Canadian Conference of Catholic Bishops in 1984 indicated that of 825 vacant parishes in Canada, 84 were entrusted to sisters. Since then the use of lay people and sisters in pastoral ministry is a growing phenomenon. Religious and laywomen are in many of these cases authorized to preside over the liturgy of the word and to administer communion from reserved elements.

The practice of ministry illustrates a trend in the Roman Catholic Church in Canada: The partnership of women and men in the mission of the Church is emphasized, and programs of diocesan renewal bring together priests and chairpersons of various parish committees—many of them women—into common projects of proclamation and service. In the Archdiocese of Montreal, for example, women with particular liturgical or pastoral responsibility may follow the same program of studies as diaconal candidates and be initiated into the order of service. It is reported to us that some clergy have resisted these developments, but other clergy and most lay people welcome them.

A recent sociological profile of the average woman in pastoral work in Quebec portrayed her as 47 years old, who in half the cases was a religious; in the other half she was a married woman with two or three children who previously had been in school for 15 years, had worked for another employer for 13 years and had been working for the Church for five years.[12]

2.7   Ministries in Specialized Settings

Laywomen in both our Communions have been appointed to hospital, correctional, military or educational chaplaincies, peace and justice ministries, Church-sponsored social agencies, resource services, Christian journalism and other situations. A growing number of women are attracted to such ministries in our country.

2.8   Education

Roman Catholic religious had founded and were running schools in New France already in the seventeenth century, and today thousands of lay and religious women as well as men teach in the various provincial confessional and secular school systems. The development of colleges and universities run by and for women provided opportunities at this level which were both scarce and restricted until the twentieth century. Most routine educational work among youth at the parish level appears to be done by women. An increasing number of women teach in Roman Catholic universities, and women began appearing on the faculties of seminaries and theological colleges in about 1970. In the three

Roman Catholic colleges in the Toronto School of Theology, for example, nine women teach as full-time faculty members. The Dominican College of Philosophy and Theology was the first pontifical faculty to appoint a woman as dean. Like male faculty in theological colleges, women faculty members are generally seen as filling not only academic but also pastoral roles in the community, and may preach at non-eucharistic services, counsel, and lead prayer.

Anglican women were by the 1880s being sent as missionaries to undertake educational work in the Northwest among settlers and indigenous peoples. Women have been prominent also in Sunday schools, which became increasingly common in Canadian Anglican parishes after the middle of the nineteenth century. On the prairies, women organized family clusters to receive Sunday school by post and caravans to the women and children of outlying areas. There are very few Anglican primary or secondary schools in Canada, but women play a full role in them. Anglican theological colleges, unlike their Roman Catholic counterparts, have found it difficult to find qualified women or men to appoint to their faculties, largely because the Anglican Church of Canada has not sufficiently encouraged or supported advanced theological study. Thus Anglican women with a basic theological degree currently are more likely to seek ordination, and relatively few proceed to doctoral studies.

2.9   Care of Those in Need

Since 1639 a commitment to the healing sciences, most frequently overseen by women, has characterized the Roman Catholic Church in Canada. A network of orphanages, hospitals and gerontology services has been developed across the country. These institutions, created by Catholic women and staffed, directed, and administered by them, offered unparalleled opportunity in Canadian society prior to the 1960s for the development and application of intellectual, administrative, and other talents. There was no other area of Canadian society which regularly prepared, called for, and expected the level of leadership by women at senior and executive positions in very complex institutions of central significance to Church and society. Frequently these facilities represented the first such institutions in their locale. In the Anglican Church of Canada, the Sisters of St. John the Divine have long had an involvement in health care, which began with the opening of a surgical hospital in Toronto in 1885. They continue to work in the area of geriatric care.

2.10   Mission Work

The Roman Catholic Church in Canada has been regarded as contributing generously to foreign missionary activities. Particularly in this century women have played a key role in this work, exercising a ministry of loving presence. Several thousand women have spent years working in other lands. Religious women especially, but during the last generation many laywomen as well, have been an integral part of this effort. They have served as catechists, health-care workers, educators, and in a wide variety of development undertakings, including the initiation of credit union and cooperative activity.

2.11   Ordained Ministries

The one area of Christian service to which Canadian Anglican but not Roman Catholic women have been admitted is ordained ministry. Since the 1890s, some Anglican women with vocations were 'set apart' to the ministry of deaconess. The 1930 Lambeth Conference recognized the 'order of deaconess is for women the one and only order of the ministry which we can recommend our branch of the Catholic Church to recognize and use'.[13] It involves a dedication to lifelong service, but not to celibacy.[14] But Lambeth Conference 1968 went further and proposed 'that those made deaconesses by laying on of hands with appropriate prayers be declared to be within the diaconate'.[15] By the early 1970s, women were being ordered to the diaconate in Canada. Some, but by no means all, of those deaconesses were willing to be ordained priests when this became canonically possible in 1975. Others retained their identity as deaconesses, while still others saw themselves as lay pastoral workers in the Church.

Serious but isolated proposals to ordain women to the Anglican priesthood can be traced to the nineteenth century. In 1928 the idea was discussed at greater length in the Anglican newspaper *The Canadian Churchman*. 'A living Church, if it is to remain alive and develop, must take risks', wrote the editor of the women's page in the newspaper. The ordination of women was proposed in a speech at the synod of the Diocese of Toronto in 1948. Momentum developed in the 1960s and early 1970s, with theological and historical studies commissioned by General Synod and other bodies, while numerous articles and books on the subject were appearing throughout English-speaking Anglicanism.

In 1975 General Synod came to the understanding that there were no canonical obstacles preventing diocesan bishops from ordaining women to the priesthood. Shortly afterward, the same General Synod adopted a 'conscience clause', whose precise meaning remains controversial, seeking to protect those not agreeing with its decision. The first ordinations took place in 1976, making Canada the first Anglican province to ordain women in a fully recognized, procedurally regular way. More recently the Church has sharply criticized the Church of England for refusing to recognize the orders of its women clergy.

In 1991 there were 275 women clergy in the Anglican Church of Canada. In some dioceses women have been nominated to the episcopate. Strains between Anglican provinces which do ordain women to the priesthood and those which do not are a matter of public record.

Ordained women have ministered in every Canadian Anglican diocese, and the ordination of women no longer appears as a serious controversy in the Anglican mainstream in Canada. Conversation has moved to new issues such as relations with Anglican provinces which do not recognize the ministries of Canadian women priests; alternative models of authority in church structures; the distinctive contributions, if any, which women may make to Christian spirituality, liturgy, and ministry; and the role of women priests in imaging God and healing women's experiences of isolation and rejection.

The Canadian Conference of Catholic Bishops has repeatedly taken leadership on questions related to women; in particular, it encouraged the formation of study groups on the topic of women in the Church which had a widespread effect in parish life in Canada, and it recommended the use of inclusive language in church communities.

But the further issue of whether women should be ordained in the Roman Catholic Church remains a question in Canada; unofficial advocacy groups take both sides on the issue.

2.12 Summary

Roman Catholics and Anglicans in Canada have lived out their faith in the same social and cultural context, but within different institutional and devotional settings. In our two Communions women have had ministries that have been very similar, and that similarity is in large part a reflection of our common Gospel and our common geography, national history and identity, Christian social conscience, and commitment to lay ministry.

In both our Communions, most women (and most men) live out their faith in their families and in their secular occupations. There have been particular opportunities for celibate women to commit themselves to lives of Christian service, either as religious or, among Anglicans, as deaconesses, since most deaconesses remained single during the course of their ministry. Women have had significant ministries in parish-based women's organizations, particularly in mission work, youth work, hospitality, fund-raising, and issues of social justice. Some women have assisted in church administration and institutional decision making; some have been teachers and school administrators; some have been appointed to specialized ministries.

All this we share. What divides us, in what we understand of the calling of women in Christian service, is the single but important issue of whether the Church is authorized to admit women to priestly ordination.

In seeking the reconciliation of Roman Catholics and Anglicans in Jesus Christ, therefore, we need to confirm and celebrate our common understanding and practice in these very large areas, but also to evaluate the reasons for our disagreement over the ordination of women. To what extent are the reasons matters of Christian doctrine, and which parts of Christian doctrine are implicated? To what extent are they, on the other hand, matters involving the enculturation of the Gospel? In order to answer these questions we will need to consider the theological implications of the role of women in our two Communions.

3. THEOLOGICAL IMPLICATIONS OF THE MINISTRIES OF WOMEN

In Canada the ministries of women have not only developed and flourished in the practice of our two Communions: In addition, they have been the subject of theological reflection. What is the significance of the service women have rendered to Christ in the past and present life of the Church? What does it mean that they have taken a significant role in evangelization, teaching, care for the poor and the sick, prophetic denunciation of injustice, and other Christian works? How should our proclamation of the Gospel through the ministries of women adopt and transform Canadian cultural insights, and how should it challenge and criticize these insights? These questions are at the center of lengthy and serious theological discussion in our two communions in Canada.

In this section we want briefly to describe the atmosphere of theological discussion on women within which our two Communions find themselves in Canada as they reflect upon these questions.

3.1 Affirmation of the Variety of Gifts Given to Women

Both of our Communions rejoice today at the recognition of the variety of gifts that the Holy Spirit has given to women as well as to men for the proclamation of the Gospel and the building up of the Church of Christ. Women have always been involved in a variety of ministries of the Church, but their contributions have not always been recognized clearly or welcomed fully. In our Churches today there is a sharp sense of the injustice of such oversight and a determination to proclaim in our practice 'there are varieties of gifts, but the same Spirit . . . varieties of service, but the same Lord' (1 Cor 12:4–5).

In our Churches, it is understood that those involved in evangelization must have an understanding of the experience of women. This includes not only positive experiences of women, but also in a special way women's experiences of poverty, sexual abuse, or prejudiced mistreatment based on their gender. In addition, including the voices of women within the voice of the Church is considered essential if the witness of the Church in our culture is to be effective in announcing, 'Now whoever is in Christ is a new creation' (2 Cor 5:7).

Canadian culture already has a very strong sense of the equality of women and men, stretching from the experience of the frontier when survival demanded that men and women work closely together—often in similar tasks—in order to accomplish whatever jobs needed doing. Any perceived failure by the Church to celebrate and serve women's equality in Christ is experienced by Canadian Christians as foreign or wrong. Archbishop Louis-Albert Vachon of Quebec (now retired) reflected a viewpoint prevalent in our Churches when, serving as a delegate for the Roman Catholic bishops at the 1983 Synod of Bishops, he commented, 'appeals of the Church to the world for the advancement of the status of women are on the point of losing all impact unless the recognition of women as full members becomes simultaneously a reality with the Church itself'.[16]

Hence there is a cultural predisposition to welcome and affirm gifts of the Spirit given to women for centuries but not always celebrated. In addition, there is a readiness not only to appreciate women's contributions to ministries they have traditionally held—such as catechetical instruction of children and care for the sick—but also to welcome women into ministries they have not held as frequently in Christian history. So, for example, the ministries of Roman Catholic and Anglican women who administer parishes, sit on church marriage tribunals, serve as prison or hospital chaplains, teach theology to divinity students, or conduct retreats are for the most part well received in our two Communions in Canada. Even people who are doubtful about such new experiences often report that the competence of a woman minister and her evident desire to serve the Gospel persuade them to recognize God's hand in her ministry and to know that women and men are 'fellow workers in Christ Jesus' (Rom 16:3).

Archbishop Vachon underlined the need for reconciliation between men and women arising out of the nature of our baptism. 'A new humanity is being realized in Jesus Christ in which internal conflicts of racial, social and sexual origin are abolished; a new humanity, responsible for bringing about its own historical and cultural existence', he said. 'In this humanity man and woman come into being and recognize each other on a basis of equality in origin and destiny, and equality in mission and involvement'.[17]

3.2   Reflection on the Meaning of the Man-Woman Distinction

Besides theological reflections on women's ministries, our Churches are also filled with discussion and scholarly research on the significance for the orders of creation and redemption that 'God created humanity in God's own image. . . . Male and female God created them' (Gn 1:27). While these reflections have different concerns and take often contradictory positions, certain themes are emerging as consensus positions within the theological community of our two Churches in Canada.

3.2.1. In the area of *theological anthropology*, theologians draw attention to the ambivalent role that the cultural stereotypes about men and women have played in the history of Christian thought on the theological meaning of gender difference. The identification of maleness with spirit and femaleness with matter, for example, which Christian thinkers appropriated from first-century neo-Platonic thinkers, is often cited as a damaging principle to use in elaborating a doctrine of creation about men and women. Such an identification led some Christian theologians in the past to conclude that men are by nature more rational, more constant, or more suited to give leadership, while women are by nature more emotional, more changeable, and less able to lead. Some used this understanding as a basis for arguments against giving women positions of leadership in the community and the Church. Today theologians in our Churches—whether they see the psychological differences between men and women as more due to nature or to culture—nevertheless are agreed in trying to avoid the use of a stereotyped list about men and women.

3.2.2. Second, theologians in Canada have reflected on the witness of the New Testament to *Jesus' treatment of women* during his earthly ministry. They have been concerned to show the openness toward the concerns and the collaboration of women that is revealed in the New Testament account of Jesus. He healed the woman with the flow of blood (Mk 5:25-34), and he included women such as Mary and Martha as well as Lazarus among his friends (Jn 11:5). He forgave the woman taken in adultery (Jn 7:53-8:11), and he revealed himself to the Samaritan woman at the well (Jn 4:7-42). Mary is praised for her faith (Lk 11:27-28) and honored in a special way by being chosen to give birth to the Savior (Lk 1:46-49), and women disciples are the first to receive the revelation of the resurrection of their Lord (Mt 28:1-8; Mk 16:1-8; Lk 23:55-24:12). The attitude of Jesus toward women is often contrasted with attitudes they experience in our society.

3.2.3. In addition to reflecting such experiences of Jesus with women, theologians in Canada in our two Churches have reflected on the *significance of the maleness of Christ* for his saving work. They have underlined the heritage we have both received from the first four ecumenical councils of the Church. Confessing the full divinity of Jesus Christ, they confess anew as well his full humanity. While not questioning the maleness of Christ, they emphasize that Christ's saving work transcends all racial, sexual, social, and economic barriers—since, in the words of the patristic axiom, 'what is not assumed is not saved'.

3.2.4. Finally, theological discussion has focused on our *understanding of God*. When continuing—with the Scriptures and the history of the Christian tradition—to use the language of *Father* to refer to the one whom Jesus called *Abba*, our two Communions in Canada strive to clarify the metaphorical character of that language. Theologians and liturgists have tried to collaborate in order to avoid the use of language about God that would so anthropomorphize God as to suggest that God is more like men than like women or that women are not made in the image of God. Hence they have emphasized, along with the major theologians of both the East and the West, that God's nature cannot be captured or exhausted by our true confessions about God.

In addition, they have reminded us that the Scriptures sometimes describe God with female imagery, for example as a woman groaning in labor (Dt 32:18) as the female figure of Wisdom (Prv 8:22-31; Job 28:20-23), as a mother weeping for her children (Jer 31:20), as a mother carrying a child in her womb (Is 46:3), as a mother nursing her child (Ps 131:2), as a midwife (Ps 22:9), as the mistress of a household (Prv 9:1-6), as a woman searching for her lost coin (Lk 15:8-10). Scripture also ascribes to God traits often stereotypically used to characterize women such as tenderness, gentleness, and the capacity for nurture. By emphasizing that God has such characteristics, our two communions hope also to criticize abuses in practice that would misuse faith in God to justify violence or unfair treatment of women in society.[18]

3.2.5. We have summarized very briefly an emerging theological consensus on theological anthropology, on Christology, and on God in relationship to the question of women.

But interest in these discussions is not limited to theologians or to church workers. Both of our Communions are filled with *widespread popular concern* about the theological understanding of women and about the practice of the Churches toward women. Popular lectures and books, media coverage, and debates over church policy about women draw an increasing number of people into discussion of these theological questions. This has become part of the atmosphere of church life for our two Communions in Canada.

3.3 The Canadian Context for the Question of the Ordination of Women

When the question of the ordination of women (to the diaconate, the presbyterate, or the episcopate) arises in our two Communions in Canada, it arises within the context we have been describing. The question about women's ordination, which has been answered differently by our two Communions, is located in the midst of this broad spectrum: the recent celebration of the wide variety of women's ministries, the affirmation of the legal equality of women in Canadian society, the shortage of ordained ministers to serve Canadian congregations, the experience of other Churches ordaining women for many decades in Canada, the widespread interest in theological questions about women, and the sense that unequal treatment of women is unjust. The location of the question of women's ordination within this context contributes toward making it a volatile and controversial topic within both of our Communions.

At the same time, the question appears as a small point within the sweep of our history of the many ministries of women. Women have had many ministries within the Church, and this experience continues in a particularly rich way within both of our Communions in Canada.

3.3.1. The similarities and differences between our two Communions in Canada in the concrete exercise of women's ministries show the complexity of the actual practice regarding the ministries of women in the Canadian Churches.

On the one hand, in the Roman Catholic Communion laywomen and members of women's religious communities have been involved in a wider variety of lay ministries for a longer time than in the Anglican Communion. In one sense, they experience this wide variety of women's ministries as nothing new, though they welcome the recent recognition being given more publicly to women's substantial involvement in such ministries. In addition, with the Roman Catholic Church—where women cannot be ordained—a large number of women have recently made themselves qualified professionally for ministries of leadership in the Church newly open to them such as chaplaincy in prisons or hospitals, administration of diocesan offices, teaching of divinity students, leadership by women's religious congregations in the work of justice, etc.

The Anglican Church, which ordains women, finds that it is not as successful in drawing its women into full-time professional lay ministries, since many of its qualified women seek ordination. Some Anglican laywomen have the perception that their ministry is not accorded sufficient authority unless they are ordained.

At the same time, the Anglican Church reports a very positive experience of the ministry by ordained women in their midst. Despite some tensions and even initial resistance by some persons to ordained women, most Anglicans report that the ordination of women is experienced as a grace of God to the Church, a proclamation of the Gospel about the full involvement of all persons in the redemptive work of Christ and a source of fresh approaches to pastoral care and decision making in the Church. The 1986 General Synod of the Anglican Church of Canada affirmed its 'positive experience in Canada with women in priesthood' and urged the Canadian bishops to carry to the Lambeth Conference 'our conviction that the priesthood of women has indeed been blessed and has enriched our common life'.[19]

Meanwhile, both of our Communions in Canada have suffered from a shortage of ordained ministers. In the Roman Catholic Communion this shortage is more pronounced, so that many Roman Catholic congregations in Canada are no longer able to celebrate the eucharist together even once a week. While lay ministers seek to respond to the needs of these congregations, the congregations are in fact denied the nourishment of the weekly eucharist; and their Church does not feel authorized to ordain the women or married men who are entrusted with all of the other ministries of leadership in their community except this one. In Canada, this situation is perceived as a growing pastoral crisis for the work of evangelization. Some Roman Catholics fear that their people will lose the experience of the centrality of the eucharist in their lives because they do not celebrate it even once a week.

3.3.2. In addition, in Canada the theological discussions about women also affect the question of women's ordination, and they show *the complexity of the theoretical question regarding the ministries of women in the Canadian Churches.*

Some Anglicans and Roman Catholics see in the ordination of women a capitulation to cultural pressures, a confusion of the Church with the world and its values. They stress that at times the Church must stand in prophetic contrast to the culture in which it finds itself, and they see the ordination of women as the failure to maintain such a countercultural position. In a culture which can confuse equality with sameness, a stand in favor of the difference between male and female roles seems a witness to the Gospel. They emphasize the differences between men and women, and in particular they draw attention to the beauty and dignity of the God-given role of motherhood.

In addition, some emphasize that a practice such as women's ordination should not be started unless and until the whole Church of Christ, including the Orthodox Church, has come to a consensus that would allow this step to be taken together. They welcome the stand taken by the Roman Catholic Church against the ordination of women, and they regret the beginning of this practice by the Anglican Church to ordain women. Why should the Roman Catholic Church seek full communion with a Church that would simply imitate the modern liberal culture in which it finds itself, they ask? While this position is held by more Roman Catholics than Anglicans in Canada, it is not absent from either of our Churches.

A second group of Roman Catholics and Anglicans, while emphasizing the specific characteristics of women, emphasizes as well the full equality of women with men. This group remains divided among themselves over the ordination of women.

A third group of Roman Catholics and Anglicans sees in the refusal to ordain women a denial of the full equality of women and men in Christ. They fear that this refusal is based on the cultural stereotypes about men and women that the Christian tradition inherited somewhat unreflectively from Greco-Roman culture rather than on a real discernment of the demands of the Gospel. In addition, they fear that the failure to ordain women may imply—though unintentionally—a soteriology that truncates the inclusiveness of Christ's saving work. Anglicans who have these views wonder why they should seek full communion with a Church that endangers these aspects of the Gospel so important for our day and culture. Anglicans and Roman Catholics who see the question this way applaud the ordination of women in the Anglican Church and regret the continuing refusal of the Roman Catholic Church to begin this practice.

3.4 The Reception of Authoritative Teaching For and Against the Ordination of Women in Canada

Both of our Communions have given official authoritative teachings to explain their practice with regard to the question of the ordination of women.

3.4.1. Some Protestant Churches began *the practice of ordaining women* in the nineteenth century. The first woman ordained in the Anglican Communion was Florence Li, who was ordained under wartime emergency conditions by Bishop R. O. Hall of Hong Kong in the Holy Catholic Church in China during World War II in 1944. Since that time some provinces of the Anglican Communion have begun to ordain women to the diaconate and the presbyterate. The Anglican Church of Canada began ordaining women as presbyters in 1976. Recently the Anglican provinces in the United States and New Zealand have each ordained a woman as bishop.

3.4.2. In 1976 in the Declaration on the Question of the Admission of Women to the Ministerial Priesthood (*Inter Insigniores*), the Congregation for the Doctrine of the Faith set out reasons for the Roman Catholic Communion's continuing practice of restricting ordination to men. While noting the dignity of women and the decisive role they have played in the Church, the declaration stated that 'the Church, in fidelity to the example of the Lord, does not consider herself authorized to admit women to priestly ordination'.[20] Noting that this is the constant tradition of the Church, the declaration explains that it is based on the attitude and practice of Jesus, who did not call women to be among the Twelve, and on the attitude and practice of the apostles, who did not confer ordination on women. When the

Church judges 'that she cannot accept certain changes', the declaration continues, 'it is because she knows that she is bound by Christ's manner of acting'.[21]

In addition, the declaration offered as an explanatory reason that 'in actions which demand the character of ordination and in which Christ himself, the author of the covenant, the bridegroom and the head of the Church, is represented, exercising his ministry of salvation—which is in the highest degree the case of the eucharist—his role (this is the original sense of the word *persona*) must be taken by a man'.[22]

3.4.3. In an explanation of the practice of the Anglican Communion that permits the ordination of women, Archbishop Robert Runcie, then-archbishop of Canterbury, wrote to John Paul II that—'although Anglican opinion is itself divided—those Churches which have admitted women to priestly ministry have done so for serious reasons'.[23]

Explaining this practice further in a letter to Cardinal Jan Willebrands, he notes the growing Anglican conviction that 'there exists in Scripture and tradition no fundamental objections to the ordination of women to the ministerial priesthood'.[24] Furthermore, Anglican provinces that ordain women argue that a substantial doctrinal reason not only justifies the ordination of women, but actually requires it. 'The fundamental principle of the Christian economy of salvation—upon which there is no question of disagreement between Anglicans and Roman Catholics—is that the Eternal Word assumed our human flesh in order that through the passion, resurrection and ascension of the Lord Jesus Christ this same humanity might be redeemed and taken up into the life of the triune Godhead', he writes. 'It is also common ground between us that the humanity taken by the Word, and now the risen and ascended humanity of the Lord of all creation, must be a humanity inclusive of women, if half the human race is to share in the redemption he won for us on the cross'.[25]

In addition, he continues, some Anglicans would go on 'to point to the representative nature of the ministerial priesthood. They would argue that priestly character lies precisely in the fact that the priest is commissioned by the Church in ordination to represent the priestly nature of the whole body and also—especially in the presidency of the eucharist— to stand in a special sacramental relationship with Christ, in whom complete humanity is redeemed and who ever lives to make intercession for us at the right hand of the Father. Because the humanity of Christ our high priest includes male and female, it is thus urged that the ministerial priesthood should now be opened to women in order the more perfectly to represent Christ's inclusive high priesthood'.

He continues, 'This argument makes no judgement upon the past, but is strengthened today by the fact that the representational nature of the ministerial priesthood is actually weakened by a solely male priesthood, when exclusively male leadership has been largely surrendered in many human societies'. Despite the tensions associated with this issue, he adds, Anglican provinces that ordain women report 'that their experience has been generally beneficial'.[26]

3.4.4. In 1986, Cardinal Jan Willebrands, president of the Pontifical Council (then called Secretariat) for Promoting Christian Unity, explained the Roman Catholic position further in a letter responding to Archbishop Runcie. 'The ordination only of men to the priesthood has to be understood in terms of the intimate relationship between Christ the redeemer and those who, in a unique way, cooperate in Christ's redemptive work', Willebrands explains. 'The priest represents Christ in his saving relationship with his body the Church. He does not primarily represent the priesthood of the whole people of God. However unworthy, the priest stands *in persona Christi*. Christ's saving sacrifice is made present in the world as a sacramental reality in and through the ministry of priests. And the sacramental ordination of men takes on force and significance precisely within this context of the Church's experience of its own identity, of the power and significance of the person of Jesus Christ, and of the symbolic and iconic role of those who represent him in the eucharist'. He noted that the topic of women's ordination 'will, of course, continue to be a matter of discussion'.[27]

3.4.5. Finally, an additional reflection on this understanding was offered by Pope John Paul II in his meditation 'On the Dignity and Vocation of Women' (*Mulieris Dignitatem*), published in 1988. In pondering the symbolic significance of Christ's self-offering, he writes, 'As the redeemer of the world, Christ is the bridegroom of the Church'. He continues, 'Since Christ in instituting the eucharist linked it in such an explicit way to the priestly service of the apostles, it is legitimate to conclude that he thereby wished to express the relationship between man and woman, between what is *feminine* and what is *masculine*. It is a relationship willed by God both in the mystery of creation and in the mystery of redemption. It is the eucharist above all that expresses the redemptive act of Christ, the bridegroom, toward the Church, the bride. This is clear and unambiguous when the sacramental ministry of the eucharist, in which the priest act *in persona Christi*, is performed by a man. This explanation confirms the teaching of the declaration *Inter Insigniores*'.[28]

3.4.6. How are these official explanations of church practice *received in Canada?* As to the Anglican statement, Anglicans among us report that most Canadian Anglicans find the theological explanation of Archbishop Runcie persuasive or at least satisfactory. While ordained Anglican women report initial resistance at times to their priestly ministry from individuals within a congregation, in general the ordination of women has been welcomed within the Anglican Church of Canada as a grace of God to the Church and a sign of the new creation in Christ.

The 1986 General Synod of the Anglican Church of Canada voted to 'reaffirm its acceptance of ordination of women to the priesthood'. Furthermore, it ruled that future candidates for ordained ministry would no longer be able to avail themselves of a clause that had earlier permitted bishops not to ordain women if their conscience did not allow it.[29] In accord with this affirmation of the value of women's ordination, the National ecutive Council of the Anglican Church of Canada at their November 1986 meeting also criticized the Church of England for its decision to deny the exercise of sacramental ministry to Anglican women ordained in Canada. 'Such a decision threatens the unity of the Anglican Communion by extending the privilege of ecclesiastical hospitality to some of our clergy and not to others', they wrote.[30]

At the same time, Anglicans are concerned about the impact of women bishops on the bonds of communion. They cannot yet know what the long-term impact will be when women become bishops in provinces of the Anglican Communion.

In regard to the explanations given by the Declaration on the Question of the Admission of Women to the Ministerial Priesthood, the correspondence of Cardinal Willebrands and 'On the Dignity and Vocation of Women', Roman Catholics among us report that the reception in their communion is more varied. On the one hand, there is in general the submission of mind and will that Roman Catholics in Canada spontaneously give to the ordinary teaching of the Magisterium. This is combined with a widespread sense of perseverance regarding this issue and a sense of loyalty to the Roman Catholic Church.

Many Roman Catholics in Canada hear in the teaching and practice of their Church on this issue a preservation of the apostolic faith, for the reasons we mentioned above. Many others do not. Speaking as delegate of the Canadian Roman Catholic bishops to the 1987 synod, Bishop Jean-Guy Hamelin of Rouyn-Noranda, Quebec, drew attention to this response: 'We know that this synod on the laity is not the appropriate forum for dealing specifically with the question of the ordination of women. But we cannot avoid underlining in this assembly that the reasoning used so far to explain the reservation of sacred orders to men has not seemed convincing, especially not to young people'.[31]

The variety of responses to official teaching and practice on this question is an emerging issue within the Roman Catholic Church in Canada. The fact that the very same practice causes scandal to some while being welcomed by others in the same Communion is a source of pain and polarization. Some Roman Catholics perceive this polarized situation as a growing pastoral problem.

4. OUR PROPOSAL FOR A WAY FORWARD: DISCERNMENT ON THE GOSPEL AND CULTURE FOR THE SAKE OF EVANGELIZATION IN CANADA

We propose that the issue of women's ordination be approached as a disputed question about the enculturation of the Gospel; and we suggest this approach in particular to the Second Anglican Roman Catholic International Commission, which is charged with considering this question.

4.1   An Urgent Question in Canada for the Mission of the Church to Worldwide Evangelization

In this perspective, the question assumes urgency, because it deals with the removal of a twofold obstacle. On the one hand, the different understandings and practice of our two Communions constitute an obstacle between us in the very close fellowship we experience in Canada in the work of evangelization. At the same time, evangelization in Canada demands a careful theology and practice about women and their gifts within the Church, as we have suggested above. Addressing the issue of women is actually part of evangelization within Canada. Hence it is urgent that we benefit from each other's experience in order to fulfill our common vocation of spreading the Gospel in this place. As 'Baptism, Eucharist and Ministry' points out when discussing the ordination of women, 'Openness to each other hold the possibility that the Spirit may well speak to one Church through the insights of another'.[32]

4.2   The Gospel and Culture

What is the significance of the experience of the growing affirmation of women's ministries in Canada? This question is part of the larger question: How is the Gospel related to cultures? We believe that the Church is called to proclaim the Gospel in every culture in such a way that the culture is taken up and transformed. The Gospel is not opposed to culture, said Pope John Paul II when he visited Canada in 1984; Christians should not accept a 'divorce between faith and culture'.[33] At the same time, they are called to 'evangelize in depth . . . culture and cultures', he said.[34] The Gospel challenges and criticizes cultural practices, calling for their reform. Christian proclamation calls every culture to repentance for its collective sins and sets forth a prophetic call that may meet resistance and hostility in a culture because of the Gospel's high demands. 'God's love extends to people of every culture', the 1988 Lambeth Conference said, 'and . . . the Gospel judges every culture according to the Gospel's own criteria of truth, challenging some aspects of culture while endorsing and transforming others for the benefit of the Church and society'.[35]

Sometimes, then, the Gospel transforms culture. Sometimes it challenges and criticizes culture. We believe that the issue of women in our culture and our Communions in Canada must be examined within this context of Gospel and culture. It is a question of the indigenization of the Gospel in Canada for the sake of the mission of the Church for the whole world: But to what is the Gospel calling us on this matter?

We agree with the comments of Bishop Hamelin: 'We must begin by facing some facts. The affirmation movement of women, with its strengths and its limitations is incontestably one of the facts that shapes social evolution in our day. In *Pacem in Terris*, Pope John XXIII invited us to see in it a "sign of the times". Are we not faced with a major development within our civilization—as massive as the industrial revolution of the nineteenth century?

'It follows that our duty is to exercise discernment. The women's movement carries some precious seeds for the humanization of culture. It also carries with it built-in risks. At present, we are right in the midst of a collective effort with openness and with tenacity. We must draw insights even from the tensions and differences of interpretation that are among us'.[36]

4.3   An Invitation to Discernment

We invite Anglicans and Roman Catholics throughout the world to join Canadian Anglicans and Roman Catholics in this process of discernment about the meaning of these developments within Canadian culture. We suspect that they have significance for the Church throughout the world; but we must discover together, under the guidance of the Holy Spirit, what exactly that significance is.

In this process of discernment each of us must wrestle with some difficult questions.

4.3.1. Anglicans must face some *difficult questions* in their dialogue with Roman Catholics and in their own internal discussions. Have they sufficiently explained their decision to ordain women in relation to the whole Church with its many cultures? If this decision has caused and continues to cause such deep divisions within their own Communion between provinces from different cultures, what does it mean for the work of evangelization throughout the world? This is even more painfully important since the Lambeth Conference of 1988 recognized the possibility of the consecration of women bishops; and in fact since then two women have been consecrated to the episcopate in the Anglican Communion.

If an initiative drastically breaks the *koinonia* in the Gospel, can it be the work of the Spirit? Or are those Anglicans right who believe that short-term strain in relationships will lead to long-term strengthening and extension of the gift of fuller communion to the whole of humanity?

In addition, Roman Catholics would be troubled if they sensed that the ordination of women was simply an affirmation of certain First World cultural emphases on individual rights. They ask the Anglican Communion: How does the decision to ordain women not simply repeat in a new key cultural presuppositions about men and women popular in North America today, presuppositions which may be no closer to the Gospel than were those operative at an earlier stage in the Greco-Roman world? Finally, they wonder whether the ordination of women increases the perception that one must be ordained in order to minister.

4.3.2. In their own process of discernment, *Roman Catholics* also face some *difficult questions*. They need to consider whether the experience of new cultural understandings of the equality of women, such as those that permeate the Canadian Church continually, could be a sign of the times to which the Roman Catholic Church must respond more fully in its understanding and practice about women.

We are aware that the Roman Catholic position is that 'it does not consider herself authorized to admit women to priestly ordination'.[37] We wonder if thought might be given to the conditions under which the Roman Catholic Church would feel authorized for such a change. We suggest that the experience of the Roman Catholic Church in Canada could contribute to such a reflection. When women assume an increasing number of ministries within our communion for the sake of Gospel, it becomes hard to explain why they should be kept from this one ministry—especially when the shortage of ordained ministers, the cultural sensitivity to the equality of women, the theological discussions about women, the positive experience of the Anglican and other Churches in ordaining women, and the impression of giving scandal by not ordaining women: All raise the question of whether the Holy Spirit might be leading us to a new enculturation of the Gospel in this place.

The urgency with which the question is perceived in Canada leads us to suspect the question might be a sign of the times with significance for the whole Church, which recognizes that 'diversity of customs and observances only adds to [the Church's] comeliness and contributes greatly to carrying out her mission'.[38] Could this be an issue which would allow a diversity of practices in recognition of diverse cultural customs?

The Roman Catholic bishops of Canada have called for [such] a re-examination of the question of the ordination of women in their response to *The Final Report* of the Anglican Roman Catholic International Commission. Noting the urgency of Christ's mandate for unity, they continue, 'We call for a concerted and wholehearted effort, under the guidance of the Spirit, to discern the mind of Christ for his entire Church today on this issue [the question of the ordination of women], so as to bring to completion our mutual recognition of orders'.[39] Speaking more generally about our two Communions in Canada, they noted that 'the Canadian experience of cultural dialogue, a long and unique one, as well as the close acquaintance of our conference with the life and work of Anglicans in Canada make us well disposed to accept their witness about their own faith. We invite others to be open to a similar experience as our journey of convergence continues'.[40]

CONCLUSION

We have tried to discuss the issue of the ministries of women—including the question of the ordination of women—as it looks from the perspective of the experience of the Anglican and Roman Catholic Communions in Canada. We have done so with a sense of the urgency that this issue poses for the work of evangelization here. It is our hope that our reflections will serve efforts to bring the Anglican Church and the Roman Catholic Church into full communion. We have learned urgency from our common Lord, to whose prayer we join our own: 'I do not pray for these only, but also for those who believe in me through their word, that they may all be one; even as thou, Father, art in me, and I in thee, that they also may be in us, so that the world may believe that thou hast sent me' (Jn 17:20-21).

Toronto and Ottawa
April 11, 1991

NOTES

1   John Paul II and Robert Runcie, Common Declaration (Oct. 2, 1989), *Origins* 19 (1989-90), pp. 316-17.

2   Ibid., p. 317.

3   Ibid.

4   Vatican II, *Lumen Gentium*, in *The Documents of Vatican II*, ed. Walter M. Abbot (New York: Guild, 1966), no. 31.

5   Anglican Roman Catholic International Commission, Ministry and Ordination, *The Final Report* (London: SPCK and Catholic Truth Society, 1982), no. 13.

6   *Lumen Gentium*, 10.

7   *The Report of the Lambeth Conference 1978* (London: CIO Publishing, 1978), Report of Section 2, p. 82.

8   *The Lambeth Conference 1968: Resolution and Reports* (New York: SPCK and Seabury Press, 1968), no. 24, p. 37.

9   Decree on the Apostolate of the Laity (*Apostolicam Actuositatem*) in *The Documents of Vatican II*, no. 9.

10   Phillip Carrington, *The Anglican Church in Canada: A History* (Toronto: Collins, 1963), p. 262.

11   *Lumen Gentium*, 31.

12   Sarah Balanger, *Portrait du personnel pastoral feminin au Québec* (Montreal: Bellarmin, 1988).

13   *The Lambeth Conference 1930: Encyclical Letter From the Bishops With Resolutions and Reports* (London: SPCK and New York: Macmillian, 1930), no. 67, p. 60.

14   Ibid., 69, pp. 60-61.

15   *The Lambeth Conference 1968: Resolutions and Reports*, no. 32, p. 39.

16   Louis-Albert Vachon, 'Male and Female Reconciliation in the Church', *Origins* 13 (1983): 334.

17   Ibid., p. 335.

18   Task Force Report to General Synod 1986 of the Anglican Church of Canada, *Violence Against Women: Abuse in Society and Church and Proposals for Change* (Toronto: Anglican Book Center, 1987), pp. 42-45; cf. Social Affairs Committee of the Assembly of Quebec Bishops, *A Heritage of Violence? A Pastoral Reflection on Conjugal Violence*, trans. Antionette Kinlough (L'Assemblée des Evêques du Quebec: Montreal, 1989).

19   Anglican Church of Canada, *Journal of the 31st General Synod* (Toronto: Anglican Church of Canada, 1986), Act 65, p. 85.

20   Congregation for the Doctrine of the Faith, 'Declaration on the Question of the Admission of Women to the Ministerial Priesthood (*Inter Insigniores*)', *Origins* 6 (1976-77): 519.

21 Ibid., p. 522.

22 Ibid.

23 Robert Runcie to John Paul II, Dec. 11, 1985, *Origins* 16 (1986): 155.

24 Robert Runcie to Jan Willebrands, Dec. 19, 1985, *Origins* 16 (1986): 156.

25 Ibid., p. 157.

26 Ibid.

27 Jan Willebrands to Robert Runcie, June 17, 1986, *Origins* 16 (1986): 160.

28 John Paul II, 'On the Dignity and Vocation of Women' (*Mulieris Dignitatem*), *Origins* 18 (1988-89): 279.

29 *Journal of the 31st General Synod*, Act 91, pp. 116-17.

30 Statement of the National Executive Council of the Anglican Church of Canada to the Officers of the General Synod of the Church of England, Minutes, November 1986.

31 Jean-Guy Hamelin, 'Access of Women to Church Positions', *Origins* 17 (1987): 347.

32 World Council of Churches, 'Ministry', *Baptism, Eucharist and Ministry* (Geneva: World Council of Churches, 1982), no. 54.

33 John Paul II 'In a Changing Society the Faith Must Learn to Speak Out and Be Lived', *Canada: Celebrating Our Faith* (Boston: Daughters of St. Paul, 1986), no. 6, p. 21.

34 John Paul II, 'In the Civil Order, Too, the Gospel Is at the Service of Harmony', *Canada: Celebrating Our Faith*, no. 22, p. 219.

35 Lambeth Conference (1988), *The Truth Shall Make You Free* (London: Church House Publishing, 1988), no. 22, p. 219.

36 Hamelin, p. 347.

37 Declaration on the Question of the Admission of Women to the Ministerial Priesthood, p. 519.

38 Decree on Ecumenism (*Unitatis Redintegratio*), 16.

39 Canadian Conference of Catholic Bishops, Response of the Canadian Conference of Catholic Bishops to the ARCIC I Final Report, *Ecumenism* (December 1987), p. 15.

40 Ibid., p. 11.

16. PASTORAL GUIDELINES FOR CHURCHES IN THE CASE OF CLERGY MOVING FROM ONE COMMUNION TO THE OTHER

Anglican–Roman Catholic Bishops Dialogue, Canada, 1991

A BRIEF HISTORY

In November 1985, the Anglican–Roman Catholic Bishops' Dialogue began to discuss the ecumenical implications of clergy moving from one Church to the other. Participants agreed that when a change is requested, it is important to make contact with the authorities in the Church from which the person comes; to assess the impact on the person and on the whole Christian community; to proceed with ecumenical courtesy.

In November of 1986, the topic was resumed with a focus on the criteria and procedures for preparing candidates for ordination.

At the November 1987 meeting, there was a further discussion of criteria and procedures as well as some consideration of discernment of vocation. It was agreed that the number of cases may increase and that guidelines would be helpful. Archbishops Antoine Hacault and Walter Jones agreed to prepare a first draft for discussion the following year.

In 1988, an outline of the proposed guidelines was discussed. The two bishops agreed to work with staff to prepare a more detailed set of guidelines.

In 1989, Archbishops Hacault and Jones presented their draft text. There was a page by page examination of the document and a number of modifications were proposed. It was agreed that these would be incorporated and that the text would be forwarded to the CCCB's (Canadian Conference of [Roman Catholic] Bishops) Ecumenism Commission and the Anglican Interchurch Interfaith Committee for comment.

At the 1990 meeting, Archbishop Hacault presented the revised text. Participants studied the document in detail in both French and English versions and made a number of revisions. Sister Donna Geernaert was asked to edit the text and circulate it prior to the 1991 meeting.

With a few changes, including the title of the English version, the revised text was approved at the meeting of November 21-23, 1991. It was agreed that the document should be forwarded to the CCCB Permanent Council and the Anglican House of Bishops. This is to be a document for the bishops' information and use rather than a formal publication such as the Pastoral Guidelines for Interchurch Marriages.

I. ORDAINED MINISTRY IN THE LIFE OF THE CHURCH

1.   In Canada over the past few years there have been instances of Anglican or Roman Catholic clergy joining the other Church and wishing to exercise an ordained ministry. Sometimes there have been unfortunate consequences, resulting in uncertainty and confusion among members of both Churches. The individuals concerned are motivated by deep personal reasons but people do not always understand what has happened or why. We hope that such transitions might not be occasions of triumphalism but will take place in ways appropriate to a relationship between two Churches which today receive each other as sister Churches in real but imperfect communion. For this reason, it will be helpful for both Churches in such cases to deal with each other openly and in a spirit of mutual respect to the world.

2.   For a quarter of a century, Anglicans and Roman Catholics have been engaged 'in a serious dialogue which, founded on the Gospels and on the ancient traditions, may lead to that unity in truth, for which Christ prayed' (Common Declaration of Pope Paul VI and Archbishop Michael Ramsey, 1966). One of the fruits of that dialogue has been growing appreciation of the ministry exercised in the other Church. In the Agreed Statement on Ministry and Ordination (Windsor, 1973) the Anglican Roman Catholic International Commission claims to have reached consensus on essential matters related to the nature of ordained ministry and its role in the life of the Church. It is in this context, far removed from the more polemical approach which often marred earlier relationships, that the question of the movement of persons in the ordained ministry from one Church to the other should be approached.

3.   Another important element in our dealing with the persons seeking admission to the ordained ministry within the other Church must be a profound respect for the conscience of those whose pilgrimage of faith has made such a move seem desirable and necessary to them. The intention of these guidelines is a pastoral one, to ensure that the procedures followed are a help and not a hindrance to individuals in clarifying the motivation and implications of their movement into the communion of the other Church. It is also important to keep in mind the needs and concerns of the church communities which are involved and in which they will eventually serve.

4.   We wish to ensure that such occasions are not disruptive of our growing ecumenical relationship. We are convinced that sensitivity to the rights of both individuals and particular Churches will not conflict with the growing appreciation of the real but imperfect communion which already exists between our Churches.

5.   There are several important reasons why pastoral guidelines are appropriate for dealing with cases of clergy moving from one Communion to the other:

(a) In both Communions the ordained ministry is a public office, representing a focus of leadership and unity within the Church. When an individual decides to move into communion with another Church it cannot avoid coming to the attention of the wider community and giving rise to questions and concerns regarding the relationship between the two Churches involved.

(b) Ordained ministry is carried out within the context of a worshiping and serving community which needs a pastor who understands it. Guidelines for the movement of ordained persons from communion with one Church into communion with the other should ensure that the person concerned is given the opportunity to become familiar with the rites and ethos of the receiving community.

(c) It is important for both the applicant and the Church to discern if those in pastoral leadership have the vocation and qualities appropriate to the exercise of ordained ministry. This is why both Churches have procedures to be followed before admitting candidates into the exercise of ordained ministry, and there are particular policies regarding the admission of persons ordained in another Church. These guidelines presuppose that such regulations are understood and followed.

(d) Persons leaving one Church for the other need to be aware of the ecumenical dialogue between us, which aims at nothing less than the restoration of full communion between sister Churches. Any move from one to the other ought to be motivated primarily by a love for the new Church, not by frustration or anger, and the bishop receiving such a person should encourage a healthy respect for the former Church and for our continuing search for reconciliation and understanding.

II. ASSISTING APPLICANTS IN DISCERNMENT OF VOCATION

A. Initial Approach

6. From a theological perspective baptism precedes ordination. That is, church membership is prior to the seeking of ordained ministry in the Church of which one is a member. Further, commitment to the doctrine and practice of the receiving Church must be broader than a single issue which may appear to have motivated the change. Although it is difficult to discern among the complexity of human motivations it is important to attend to the difference between opportunism and spiritual growth. Applicants will also need to become used to the similarities and differences which characterize the two Churches. It may, therefore, be appropriate for them to spend two or three years as a practicing member of the receiving Church and have the opportunity of learning its ethos before either ordination or reception into ordained ministry.

7. Before leaving one Church for another it would be helpful to bring closure to the earlier relationship. Among other things, the person should be encouraged to contact the former bishop and be informed that the receiving bishop will want to talk with the former bishop.

8. In both Churches there are procedures for helping individuals discern their vocation, and to identify right intention and the possession of the spiritual, moral, personal,

and social qualities integral to the exercise of ordained ministry. Applicants who have been ordained in the other Church should be asked to give careful consideration to: (a) their commitment to the receiving Church, (b) signs of vocation specific to that Church, and (c) for those entering the Roman Catholic Church, the significance of the link between celibacy and the priesthood.

The Call to Celibacy or Marriage

9.   Both Churches acknowledge that marriage, celibacy, and priesthood are all gifts of God. There is, however, a difference of approach between the two Churches in the link recognized between celibacy and priesthood.

(a)   A married priest moving from the Anglican tradition into the Roman Catholic Church needs to be aware that the majority of his colleagues in the presbyterium will be celibate and that the Roman Catholic Church is committed to the principle of linking celibacy and priesthood. Under certain circumstances permission can be granted for married men to be ordained, but the basic model is renunciation of marriage for the sake of the Kingdom.

(b)   In the case of someone coming to the Anglican Church from the Roman Catholic tradition the Anglican bishop will want to discern that the applicant is not making the change solely out of a desire for marriage. He will also want to be sure that any marriage that exists is firmly established before ordination or reception into ordained ministry. It should also be noted that while the Anglican tradition recognizes that some may discern a call to celibacy, this is not a qualification for ordained ministry.

Signs of Vocation

(a) Subjective Perception

10. An exploration of the applicant's own sense of vocation should include such matters as:

(a)   a brief autobiographical statement including a description of the persons, events, and institutions which have shaped the applicant's development in either a positive or negative manner; (b) a history of the candidate's vocational and spiritual development; (c) an appraisal of the candidate's personal and professional strengths; (d) an assessment of the applicant's relationship to the Church at this stage of spiritual and emotional development; (e) a description of the applicant's personal and vocational goals; (f) the applicant's perception of authority and the way the applicant sees himself exercising it; (g) motivation or desire for change at the present stage of personal and vocational development; (h) hopes and dreams for the future.

(b)   Authority's Assessment

11. In both our traditions it is the bishop who carries ultimate responsibility, upon informed recommendation, for making an assessment of the applicant's suitability for ordination. Both Churches also have structures to help the bishop make such an informed decision: the presbyterium or Council of Priests, the seminary team, the Advisory Committee on Postulants for Ordination, etc. Appropriate assessment procedures should be followed. It may be important to explore attitudes toward both authority and colleagues in ministry. It is important that underlying differences with the position of the former Church on such matters as celibacy or the ordination of women do not reflect negative attitudes toward authority which could make it difficult for the person to adjust to life in the new Church.

(c)   Community Discernment

12. Although both traditions see the ordained ministry as having a distinctive role which is not simply 'an extension of the common Christian priesthood but belongs to another realm of the gifts of the Spirit' *(Ministry and Ordination*, para. 13), they would also agree that the priesthood is exercised in and for the sake of the Christian community. As part of his ministry of oversight the bishop has a particular obligation to ensure that the community is served by clergy who understand its ethos and are sensitive to its needs. For this reason it is important for lay members of the Church to be involved in the assessment of the candidate's capacity to function as an ordained minister in the new context according to the disciplines of the respective Churches.

B. Communication Between Bishops

13. The movement of clergy between our Churches implies a responsibility on the part of the Church a well as the individual. Anglican and Roman Catholic bishops in Canada have been in dialogue for considerable time and sufficient mutual confidence has been built up so that they should be in contact as early as possible when one or the other is approached by clergy wanting to move from one Church to the other. Questions to be discussed will include: (1) the personality of the candidate; (2) the authenticity of the candidate's earlier calling to ordained ministry and in the case of one leaving the Roman Catholic Church, his vocation to the celibate life; (3) the candidate's capacity as a pastor in the community that is being left; and (4) any other information that will be of assistance to both the individual and the receiving Church.

14. The financial situation of the candidate should be part of the conversation between the bishops. What, for example, does a person do during the waiting period? The need could be especially acute if the individual concerned is married and has a family.

15. It may also be necessary for the two bishops to discuss the question of publicity and media interest in the movement of a particular priest. A competitive approach does not accurately reflect the relationship which our two Churches now enjoy. Instead, cooperation between the respective bishops can be a living demonstration of the search for unity and reconciliation in which both Churches are currently engaged. Consideration should be given to a joint announcement or to a coordinated response. Applicants themselves should be discouraged from making statements.

III. FOLLOWING APPROPRIATE PROCEDURES

16. Bishops should be aware of the procedure applicable in the sister Church for the reception of those ordained in another tradition. Guidelines should be shared where available and differences in procedure should be respected. Through dialogue, in an atmosphere of mutual regard and respect the reasons behind particular requirements can be clarified and their intention understood. As a result of this process, it is to be hoped that if there are any aspects of our respective procedures which could give rise to offence, they will be modified insofar as the competence of the leadership of our respective Churches is able to do so.

17. One area of difference is a disparity in practice regarding ordination or reordination. A bishop of the Roman Catholic Church will be required by its discipline to ordain a person ordained according to the rites of the Anglican Church. On the other hand, a priest lawfully ordained in the Roman Catholic Church would normally be received, rather than ordained, on admission into ordained ministry in the Anglican Church. This will continue to be a source of pain and misunderstanding as long as our two Churches do not mutually recognize each other's ordinations. The recognition of each other's ministries and the restoration of full communion continues to be the objective of the dialogue being carried out by the Anglican Roman Catholic International Commission and by a variety of regional and national dialogues.

IV. PASTORAL SUPPORT FOR THOSE IN TRANSITION

18. Just as a newly ordained person needs time and support to become comfortable with life in the ordained ministry, this need should not be overlooked for the person in transition. Special consideration should be given to pastoral support during the first year or two after an individual has been ordained or received into ordained ministry in the other Church. The bishop should appoint a capable team including a priest and some lay people who will meet regularly with the person concerned in order to serve as a source of support and provide continued formation in ordained ministry in the new Church.

19. Individual circumstances will call for flexibility. The nature and duration of the person's experience in the former Church, as well as his understanding of the receiving Church should be taken into account in the planning of early placements. For the common good, the person concerned should usually not be placed in the same area that was served in prior to the change. Such early service will often take place in a non-parish setting or as an assistant to the pastor of a parish to give the person an opportunity to adapt and better equip himself to serve the people of the Church with which he has now identified.

20. We are aware this document focuses primarily on those moving from priesthood in one Church to priesthood in the other. Other circumstances of transition can be envisioned, including the deacon or lay person who may feel called to seek priesthood in the other Church. We believe that if the same principles of ecumenical and pastoral sensitivity are applied these also can be occasions of growth and understanding.

21. The Church is called to proclaim the reconciling love of God in Christ, to be a people among whom this love is manifested and the instrument through which salvation is offered to all. It is this priesthood of the whole Church which the ordained ministry seeks to serve. May God guide and nurture all men and women in their various ministries within the community of the faithful.

> *The gifts he gave were that some would be*
> *apostles, some prophets, some evangelists,*
> *some pastors and teachers, to equip the saints*
> *for the work of ministry, for building up the*
> *body of Christ, until all of us come to the*
> *unity of the faith and of the knowledge of the*
> *Son of God, to maturity, to the measure of the*
> *full stature of Christ.*
> (Eph 4.11-13 [N.R.S.V.])

November 1991

17. AGREED STATEMENT ON INFALLIBILITY

Anglican-Roman Catholic Dialogue, Canada, 1992

1. God alone is essentially and inalienably infallible, incapable of deceiving or being deceived.

2. The Church as a whole can be said to be infallible in the analogical sense that, by God's grace, it will never deceive or err so gravely concerning the truths of the Gospel that the message of salvation is lost to humankind. To speak of 'infallibility' in this sense is not to claim that either the institutions of the Church or even the majority of its members are immune from error. It is simply to assert that the Church can be confident in the sufficiency of the Holy Spirit, who will safeguard the faith and enable the Church to fulfill its mission. The Church puts its trust in God who will not allow it to fall totally away from the path of salvation.

3. The truths of the Gospel thus 'infallibly' preserved enlighten the whole people of God. By virtue of their participation in the prophetic ministry of Jesus Christ, all persons and institutions of the Church are called to express and preserve these truths in appropriate ways. However, we must recognize also a special sign of God's grace in preserving the Church from error at times of crisis or when fundamental matters of faith are in question: this sign occurs when the institutions which serve the universal fellowship (i.e., council and/or primate) are enabled to articulate these truths faithfully to Scripture and in a way that commends itself to the whole Church, thus equipping the Church to meet the challenge. Such pronouncements, by virtue of their foundation in Scripture and their appropriateness to the need of the time, give the first embodiment to a renewed agreement in the truth to which they summon the whole of the Church. The 'formal authority' of such pronouncements helps the Church to meet the threat of error and gives it confidence in proclaiming the Gospel: but it must always defer to the 'material authority' of Scripture, in fidelity to which the pronouncements were formulated.

III

THE PEOPLE OF GOD AND PASTORAL CARE

THE THEOLOGICAL TEXTS PRESENTED IN THE PRECEDING SECTIONS have profound implications for the daily life and worship of our people. This section brings together texts from the dialogues, international and national, that concern ethical, pastoral, and spiritual issues that separate our two Churches. The theological core of our faith and the daily pastoral lives of our people are both integral elements in building communion.

In some places and cultures the question has been raised, 'Do ethical differences in church and society not generate greater tension than the historic theological differences?' ARCIC II has grappled with this question and provided an important text, demonstrating that much more unites our Churches than divides us. Issues on which we differ need not, finally, be church dividing. The United States dialogue has seriously studied the ARCIC II text and raised points that should contribute to the international conversation, especially as it begins the still unfinished consideration of authority.

In Canada the bishops of the two Churches engage in regular dialogue. They encourage their people by providing guidelines. The two texts here are directed especially to interchurch families and seek to give guidance in a relationship fraught with difficulty. Their guidelines for interchurch families, which relies on the international work (Vischer, 1984), could be used widely to support couples and those who minister to them.

Theological reflection always has pastoral and local implications. Likewise, theological dialogues are responsive to the questions and needs generated in the variety of cultural and pastoral situations in which the Churches find themselves. These documents are an important link between the vision of the Church and its lived embodiment in the human lives of our communities.

18. LIFE IN CHRIST: MORALS, COMMUNION, AND THE CHURCH

Anglican Roman Catholic International Commission, 1994

PREFACE BY THE CO-CHAIRMEN

As we reach the end of ten years in the life of ARCIC II, it may be opportune to recall the words of Pope John Paul II and Archbishop Robert Runcie in their Common Declaration at Canterbury in May 1982.

> The new International Commission is to continue the work already begun; to examine, especially in the light of our respective judgements on *The Final Report*, the outstanding doctrinal differences which still separate us; with a recognition of the ministries of our Communions, and to recommend what practical steps will be necessary when, on the basis of our unity in faith, we are able to proceed to the restoration of full communion. We are well aware that this new Commission's task will not be easy but we are encouraged by our reliance on the grace in the ecumenical movement of our time.

We repeat these words in order to assure both our Communions that the work of the Commission, however long or difficult it may be, must continue and is continuing.

Among the many international dialogues, bilateral and multilateral, between divided Christians, the Anglican Roman Catholic International Commission is the first to have directly attempted the subject of morals. We have prepared this statement in response to requests from authorities of both our Communions. These requests have given voice to a widespread belief that Anglicans and Roman Catholics are as much, if not more, divided on questions of morals as on questions of doctrine. This belief in turn reflects the profound and true conviction that authentic Christian unity is as much a matter of life as of faith. Those who share one faith in Christ will share one life in Christ. Hence the title of this statement: *Life in Christ. Morals, Communion, and the Church*.

The theme of this statement was already adumbrated in our previous work on *Church as Communion*. In describing the 'constitutive elements essential for visible communion of the Church', we wrote, 'Also constitutive of life in communion is acceptance of the same basic moral values, the sharing of the same vision of humanity created in the image of God and re-created in Christ, and the common confession of the one hope in the final consummation of the Kingdom of God' (44, 45).

As Christians we seek a common life not for our own sakes only, but for the glory of God and the good of humankind. In the face of the world around us, the name of God is profaned whenever those who call themselves Christians show themselves divided in their witness to the objective moral demands which arise from our life in Christ. Our search for communion and unity in morals as in faith is therefore a form of the Lord's own prayer to his Father:

Hallowed be thy name,
thy Kingdom come,
thy will be done,
on earth as it is in heaven.

✠ **CORMAC MURPHY-O'CONNOR**
✠ **MARK SANTER**
Venice, 5 September 1993

A. INTRODUCTION

1.   There is a popular and widespread belief that the Anglican and Roman Catholic Communions are divided most sharply by their moral teaching. Careful consideration has persuaded the Commission that, despite existing disagreement in certain areas of practical and pastoral judgement, Anglicans and Roman Catholics derive from the Scriptures and Tradition the same controlling vision of the nature and destiny of humanity and share the same fundamental moral values. This substantial area of common conviction calls for shared witness, since both Communions proclaim the same Gospel and acknowledge the same injunction to mission and service. A disproportionate emphasis on particular disagreements blurs this important truth and can provoke a sense of alienation. There is already a notable convergence between the two Communions in the witness they give, for example, on war and peace, euthanasia, freedom and justice, but exaggeration of outstanding differences makes this shared witness—a witness which could give direction to a world in danger of losing its way—more difficult to sustain and at the same time hinders its further development. Such a shared witness is, in today's society, urgent. It is also, we believe, possible. The widespread assumption, therefore, that differences of teaching on certain particular moral issues signify an irreconcilable divergence of understanding, and therefore present an insurmountable obstacle to shared witness, needs to be countered. Even on those particular issues where disagreement exists, Anglicans and Roman Catholics, we shall argue, share a common perspective and acknowledge the same underlying values. This being so, we question whether the limited disagreement, serious as it is, is itself sufficient to justify a continuing breach of communion.

2.   In presenting this statement on morals, we are responding, not simply to popular concern, but also to requests from the authorities of both Communions. In the past, ecu-

menical dialogue has concentrated on matters of doctrine. These are of primary importance and work here still remains to be done. However, the Gospel we proclaim cannot be
divorced from the life we live. Questions of doctrine and of morals are closely inter-
connected, and differences in the one area may reflect differences in the other. Common to
both is the matter of authority and the manner of its exercise. Although we shall not here
be addressing the issue of authority directly, nevertheless we hope that an understanding
of the relationship between freedom and authority in the moral life may contribute to our
understanding of their relationship in the life of the Church.

3. In what follows we shall attempt to display the basis and shape of Christian moral
teaching and to show that both our Communions apprehend it in the same light. We begin
by reaffirming our common faith that the life to which God, through Jesus Christ, calls
women and men is nothing less than participation in the divine life, and we spell out some
of the characteristics and implications of our shared vision of life in Christ. We go on to
remind ourselves of our common heritage and of the living tradition through which both
Communions have sought to develop a faithful and appropriate response to the good news
of the Gospel. Next we review the ways in which this tradition has diverged since the break
in communion, at the same time drawing attention to signs of a new convergence, not
least in our emphasis on the common good. We fasten upon the two particular issues of
marriage after divorce and contraception—issues upon which the two Communions have
expressed their disagreement in official documents and pastoral practice—in order to determine as precisely as we can the nature and extent of our moral disagreement and to relate
it to our continuing agreement on fundamental values. In our last section we return to the
theme of communion and, in the light of what has gone before, show how communion
determines both the structure of the moral order and the method of the Church's discernment and response. Finally, we reaffirm our belief that differences and disagreements are
exacerbated by a continuing breach of communion, and that integrity of moral response
itself requires a movement towards full communion. We conclude by suggesting steps by
which we may move forward together along this path to the greater glory of God and the
well-being of God's world.

B. SHARED VISION

4.   The Christian life is a response in the Holy Spirit to God's self-giving in Jesus
Christ. To this gift of himself in incarnation, and to this participation in the divine life, the
Scriptures bear witness (cf. 1 Jn 1:1-3; 2 Pt 1:3-4). Made in the image of God (cf. Gn 1:27),
and part of God's good creation (cf. Gn 1.31), women and men are called to grow into the
likeness of God, in communion with Christ and with one another. What has been entrusted
to us through the incarnation and the Christian tradition is a vision of God. This vision of
God in the face of Jesus Christ (cf. 2 Cor 4:6; compare Gn 1:3) is at the same time a vision
of humanity renewed and fulfilled. Life in Christ is the gift and promise of new creation

(cf. 2 Cor. 5:17), the ground of community, and the pattern of social relations. It is the shared inheritance of the Church and the hope of every believer.

5. God creates human beings with the dignity of persons in community, calls them to a life of responsibility and freedom, and endows them with the hope of happiness. As children of God, our true freedom is to be found in God's service, and our true happiness in faithful and loving response to God's love and grace. We are created to glorify and enjoy God, and our hearts continue to be restless until they find in God their rest and fulfilment.

6. The true goal of the moral life is the flourishing and fulfilment of that *humanity* for which all men and women have been created. The fundamental moral question, therefore, is not 'What ought we to do?', but 'What kind of persons are we called to become?' For children of God, moral obedience is nourished by the hope of becoming like God (cf. 1 Jn 3:1-3).

7. True personhood has its origins and roots in the life and love of God. The mystery of the divine life cannot be captured by human thought and language, but in speaking of God as Trinity in Unity, Father, Son, and Holy Spirit, we are affirming that the Being of God is a unity of self-communicating and interdependent relationship. Human persons, therefore, made in this image, and called to participate in the life of God, may not exercise a freedom that claims to be independent, willful, and self-seeking. Such a use of freedom is a distortion of their God-given humanity. It is sin. The freedom that is properly theirs is a freedom of responsiveness and interdependence. They are created for communion, and communion involves responsibility, in relation to society and nature as well as to God.

8. Ignorance and sin have led to the misuse and corruption of human freedom and to delusive ideas of human fulfilment. But God has been faithful to his eternal purposes of love and, through the redemption of the world by Jesus Christ, offers to human beings participation in a new creation, recalling them to their true freedom and fulfilment. As God remains faithful and free, so those who are in Christ are called to be faithful and free, and to share in God's creative and redemptive work for the whole of creation.

9. The new life in Christ is for the glorification of God. Living in communion with Christ, the Church is called to make Christ's words its own. 'I have glorified you on earth' (cf. Jn 17.4). The new life has also been entrusted to the Church for the good of the whole world (cf. *Church as Communion*, 18). This life is for everyone and embraces everyone. In seeking the common good, therefore, the Church listens and speaks not only to the faithful, but also to women and men of goodwill everywhere. Despite the ambiguities and evils in the world, and despite the sin that has distorted human life, the Church affirms the original goodness of creation and discerns signs and contours of an order that continues to reflect the wisdom and goodness of the Creator. Nor has sin deprived human beings of all perception of this order. It is generally recognised, for example, that torture is intrinsically wrong, and that the integration of sexual instincts and affections into a lifelong relationship of married love and loyalty constitutes a uniquely significant form of human flour-

ishing and fulfilment. Reflection on experience of what makes human beings, singly and together, truly human gives rise to a natural morality, sometimes interpreted in terms of natural justice or natural law, to which a general appeal for guidance can be made. In Jesus Christ this natural morality is not denied. Rather, it is renewed, transfigured, and perfected, since Christ is the true and perfect image of God.

10. Christian morality is one aspect of the life in Christ which shapes the tradition of the Church, a tradition which is also shaped by the community which carries it. Christian morality is the fruit of faith in God's Word, the grace of the sacraments, and the appropriation, in a life of forgiveness, of the gifts of the Spirit for work in God's service. It manifests itself in the practical teaching and pastoral care of the Church and is the outward expression of that continual turning to God whereby forgiven sinners grow up together into Christ and into the mature humanity of which Christ is the measure and fullness (cf. Eph. 4:13). At its deepest level, the response of the Church to the offer of new life in Christ possesses an unchanging identity from age to age and place to place. In its particular teachings, however, it takes account of changing circumstances and needs, and in situations of unusual ambiguity and perplexity it seeks to combine new insight and discernment with an underlying continuity and consistency.

11. Approached in this light the fundamental questions with which a Christian morality engages are such as these.

- What are persons called to be, as individuals and as members one of another in the human family?
- What constitutes human dignity, and what are the social as well as the individual dimensions of human dignity and responsibility?
- How does divine forgiveness and grace engage with human finitude, fragility, and sin in the realisation of human happiness?
- How are conditions and structures of human life related to the goal of human fulfilment?
- What are the implications of the creatureliness which human beings share with the rest of the natural world?

At this fundamental level of inquiry and concern, we believe, our two Communions share a common vision and understanding. To affirm our agreement here will prove a significant step toward the recovery of full communion. It will put in proper perspective any disagreement that may continue to exist in official teaching and pastoral practice on particular issues, such as divorce and contraception. The crisis of the modern world is more than a crisis of sexual ethics. At stake is our humanity itself.

C. COMMON HERITAGE

1. A Shared Tradition

12. Anglicans and Roman Catholics are conscious that their respective traditions, rooted in a shared vision, stem from a common heritage, which in spite of stress and strain, within and without, shaped the Church's life for some fifteen hundred years. Drawing upon the faith of Israel, this common heritage springs from the conversion of the disciples to faith in Jesus Christ and their mission to share that faith with others. Fullness of life in Christ in the kingdom of God is its goal. It is also the norm by which the tradition in all its varied manifestations is to be judged. Any manifestation that no longer has the power to nurture and sustain the new life in Christ is thereby shown to be corrupt. Anglicans and Roman Catholics firmly believe that their respective traditions continue to nourish and support them in their daily discipleship, but they are aware of the impairment to their common heritage caused by the breach in their communion, and they look forward to the time when both traditions will again flow together for their mutual enrichment and for their common witness and service to the world.

13. The shared tradition was richly woven from many strands. These include faith in God, Father, Son, and Holy Spirit, publicly professed in baptism; a common life, founded on love, centered in eucharistic prayer and worship, expressed in service; the teaching and nourishment of the Scriptures; an ordered leadership, entrusted with guarding and guiding the tradition through the conflicts of history; a sense of discipleship, manifested in the lives of the saints and acknowledged by devotion and piety; the proscription of deeds that undermine the values of the Gospel and threaten to destroy the new life in Christ; ways of reconciliation, by which sinners may be brought back into communion with God and with one another. At the same time the tradition drew upon the inherited wisdom and culture of the world in which it was embedded.

14. This common tradition carried with it a 'missionary imperative'—a call to preach the Gospel, to live the life of the Gospel in the world, and to work out a faithful and fruitful response to the Gospel in encounter with different cultures. Both Anglicans and Roman Catholics have understood the missionary task in this way, and both have been eager to fulfil the claims of their earthly citizenship (cf. Rom 13:4-5), while remembering that they are citizens of heaven (cf. Phil 3:20). They have attempted to carry out Christ's missionary injunction accordingly, though sometimes they have interpreted their involvement in the cultural life of the world in very different ways. In their engagement with culture they have been led to give careful thought to the practical expression of the new life in Christ and to provide specific teaching on some of its moral and social aspects.

15. This openness to the world, which has characterised both our traditions, has shaped the pattern of life which these traditions have sustained. It is not the life of an inwardly pious and self-regarding group, withdrawn from the world and its conflicts. It is, rather, a life to be lived out amidst the ambiguities of the world and its conflicts. Yet it is also a

pilgrim life which, while seeking the welfare of the world, has a destiny which transcends the present age. Admittedly, this involvement with the world has from time to time led the Church into compromise and alliance with corrupt principalities and powers. At other times, however, co-operation with secular authorities has borne good fruit, and the conviction that the Church is called to live in the world and to work for the salvation of the world has remained strong. Thus, while both our Communions retain painful memories of occasions of betrayal and sin, both put their trust, not in human strength, but in the saving power of God.

16. Both our traditions draw their vision from the Scriptures. To the Scriptures, therefore, we now turn, to discover the origins of our common heritage in the Gospel of Jesus Christ and the faithful response of the Christian community.

2. The Pattern of Our Life in Christ

17. The good news of the Gospel is the coming of the kingdom of God (cf. Mk 1:15), the redemption of the world by our Lord Jesus Christ (cf. Gal 4:4-5), the forgiveness of sins and new life in the Spirit (cf. Acts 2:38), and the hope of glory (cf. Col 1:27).

18. The redemption won by Jesus Christ carries with it the promise of a new life of freedom from the domination of sin (cf. Rom 6:18). Through his dying on the cross Christ has overcome the powers of darkness and death, and through his rising again from the dead he has opened the gates of eternal life (cf. Heb 10:19-22). No longer are men and women alienated from God and from one another, enslaved by sin, abandoned to despair and destined to destruction (cf. Eph 2:1-12). The entail of sin has been broken and humanity set free—free to enter upon the liberty and splendour of the children of God (cf. Rom 6:23; 8:21).

19. The liberty promised to the children of God is nothing less than participation, with Christ and through the Holy Spirit, in the life of God. The gift of the Spirit is the pledge and first instalment of the coming kingdom (cf. 2 Cor 1:21-22). Patterned according to Christ, the Wisdom of God, and empowered by the Holy Spirit of God, the Church is called not only to proclaim God's kingdom, but also to be the sign and firstfruits of its coming. The unity, holiness, catholicity, and apostolicity of the Church derive their meaning and reality from the meaning and reality of God's kingdom. They reflect the fullness of the life of God. They are signs of the universal love of God, Father, Son, and Holy Spirit, the love poured out upon the whole creation. Hence the life of the Church, the body of Christ, the community of the Holy Spirit, is rooted and grounded in the eternal life and love of God.

20. It is this patterning power of the kingdom that gives the Church its distinctive character (cf. Rom 14:17). The new humanity, which the Gospel makes possible, is present in the community of those who, already belonging to the new world inaugurated by the resurrection, live according to the law of the Spirit written in their hearts (cf. Jer 31:33).

However, the Church has always to become more fully what its title deeds proclaim it to be. It exists in the 'between-time', between the coming of Christ in history and his coming again as the Christ of glory. Insofar as it remains in the world, it too has to learn obedience to its living Lord, and to work out in its own life in community the matter and manner of its discipleship.

21. The earliest disciples devoted themselves to the 'apostles' teaching and fellowship, the breaking of bread and prayers' (Acts 2:42). In the portrayal of this communion the disciples were said to have had 'all things in common', selling their possessions and sharing their goods 'as any had need' (Acts 2:44-45). This striking example of community care and concern has, down the ages, prompted a critique of every form of society based on the unbridled pursuit of wealth and power. It has challenged Christians to use their gifts and resources to equip God's people for the work of service (cf. Eph 4:12). Its deep significance is disclosed in the claim that the whole company of believers was 'of one heart and soul . . . and everything they owned was held in common' (Acts 4:32).

22. This communion in heart and soul is inspired by the Holy Spirit and manifested in a life patterned according to the mind of Christ. As Paul puts it, 'if there is any encourage-ment in Christ, any incentive of love, any participation in the Spirit, any affection and sympathy, complete my joy by being of the same mind, having the same love, being in full accord and of one mind . . . that same mind which was in Christ Jesus' (Phil 2:1-2:5). The distinctive mark of the mind of Christ, Paul goes on to explain, is humble obedience and self-emptying love (cf. Phil 2:7-8).

3. The Mind of Christ

23. The mind of Christ remains in the Church through the presence of the Paraclete/Spirit (cf. Jn 14:26). It is mediated through the remembered teaching of Jesus and the prayerful discernment of the body of Christ and its members, and gives shape and direction to the practical life of Christian community. This teaching is expressed in Jesus' summary of the Law in the twofold commandment of love (cf. Mt 5:3-12, 21-48). It has a dual focus in the radical command 'Love your enemies' (cf. Mt 5:43) and the new commandment 'Love one another as I have loved you' (cf. Jn 13:34). The mind of Christ, so disclosed, determines the character of renewed humanity, forms the pattern of Christian obedience, and establishes the universe of shared moral values. In this important sense there is a givenness within the Christian response, which the changes of history and culture cannot impair.

24. The mind of Christ, who is the Way as well as the Truth and the Life (cf. Jn 14:6; Mt 7:14), also shapes the process by which Christians approach the challenge of new and complex moral and pastoral problems. Because they worship the same God and follow the same Lord, with the guidance of the Holy Spirit they approach these problems with similar resources and concerns. The method of arriving at practical decisions may vary, but under-

lying any differences of method there is a shared understanding of the need to use practical reason in interpreting the witness of the Scriptures, tradition, and experience.

25. The mind of Christ also exposes the continuing threat of sin—sins of ignorance and neglect as well as deliberate sins. A knowing and willing disregard of the pattern of life which Christ sets before us is deliberate sin. But people can also drift into sin without any perception of what they are doing. Distorted structures of common life prompt a sinful response. Habits of sin then dull the conscience, until sinners come to prefer darkness to light. So solidarity in sin threatens to disrupt the fellowship of the Holy Spirit.

26. In Christ freedom and order are mutually supportive. The obedience of Christian discipleship is neither the mechanical application of regulation and rule, nor the willful decision of arbitrary choice. In the freedom of a faithful and obedient response the disciples of Christ seek to discern Christ's mind rather than express their own. In exercising its authority to remit and retain sins (cf. Jn 20:23), the Church has a twofold task of guarding against the power of sin to destroy the life of the community, and of fostering the freedom of its members to discern what is 'good and acceptable and perfect' (Rom 12:2).

4. Growing up into Christ

27. The salvation which God has secured for us once and for all, through the death and resurrection of Jesus Christ, he has now to secure in us and with us through the power of the Holy Spirit. We have to become what, in Christ, we already are. We have to 'grow up in every way into him who is the head, into Christ' (Eph 4:15). We have to 'work out (our) own salvation with fear and trembling; for God is at work in (us), both to will and to work for his good pleasure' (Phil 2:12-13).

28. The lived response of the Church to the grace of God develops its own shape and character. The pattern of this response is fashioned according to the mind of Christ; the raw material is the stuff of our everyday world. In Johannine language, believers are still 'in' the world, but are not 'of' the world (cf. Jn 17:13-14). In Pauline language, they continue to live 'in the body' (2 Cor 5:6), but no longer 'in the flesh' (Rom 8:9). Christians are to continue in their secular roles and relationships according to the accepted social codes of behaviour, but are to do so as 'in the Lord' (cf. Eph 5:21-6:11; Col 3:18-4:1). Their new intention and motivation, while affirming the need for these social structures, contain the seeds of radical critique and reappraisal.

29. The fidelity of the Church to the mind of Christ involves a continuing process of listening, learning, reflecting, and teaching. In this process every member of the community has a part to play. Each person learns to reflect and act according to conscience. Conscience is informed by, and informs, the tradition and teaching of the community. Learning and teaching are a shared discipline, in which the faithful seek to discover together what obedience to the gospel of grace and the law of love entails amidst the moral implications of the Gospel which calls for continuing discernment, constant repentance, and 'renewal of

the mind' (Rom 12:2), so that through discernment and response men and women may become what in Christ they already are.

30. As part of its missionary imperative and pastoral care, the Church has not only to hand on from generation to generation its understanding of life in Christ, but also from time to time to determine how best to reconcile and support those members of the community who have, for whatever reason, failed to live up to its moral demands. Its aim is twofold: on the one hand, both to minimise the harm done by their falling away and to maintain the integrity of the community; and on the other, to restore the sinner to the life of grace in the fellowship of the Church.

5. Discerning the Mind of Christ

31. Christian morality is an authentic expression of the new life lived in the power of the Holy Spirit and fashioned according to the mind of Christ. In the tradition common to both our Communions, discerning the mind of Christ is a patient and continuing process of prayer and reflection. At its heart is the turning of the sinner to God, sacramentally enacted in baptism and renewed through participation in the sacramental life of the Church, meditation on the scriptures, and a life of daily discipleship. The process unfolds through the formation of a character, individual and communal, that reflects the likeness of Christ and embodies the virtues of a true humanity (cf. Gal 5:19-24). At the same time shared values are formulated in terms of principles and rules defining duties and protecting rights. All this finds expression in the common life of the Church as well as in its practical teaching and pastoral care.

32. The teaching developed in this way is an essential element in the process by which individuals and communities exercise their discernment on particular moral issues. Holding in mind the teaching they have received, drawing upon their own experience, and exploring the particularities of the issue that confronts them, they have then to decide what action to take in these circumstances and on this occasion. Such a decision is not only a matter of deduction. Nor can it be taken in isolation. It also calls for detailed and accurate assessment of the facts of the case, careful and consistent reflection and, above all, sensitivity of insight inspired by the Holy Spirit.

6. Continuity and Change

33. Guided by the Holy Spirit, believer and believing community seek to discern the mind of Christ amidst the changing circumstances of their own histories. Fidelity to the Gospel, obedience to the mind of Christ, openness to the Holy Spirit—these remain the source and strength of continuity. Where there has been an actual break in communion, this difference cannot but be the more pronounced, giving rise to the impression, often mistaken, that there is some fundamental disagreement of understanding and approach.

34. Moral discernment is a demanding task both for the community and for the individual Christian. The more complex the particular issue, the greater the room for disagreement. Christians of different Communions are more likely to agree on the character of the Christian life and the fundamental Christian virtues and values. They are more likely to disagree on the consequent rules of practice, particular moral judgements, and pastoral counsel.

35. In this chapter we have been concerned to reaffirm the heritage which Anglicans and Roman Catholics share together. We believe that the elements of this heritage provide the basis for a common witness to the world. But since the Reformation the traditions of our two Communions have diverged, and there are now differences between them which we must acknowledge and face with honesty and patience. Left unacknowledged, they remain a threat to any common task we might undertake. Faced together with honesty and integrity, they will, we believe, be seen at a deeper level to reflect different aspects of a living whole.

D. PATHS DIVERGE

36. For some fifteen centuries the Church in the West struggled to maintain a single, living tradition of communion in worship, faith, and practice. In the sixteenth century, however, this web of shared experience was violently broken. Movements for reform could no longer be contained within the one Communion. The Roman Catholic Church and the Churches of the Reformation went their different ways and fruits of shared communion were lost. It is in this context of broken communion and diverging histories that the existing differences between Anglicans and Roman Catholics on matters of morality must be located if they are to be rightly understood.

37. These differences, we believe, do not derive from disagreement on the sources of moral authority or on fundamental moral values. Rather, they have arisen from the different emphases which our two Communions have given to different elements of the moral life. In particular, differences have occurred in the ways in which each, in isolation from the other, has developed its structures of authority and has come to exercise that authority in the formation of moral judgement. These factors, we believe, have contributed significantly to the differences that have arisen in a limited number of important moral issues. We cannot, of course, hope to do justice to the complex histories that have shaped our two Communions and given to each its distinctive ethos. However, we wish to draw attention to two strands in our histories which, for present purposes, are of special significance. First, structures of government and the voice of the laity; and secondly, processes of moral formation and individual judgement.

1. Structures of Government and the Voice of the Laity

38. At the Reformation the Church of England abjured papal supremacy, acknowledged the Sovereign as its Supreme Governor (cf. Article 37), and adopted English as the

language of its liturgy (cf. Article 24). Thus the life of the Church, the culture of the nation, and the law of the land were inextricably combined. In particular, the lay voice was given, through Parliament, a substantial measure of authority in the affairs of the Church. With the growth of the Anglican Communion as a world-wide body, patterns of synodical government developed in which laity, clergy, and bishops shared the authority of government, the bishops retaining a special voice and responsibility in safeguarding matters of doctrine and worship.

39. As the Anglican Communion has spread, provinces independent of the Church of England have come into being, each with its own history and culture. English culture has become less and less of a common bond as other cultures have exercised an increasing influence. Each province is responsible for the ordering of its own life and has independent legislative and juridical authority; yet each continues in communion with the Church of England and with one another. Every ten years since 1867 the bishops of the Anglican Communion have met together at Lambeth at the invitation of the Archbishop of Canterbury, to whom they continue to ascribe a primacy of honor. The resolutions of their conferences have a high degree of authority, but they do not become the official teaching of the individual provinces until these have formally ratified them. In recent times regular meetings of the Primates of the Anglican Communion, as well as of the Anglican Consultative Council, in which laity, clergy, and bishops are all represented, have contributed to this network of dispersed authority. Whether existing instruments of unity in the Anglican Communion will prove adequate to the task of preserving full communion between the provinces, as they develop their moral teaching in a rapidly changing and deeply perplexing world, remains to be seen.

40. The Reformation and its aftermath also had repercussions in the government of the Roman Catholic Church. Some of the European rulers who maintained allegiance to Rome found this relationship strained and frustrating, especially since, in certain areas, the papacy also exercised temporal power. The Church reacted strongly, however, to any attempt by a secular power to arrogate to itself prerogatives that it believed were rightfully its own. This concern of the Church to uphold its independence from the state, together with its need to reaffirm and strengthen its unity in the face of divisive forces, lent to the papal office a renewed significance, and provided the context for the solemn definition of the first Vatican Council which clarified the universal jurisdiction of the Bishop of Rome and his infallibility.

41. A further development in the Roman Catholic Church since Vatican I has clarified the teaching role of the college of bishops in communion with its head, the bishop of Rome. Bishops are not only the chief teachers in their own diocese, but they also share responsibility for the teaching of the whole Church. For Roman Catholics, government and teaching continue to be the prerogative of the episcopal office. Their experience has been that these structures of authority have served the Church well in maintaining a fundamental unity of moral teaching.

42. There has also been a significant development in the Roman Catholic Church in the ways by which the laity participate in the discernment and articulation of the Church's faith. Lay persons have taken on new roles in liturgy, catechesis, and pastoral work, and have come to be involved with their pastors in a variety of consultative and advisory bodies at parochial, diocesan, and national levels. This collaboration has been enhanced by their involvement in theological education.

2. Processes of Moral Formation and Individual Judgement

43. After the breakdown in communion, Anglicans and Roman Catholics continued to develop, in related but distinctive ways, their common tradition of moral theology and its application by a process of casuistry to specific moral problems. This process has its roots in the New Testament and in the writings of the church Fathers. In the late Middle Ages, however, certain widespread philosophical views diverted attention from the controlling moral vision and concentrated on the obligations of the individual will and the legality of particular acts. What is intended to be a painstaking search for the will of God in the complex circumstances of daily life ran the danger of becoming either meticulous moralism or a means of minimising the challenge of the Gospel.

44. Developments in Roman Catholic moral theology after the Council of Trent were not altogether free from this danger. In the seventeenth century papal authority countermanded both rigorism and laxity. It sought to re-establish a vision of the moral life which respected the demands of the Gospel while, at the same time, acknowledging the costliness of discipleship and the frailties of the human condition. During this and subsequent periods, moral theology and spiritual theology were treated as two disciplines, the former tending to restrict itself to the minimal requirements of Christian obedience. In the second half of the present century the Roman Catholic Church, in its desire to set the moral life within a comprehensive vision of life in the Spirit, has witnessed a renewal of moral theology. There has been a return to the Scriptures as the central source of moral insight. Older discussions, based on the natural law, with the scriptures cited solely for confirmation, have been integrated into a more personalistic account of the moral life, which itself has been grounded in the vocation of all human persons to participate in the life of God. An emphasis on the community of persons has led to significant developments, not only in the Church's teaching on personal relationships, but also in its teaching on the economic and social implications of the common good.

45. The Anglican tradition of moral theology has been varied and heterogeneous. In the seventeenth century Anglican theologians of both catholic and puritan persuasion produced comprehensive works of 'practical divinity'. Drawing on the scholastic tradition, and determined to hold together the moral and spiritual life, they developed this tradition within a context of Christian vocation of personal holiness. Thus they rejected any approach to the moral life that smacked of moral laxity, and mistrusted any casu-

istry that, in the details of its analysis of the moral act, threatened to destroy an integral spirit of genuine repentance and renewal. In subsequent centuries the practice of casuistry fell largely into disuse, to be replaced by teaching on 'Christian ethics'. The aim of this discipline was to set forth the ideal character and pattern of the Christian life and so to prepare Christians for making their own decisions how best to realise that ideal in their own circumstances. The present century has seen a renewal among Anglicans of the discipline of moral theology, sustained by a growing recognition of the need for systematic reflection on the difficult moral issues raised by new technologies, the limits of natural resources, and the claims of the natural environment. In recent times, in response to widespread appeals for guidance on issues of public and social morality, representatives of Christian bodies and other persons of good will have been brought together to study these issues and to suggest how society might best respond to them for the sake of the common good.

46. Anglicans and Roman Catholics have both used a variety of means to strengthen Christian discipleship in its moral dimension. These have included preaching, regular use of catechisms, and public recitation of the Commandments. In one matter of special significance, however, the Reformation and the consequent Counter-Reformation moved the Church of England and the Roman Catholic Church in different directions. The Reformers' emphasis on the direct access of the sinner to the forgiving and sustaining Word of God led Anglicans to reject the view that private confession before a priest was obligatory, although they continued to maintain that it was a wholesome means of grace, and made provision for it in the *Book of Common Prayer* for those with an unquiet and sorely troubled conscience. While many Anglicans value highly the practice of private confession to a priest, others believe with equal sincerity that it is for them unhelpful and unnecessary. It is sufficient for themselves, they say, that the Word of God, expressed in the Scriptures and appropriated in the power of the Holy Spirit, speaks authoritatively to their conscience, offering both assurance of forgiveness and practical guidance. For both those who do, and for those who do not, confess their sins privately, general confession and absolution by the priest remains an integral part of the regular Anglican liturgy, a ministry designed to cover both individual and corporate sin. Furthermore, Anglicans often turn to their pastors and advisors, lay and ordained, for moral and spiritual counsel.

47. The Roman Catholic Church, on the other hand, has continued to emphasise the sacrament of penance and the obligation, for those conscious of serious sin, of confessing their sins privately before a priest. Indeed, the renewal of private confession was a major concern of the Council of Trent. Since Vatican II the development of the ministry of forgiveness and healing has led to new forms of sacramental reconciliation, both individual and communal. For centuries the discipline of the confession of sins before a priest has provided an important means of communicating the Church's moral teaching and nurturing the spiritual lives of penitents.

3. Moral Judgement and the Exercise of Authority

48. Reflection on the divergent histories of our two Communions has shown that their shared concern to respond obediently to God's Word and to foster the common good has nevertheless resulted in differing emphases in the ways in which they have nurtured Christian liberty and authority. Both Communions recognise that liberty and authority are essentially interdependent, and that the exercise of authority is for the protection and nurture of liberty. It cannot be denied, however, that there is a continuing temptation which the continued separation of our two Communions serves only to accentuate—to allow the exercise of authority to lapse into authoritarianism and the exercise of liberty to lapse into individualism.

49. All moral authority is grounded in the goodness and will of God. Our two Communions are agreed on this principle and on its implications. Both our Communions, moreover, have developed their own structures and institutions for the teaching ministry of the Church, by which the will of God is discerned and its implications for the common good declared. Our Communions have diverged, however, in their views of the ways in which authority is most fruitfully exercised and the common good best promoted. Anglicans affirm that authority needs to be dispersed rather than centralised, that the common good is better served by allowing to individual Christians the greatest possible liberty of informed judgement, and that therefore official moral teaching should as far as possible be commendatory rather than prescriptive and binding. Roman Catholics, on the other hand, have, for the sake of common good, emphasised the need for a central authority to preserve unity and to give clear and binding teaching.

4. Differing Emphases, Shared Perspectives

50. In our conversations together we have made two discoveries: first, that many of the preconceptions that we brought with us concerning each other's understanding of moral teaching and discipline were often little more than caricatures; and secondly, that the differences which actually exist between us appear in a new light when we consider them in their origin and context.

51. Some of these differences lend themselves to misperception and caricature. It is not true, for instance, that Anglicans concern themselves solely with liberty, while Roman Catholics concern themselves solely with law. It is not true that the Roman Catholic Church has predetermined answers to every moral question, while the Anglican Church has no answers at all. It is not true that Roman Catholics always agree on moral issues, nor that Anglicans never agree. It is not true that Anglican ethics is pragmatic and unprincipled, while Roman Catholic moral theology is principled but abstract. It is not true that Roman Catholics are always more careful of the institution in their concern for the common good, while Anglican moral teaching is utilitarian. Caricature, we may grant, is never totally

contrived; but caricature it remains. In fact, there is good reason to hope that, if they can pray, think, and act together, Anglicans and Roman Catholics, by emphasising different aspects of the moral life, may come to complement and enrich each other's understanding and practice of it.

52. Nevertheless, differences there are and differences they remain. Both Anglicans and Roman Catholics are accustomed to using the concept of law to give character and form to the claims of morality. However, this concept is open to more than one interpretation and use, so causing real and apparent differences between our two traditions. For example, a notable feature of established Roman Catholic moral teaching is its emphasis on the absoluteness of some demands of the moral law and the existence of certain prohibitions to which there are no exceptions. In these instances, what is prohibited is intrinsically disordered and therefore objectively wrong. Anglicans, on the other hand, while acknowledging the same ultimate values, are not persuaded that the laws as we apprehend them are necessarily absolute. In certain circumstances, they would argue, it might be right to incorporate contextual and pastoral considerations in the formulation of a moral law, on the grounds that fundamental moral values are better served if the law sometimes takes into account certain contingencies of nature and history and certain disorders of the human condition. In so doing, they do not make the clear-cut distinction, which Roman Catholics make, between canon law, with its incorporation of contingent and prudential considerations, and the moral law, which in its principles is absolute and universal. In both our Communions, however, there are now signs of a shift away from a reliance on the concept of law as the central category of providing moral teaching. Its place is being taken by the concept of 'persons-in-community'. An ethic of response is preferred to an ethic of obedience. In the desire to respond as fully as possible to the new law of Christ, the primacy of persons is emphasised above the impersonalism of a system of law, thus avoiding the distortions of both individualism and utilitarianism. The full significance of this shift of emphasis is not yet clear, and its detailed implications have still to be worked out. It should be emphasised, however, that whatever differences there may be in the way in which they express the moral law, both our traditions respect the consciences of persons in good faith.

53. We hope we have said enough in this chapter to explain how a deeper understanding of our separated histories has enabled us to appreciate better the real character of our divergences, and has persuaded us that it has been our broken communion, more than anything else, that has exacerbated our disagreements. In recent times there has been a large measure of cross-fertilisation between our two traditions. Both our Communions, for example, have shared in the renewal of biblical, historical, and liturgical studies, and both have participated in the ecumenical movement. Our separated paths have once again begun to converge. It is in the conviction that we also possess a shared vision of Christian discipleship and a common approach to the moral life, that we take courage now to look directly at our painful disagreement on two particular moral issues.

E. AGREEMENT AND DISAGREEMENT

54. The moral issues on which the Anglican and Roman Catholic Communions have expressed official disagreement are the marriage of a divorced person during the life-time of a former partner; and the permissible methods of controlling conception. There are other issues concerning sexuality on which Anglican and Roman Catholic attitudes and opinions appear to conflict, especially abortion and the exercise of homosexual relations. These we shall consider briefly at the end of this section; but because of the official nature of the disagreement on the former two issues, we shall concentrate on them.

1. Human Sexuality

55. Before considering the points of disagreement, we need to emphasise the extent of our agreement. Both our traditions affirm with Scripture that human sexuality is part of God's good creation (cf. Gn 1:27; see further Gn 24; Ruth 4; the Song of Songs; Eph 5:21-32; etc.). Sexual differentiation within the one human nature gives bodily expression to the vocation of God's children to inter-personal communion. Human sexuality embraces the whole range of bodily, imaginative, affective, and spiritual experiences. It enters into a person's deepest character and relationships, individual and social, and constitutes a fundamental mode of human communication. It is ordered towards the gift of self and the creation of life.

56. Sexual experience, isolated from the vision of the full humanity to which God calls us, is ambivalent. It can be as disruptive as it can be unitive, as destructive as it can be creative. Christians have always known this to be so (cf. Mt 5.28). They have therefore recognised the need to integrate sexuality into an ordered pattern of life, which will nurture a person's spiritual relationships both with other persons and with God. Such integration calls for the exercise of the virtue traditionally termed chastity, a virtue rooted in the spiritual significance of bodily existence (cf. 1 Thes 4:1-8; Gal 5:23; Cor 6:9, 12-20).

57. Both our traditions offer comparable accounts of chastity, which involves the ordering of the sexual drive either towards marriage or in a life of celibacy. Chastity does not signify the repression of sexual instincts and energies, but their integration into a pattern of relationships in which a person may find true happiness, fulfilment, and salvation. Anglicans and Roman Catholics agree that the new life in Christ calls for a radical break with the sin of sexual self-centredness, which leads inevitably to individual and social disintegration. The New Testament is unequivocal in its witness that the right ordering and use of sexual energy is an essential aspect of life in Christ (cf. Mk 10:9; Jn 8:11; 1 Cor 7:1; Pt 3:1-7; Heb 13:4), and this is reiterated throughout the common Christian tradition, including the time since our two Communions diverged.

58. Human beings, male and female, flourish as persons in community. Personal relationships have a social as well as a private dimension. Sexual relationships are no exception. They are bound up with issues of poverty and justice, the equality and dignity of women

and men, and the protection of children. Both our traditions treat of human sexuality in the context of the common good, and regard marriage and family life as institutions divinely appointed for human well-being and happiness. It is in the covenanted relationship between husband and wife that the physical expression of sexuality finds its true fulfilment (cf. Gn 2:18-25), and in the procreation and nurturing of children that the two persons together share in the life-giving generosity of God (cf. Gn 1:27-29).

2. Marriage and Family

59. Neither of our two traditions regards marriage as a human invention. On the contrary, both see it as grounded by God in human nature and as a source of community, social order, and stability. Nevertheless, the institution of marriage has found different expression in different cultures and at different times. In our own time, for instance, we are becoming increasingly aware that some forms, far from nurturing the dignity of persons, foster oppression and domination, especially of women. However, despite the distortions that have affected it, both our traditions continue to discern and uphold in marriage a God-given pattern and significance.

60. Marriage gives rise to enduring obligations. Personal integrity and social witness both require a life-long and exclusive commitment, and the 'good' which marriage embodies includes the reciprocal love of husband and wife, and the procreation and raising of children. When these realities are disregarded, a breakdown of family life may ensue, carrying with it a heavy burden of misery and social disintegration. The word 'obligation', however, is inadequate to express the profound personal call inherent in the Christian understanding of marriage. Both our traditions speak of marriage as a 'vocation to holiness' (Lambeth 1958, Resolution 112 as quoted in Lambeth 1968, Resolution 22), as involving an 'integral vision of . . . vocation' (*Familiaris Consortio*, 32). When God calls women and men to the married estate, and supports them in it, God's love for them is creative, redemptive, and sanctifying (cf. Lambeth, ibid.).

61. The mutual pact, or covenant, made between the spouses (cf. *Gaudium et Spes*, 47-52, and *Final Report on the Theology of Marriage and its Application to Mixed Marriages*, 1975, 21) bears the mark of God's own abundant love (cf. Hos 2:19-21). Covenanted human love points beyond itself to the covenantal love and fidelity of God and to God's will that marriage should be a means of universal blessing and grace. Marriage, in the order of creation, is both sign and reality of God's faithful love, and thus it has a naturally sacramental dimension. Since it also points to the saving love of God, embodied in Christ's love for the Church (cf. Eph 5:25), it is open to a still deeper sacramentality within the life and communion of Christ's own Body.

62. So far, we believe, our traditions agree. Further discussion, however, is needed on the ways in which they interpret this sacramentality of marriage. The Roman Catholic tradition, following the common tradition of the West, which was officially promulgated

by the Council of Florence in 1439, affirms that Christian marriage is a sacrament in the order of redemption, the natural sign of the human covenant having been raised by Christ to become a sign of the irrevocable covenant between himself and his Church. What was sacramental in the order of creation becomes a sacrament of the Church in the order of redemption. When solemnised between two baptised persons, marriage is an effective sign of redeeming grace. Anglicans, while affirming the special significance of marriage within the Body of Christ, emphasise a sacramentality of marriage that transcends the boundaries of the Church. For many years in England after the Reformation, marriages could be solemnised only in church. When civil marriage became possible, Anglicans recognised such marriages, too, as sacramental and graced by God, since the state of matrimony had itself been 'adorned and beautified' by Christ by his presence at the marriage at Cana of Galilee (cf. *BCP 1662, Introduction to the Solemnization of Matrimony*). From these considerations it would appear that, in this context, Anglicans tend to emphasise the breadth of God's grace in creation, while Roman Catholics tend to emphasise the depth of God's grace in Christ. These emphases should be seen as complementary. Ideally, they belong together. They have, however, given rise to differing understandings of the conditions under which the sacramentality of a marriage is fulfilled.

63. The vision of marriage as a fruitful, life-long covenant, full of the grace of God, is not always sustained in the realities of life. Its very goodness, when corrupted by human frailty, self-centredness and sin, gives rise to pain, despair, and tragedy, not only for the couple immediately involved in marital difficulty or breakdown, but also for their children, the wider family, and the social order. Faced with such situations, the Church endeavors to minister the grace and discipline of Christ himself. Anglicans and Roman Catholics have both sought to act in obedience to the teaching of Christ. However, in their separation their practice and pastoral discipline came to differ and diverge. In order to elucidate the significance of such differences and divergences we shall now turn to the two issues on which disagreement has been officially voiced, namely, marriage after divorce, and contraception.

3. Marriage After Divorce

64. Before the break in communion in the sixteenth century, the Church in the West had come to derive a doctrine of indissolubility from its interpretation of the teaching of Jesus concerning marriage. The official Church teaching included two affirmations: not only was it the case that the marriage bond *ought not* to be dissolved; but it was also the case that it *could not* be dissolved. At the Reformation, continental Protestant Reformers interpreted the teaching of Jesus (cf. Mt 5:32; 19:9) differently, and urged that divorce was permissible on grounds of adultery or desertion. The Council of Trent, on the other hand, reaffirmed the teaching, first, that the marriage bond could not be dissolved, even by adultery and secondly, that neither partner, not even the innocent one, could contract a second marriage during the life-time of the other.

(a) The Anglican Communion

65. The development of a distinctive marriage discipline within Anglicanism can be understood only in the context of the development of diverse civil jurisdictions. This is true both of the Church of England and of other Anglican provinces. At the time of the Reformation the Church of England passed no formal resolution on marriage and divorce. It never officially accepted the teaching of the continental Reformers, but despite attempts to introduce an alternative discipline, held to the older belief and practice. Revisions of Canon Law in 1597 and 1604 established no change in teaching or discipline, although, in the centuries that followed, theological opinion varied and even in practice was not completely uniform. Up to the middle of the nineteenth century divorce, with the consequent freedom to marry again, was available only to the rich and influential few by Act of Parliament. In 1857, when matrimonial matters were transferred from ecclesiastical to civil jurisdiction, divorce on grounds of adultery was legalised. Although clergy were given the right to refuse to solemnise the marriage of a divorced person in the lifetime of a former partner, the Church of England as a whole came to accept *de facto* the new state of affairs: marriages after divorce occurred, but the Church refused to give official approval to their solemnisation.

66. As Anglican provinces were inaugurated outside England, each had to formulate its own pastoral marriage discipline in the light of local civil law and marriage customs. In an attempt to secure a coherent policy among the provinces, the Lambeth Conference of 1888 reaffirmed the life-long intention of the marriage covenant, but accepted that the clergy should not be instructed to refuse the sacraments to those who were remarried 'under civil sanction'. It left open the question whether or not the innocent party was free to enter a second marriage. Since then, theological opinion has varied. Some Anglicans have continued to hold the traditional view of indissolubility. Others have argued that, once the married relationship has been destroyed beyond repair, the marriage itself is as if dead, the vows have been frustrated and the bond has been broken. The Lambeth Conference of 1978 reaffirmed the 'first-order principle' of life-long union, but it also acknowledged a responsibility for those for whom '*no* course *absolutely* consonant with the first-order principle of marriage as a life-long union may be available' (Resolution 34). Subsequent practice has varied. Different provinces of the Anglican Communion have devised different marriage disciplines. Among some of them permission is granted, on carefully considered pastoral grounds, for a marriage after divorce to be solemnised in church, although even in these cases practice varies concerning the precise form the complete service takes. In other cases, after a civil ceremony, a service of prayer and dedication may be offered instead. The practical decision normally lies with the bishop and the bishop's advisers.

(b) The Roman Catholic Church

67. In the period following the breach of communion, the Roman Catholic Church continued to uphold the doctrine of indissolubility reaffirmed at Trent. At the same time it developed a complex system of jurisprudence and discipline to meet its diverse practical and pastoral needs and to provide a supportive role for those whose faith was threatened by a destructive marital relationship.

68. A distinction is made between marriages that are sacraments—those in which both partners are baptised—and marriages that are not sacraments ('natural marriages')—those in which one or both partners are unbaptised. In Roman Catholic teaching both forms of marriage are in principle indissoluble. A sacramental marriage which has been duly consummated cannot be dissolved by any human power, civil or ecclesiastical. Where such a marriage, however, has not been consummated, it can be dissolved. On the other hand, it has come to be accepted that a non-sacramental marriage, whether consummated or not, can in certain cases be dissolved.

69. The history of these matters is long and complex. In his first letter to the Corinthians, St. Paul deals with the case of a married couple, one of whom is a believer, the other a non-believer. If the non-believer refuses to stay with the believer, then, he says, 'the brother or sister is not bound' (1 Cor 7:15; cf. 12-15). This was later interpreted in Canon Law to mean that the partner who had become a Christian was free to leave an unbelieving spouse who was unwilling to continue married life 'in peace', and to marry again. There are several references to this 'Pauline text' in the writings of the early church Fathers dealing with the dissolution of marriage. It became part of church legislation in 1199, but was fully clarified only in the Code of Canon Law of 1917. It is still part of Roman Catholic practice (cf. *Codex Iuris Canonici* [CIC] Can. 1143).

70. The exercise of the 'Pauline privilege' is not the only occasion when the power to dissolve a marriage is invoked. In the course of the missionary expansion of the Church other situations have prompted similar action. From 1537 popes used their powers to dissolve the natural marriages of inhabitants of Africa and the Indies who wished to convert to the Catholic faith. In 1917 this practice 'in favour of the faith' (or, as it is sometimes called, the 'Petrine privilege') was extended to other parts of the world and applied to similar situations. The 'privilege of the faith' is still recognised today, and subject to certain conditions, a dissolution of a non-sacramental marriage may, by way of exception, be granted on these grounds by the Holy See.

71. Other elements in Roman Catholic doctrine and practice have been prompted by particular practical problems. For example, it was the problem of clandestine marriages, valid but not proved to be so, that prompted the Council of Trent to promulgate the decree *Tametsi* (1563). This required that marriages be celebrated before the pastor (or another priest delegated by him or the ordinary) and two or three witnesses. With certain modifications, this 'form' is still binding, and failure to observe it, without due dispensation, ren-

ders a marriage null and void (cf. CIC Can. 1108). A partner to such a union, therefore, is not considered in Canon Law to be held by a marital bond and is free to contract a valid marriage. In the case of an intended marriage between a Roman Catholic and a person who is not a Roman Catholic, the Church today often grants a dispensation from the 'form', out of respect for the beliefs, conscience, and family ties of the person concerned.

72. Another development in Roman Catholic jurisprudence concerns the practice of annulment, that is, the declaration of the fact that a true marriage never existed. The marriage contract requires full and free consent. If this is lacking, there can be no marriage. It has always been recognised that there can be no marriage if a person is forced to enter it against his or her will. More recent reflection has analysed in greater depth the nature of consent. It is now recognised that there may be serious psychological as well as physical defects. If such defects can be demonstrated to have existed when verbal consent was exchanged, it can be declared, according to Roman Catholic teaching, that there was never a marriage at all (cf. CIC Can.1095). Serious defect is also present if, at the time of exchanging consent, there is a deliberate rejection of some element essential to marriage (cf. CIC Can. 1056; 1101, para. 2).

(c) The Situation Today

73. Clearly there are differences of discipline and pastoral practice between Anglicans and Roman Catholics. Some of the factors in our traditions are the result of responses to contingent historical circumstances, for example, the Roman Catholic Church's requirement of the 'form' for valid marriage. However, other elements have deeper roots. When we explore our differences it is to these, in particular, that we must direct our attention. Before doing so, however, it is important to note that both Communions make provision for marital separation, without excluding the persons concerned, even after civil divorce, from the eucharist.

74. In accord with the western tradition, Anglicans and Roman Catholics believe that the ministers of the marriage are the man and woman themselves, who bring the marriage into being by making a solemn vow and promise of life-long fidelity to each other. Anglicans and Roman Catholics both regard this vow as solemn and binding. Anglicans and Roman Catholics both believe that marriage points to the love of Christ, who bound himself in an irrevocable covenant to his Church, and that therefore marriage is in principle indissoluble. Roman Catholics go on to affirm that the unbreakable bond between Christ and his Church, signified in the union of two baptised persons, in its turn strengthens the marriage bond between husband and wife and renders it absolutely unbreakable, except by death. Other marriages can, in exceptional circumstances, be dissolved. Anglicans, on the other hand, do not make an absolute distinction between marriages of the baptised and other marriages, regarding all marriages as in some sense sacramental. Some Anglicans hold that all marriages are therefore indissoluble. Others, while holding that all marriages

are indeed sacramental and are in principle indissoluble, are not persuaded that the marriage bond, even in the case of marriage of the baptised, can never in fact be dissolved.

75. Roman Catholic teaching that, when a sacramental marriage has been consummated, the covenant is irrevocable, is grounded in its understanding of sacramentality, as already outlined. Further, its firm legal framework is judged to be the best protection for the institution of marriage, and thus best to serve the common good of the community, which itself redounds to the true good of the persons concerned. Thus Roman Catholic teaching and law uphold the indissolubility of the marriage covenant, even when the human relationship of love and trust has ceased to exist and there is no practical possibility of recreating it. The Anglican position, though equally concerned with the sacramentality of marriage and the common good of the community, does not necessarily understand these in the same way. Some Anglicans attend more closely to the actual character of the relationship between husband and wife. Where a relationship of mutual love and trust has clearly ceased to exist, and there is no practical possibility of remaking it, the bond itself, they argue, has also ceased to exist. When the past has been forgiven and healed, a new covenant and bond may in good faith be made.

76. Our reflections have brought to the fore an issue of considerable importance. What is the right balance between regard for the person and regard for the institution? The answer must be found within the context of our theology of communion and our understanding of the common good. For the reasons which have been explained, in the Roman Catholic Church the institution of marriage has enjoyed the favour of the law. Marriages are presumed to be valid unless the contrary case can be clearly established. Since Vatican II renewed emphasis has been placed upon the rights and welfare of the individual person, but tensions still remain. A similar tension is felt by Anglicans, although pastoral concern has sometimes inclined them to give priority to the welfare of the individual person over the claims of the institution. History has shown how difficult it is to achieve the right balance.

77. Our shared reflections have made us see more clearly that Anglicans and Roman Catholics are at one in their commitment to following the teaching of Christ on marriage; at one in their understanding of the nature and meaning of marriage; and at one in their concern to reach out to those who suffer as a result of the breakdown of marriage. We agree that marriage is sacramental, although we do not fully agree on how, and this affects our sacramental discipline. Thus, Roman Catholics recognise a special kind of sacramentality in a marriage between baptised persons, which they do not see in other marriages. Anglicans, on the other hand, recognise a sacramentality in all valid marriages. On the level of law and policy, neither the Roman Catholic nor the Anglican practice regarding divorce is free from real or apparent anomalies and ambiguities. While, therefore, there are differences between us concerning marriage after divorce, to isolate those differences from this

context of far-reaching agreement and to make them into an insuperable barrier would be a serious and sorry misrepresentation of the true situation.

4. Contraception

78. Both our traditions agree that procreation is one of the divinely intended 'goods' of the institution of marriage. A deliberate decision, therefore, without justifiable reason, to exclude procreation from a marriage is a rejection of this good and a contradiction of the nature of marriage itself. On this also we agree. We are likewise at one in opposing what has been called a 'contraceptive mentality', that is, a selfish preference for immediate satisfaction over the more demanding good of having and raising a family.

79. Both Roman Catholics and Anglicans agree, too, that God calls married couples to 'responsible parenthood'. This refers to a range of moral concerns, which begins with the decision to accept parenthood and goes on to include the nurture, education, support, and guidance of children. Decisions about the size of a family raise many questions for both Anglicans and Roman Catholics. Broader questions concerning the pressure of population, poverty, the social and ecological environment, as well as more directly personal questions concerning the couple's material, physical, and psychological resources, may arise. Situations exist in which a couple would be morally justified in avoiding bringing children into being. Indeed, there are some circumstances in which it would be morally irresponsible to do so. On this our two Communions are also agreed. We are not agreed, however, on the methods by which this responsibility may be exercised.

80. The disagreement may be summed up as follows. Anglicans understand the good of procreation to be a norm governing the married relationship as a whole. Roman Catholic teaching, on the other hand, requires that each and every act of intercourse should be 'open to procreation' (cf. *Humanæ Vitæ*, 11). This difference of understanding received official expression in 1930. Before this, both Churches would have counseled abstinence for couples who had a justifiable reason to avoid conception. The Lambeth Conference of Anglican bishops, however, resolved in 1930 that 'where there is a clearly felt moral obligation to limit or avoid parenthood, and where there is a morally sound reason for avoiding complete abstinence . . . other methods may be used' (Resolution 15). The encyclical of Pope Pius XI (*Casti Connubii*, 1930), which was intended among other things as a response to the Lambeth resolution, renewed the traditional Roman Catholic position. In 1968 the teaching was further developed and clarified in Pope Paul VI's encyclical, *Humanæ Vitæ*. The Lambeth Conference of 1968 reaffirmed the position that had been taken by the 1958 Lambeth Conference. The Roman Catholic position has been frequently reaffirmed since, for example, in the documents *Familiaris Consortio*, 1981, and *Catechism of the Catholic Church*, 1992. This teaching belongs to the ordinary magisterium calling for 'religious assent'.

81. The immediate point at issue in this controversy would seem to concern the moral integrity of the act of marital intercourse. Both our traditions agree that this involves the

two basic 'goods' of marriage, loving union and procreation. Moral integrity requires that husband and wife respect both these goods together. For Anglicans, it is sufficient that this respect should characterise the married relationship as a whole; whereas for Roman Catholics, it must characterise each act of sexual intercourse. Anglicans understand the moral principle to be that procreation should not arbitrarily be excluded from the continuing relationship; whereas Roman Catholics hold that there is an unbreakable connexion, willed by God, between the two 'goods' of marriage and the corresponding meanings of marital intercourse, and that therefore they may not be sundered by any direct and deliberate act (cf. *Humanæ Vitæ*, 12).

82. The Roman Catholic doctrine is not simply an authoritative statement of the nature of the integrity of the marital act. The whole teaching on human love and sexuality, continued and developed in *Humanæ Vitæ*, must be taken into account when considering the Roman Catholic position on this issue. The definition of integrity is founded upon a number of considerations: a way of understanding human fruitfulness and divine creativity; the special vocation of the married couple; and the requirements of the virtue of marital chastity. Anglicans accept all of these considerations as relevant to determining the integrity of the marital relationship and act. Thus they share the same spectrum of moral and theological considerations. However, they do not accept the arguments Roman Catholics derive from them, nor the conclusions they draw from them regarding the morality of contraception.

5. Other Issues

83. So far in this section we have argued that our disagreements in the areas of marriage, procreation, and contraception, areas in which our two Communions have made official but conflicting pronouncements, are on the level of derived conclusions rather than fundamental values. However, as we observed earlier, there are other important issues in the area of sexuality where no official disagreement has been expressed between our two Communions, but where disagreement is nonetheless perceived to exist. Although Anglicans and Roman Catholics may often achieve a common mind and witness on many issues of peace and social justice, nevertheless, it is said, their teaching is irreconcilable on such matters as abortion and homosexual relations. What is more, there are other difficult and potentially divisive issues in the offing, as scientific and technological expertise develops the unprecedented power to manipulate the basic material, not only of the environment, but also of human life itself.

84. This is not the time or place to discuss such further issues in detail. However, confining ourselves to the two issues of abortion and homosexual relations, we would argue that, in these instances too, the disagreements between us are not on the level of fundamental moral values, but on their implementation in practical judgements.

85. Anglicans have no agreed teaching concerning the precise moment from which the new human life developing in the womb is to be given the full protection due to a human person. Only some Anglicans insist that in all circumstances, and without exception, such protection must extend back to the time of conception. Roman Catholic teaching, on the other hand, is that the human embryo must be treated as a human person from the moment of conception (cf. *Donum Vitæ*, 1987, and *Declaration on Procured Abortion*, 1974). Difference of teaching on this matter cannot but give rise to difference of judgement on what is morally permissible when a tragic conflict occurs between the rights of the mother and the rights of the fetus. Roman Catholic teaching rejects all direct abortion. Among Anglicans the view is to be found that in certain cases direct abortion is morally justifiable. Anglicans and Roman Catholics, however, are at one in their recognition of the sanctity, and right to life, of all human persons, and they share an abhorrence of the growing practice in many countries of abortion on grounds of mere convenience. This agreement on fundamentals is reflected both in pronouncements of bishops and in official documents issued by both Communions (cf. *Catechism of the Catholic Church*, 1992, 2270, and *Lambeth Conference Report*, 1930, 16 and 1978, 10).

86. We cannot enter here more fully into this debate, and we do not wish to underestimate the consequences of our disagreement. We wish, however, to affirm once again that Anglicans and Roman Catholics share the same fundamental teaching concerning the mystery of human life and the sanctity of the human person. They also share the same sense of awe and humility in making practical judgements in this area of profound moral complexity. Their differences arise in the way in which they develop and apply fundamental moral teaching. What we have said earlier about our different formulations of the moral law is here relevant (see para. 52). For Roman Catholics, the rejection of abortion is an example of an absolute prohibition. For Anglicans, however, such an absolute and categorical prohibition would not be typical of their moral reasoning. That is why it is important to set such differences in context. Only then shall we be able to assess their wider implications.

87. In the matter of homosexual relationships a similar situation obtains. Both our Communions affirm the importance and significance of human friendship and affection among men and women, whether married or single. Both affirm that all persons, including those of homosexual orientation, are made in the divine image and share the full dignity of human creatureliness. Both affirm that a faithful and lifelong marriage between a man and a woman provides the normative context for a fully sexual relationship. Both appeal to Scripture and the natural order as the sources of their teaching on this issue. Both reject, therefore, the claim, sometimes made, that homosexual relationships and married relationships are morally equivalent, and equally capable of expressing the right ordering and use of the sexual drive. Such ordering and use, we believe, are an essential aspect of life in Christ. Here again our different approaches to the formulation of law are relevant (cf.

para. 52). Roman Catholic teaching holds that homosexual activity is 'intrinsically disordered', and concludes that it is always objectively wrong. This affects the kind of pastoral advice that is given to homosexual persons. Anglicans could agree that such activity is disordered; but there may well be differences among them in the consequent moral and pastoral advice they would think it right to offer to those seeking their counsel and direction.

88. Our two Communions have in the past developed their moral teaching and practical and pastoral disciplines in isolation from each other. The differences that have arisen between them are serious, but careful study and consideration has shown us that they are not fundamental. The urgency of the times and the perplexity of the human condition demand that they now do all they can to come together to provide a common witness and guidance for the well-being of humankind and the good of the whole creation.

F. TOWARDS SHARED WITNESS

89. We have already seen how divergence between Anglicans and Roman Catholics on matters of practice and official moral teaching has been aggravated, if not caused, by the historic breach of communion and the consequent breakdown in communication. Separation has led to estrangement, and estrangement has fostered misperception, misunderstanding, and suspicion. Only in recent times has this process been reversed and the first determined steps taken along the way to renewed and full communion.

90. The theme of communion illumines, we believe, not only the reality of the Church as a worshiping community, but also the form and fullness of Christian life in the world. Indeed, since the Church is called in Christ to be a sign and sacrament of a renewed humanity, it also illumines the nature and destiny of human life as such. As ARCIC has affirmed in *Church as Communion*:

To explore the meaning of communion is not only to speak of the Church but also to address the world at the heart of its deepest need, for human beings long for true community in freedom, justice and peace and for respect of human dignity (para. 3).

In this final section, therefore, we return once again to the theme of communion and consider the light it sheds both on the moral order and on the Church's moral response.

1. Communion and the Moral Order

91. Communion, we have argued, is a constitutive characteristic of a fully human life, signifying 'a relationship based on participation in a shared reality' (cf. *Church as Communion*, para. 12). From this perspective the moral dimension of human life is itself perceived to be fundamentally relational, determined both by the nature of the reality in which it participates and by the form appropriate to such participation.

92. Participation of human beings in the life of God, in whom they live and move and have their being (cf. Acts 17.28), is grounded in their creation in God's image (cf. *Church as Communion*, 6). The fundamental relationship in which they stand, therefore, is their relationship to God, Creator and goal of all that is, seen and unseen. Created and sustained in this relationship, they are drawn towards God's absolute goodness, which they experience as both gift and call. Moral responsibility is a gift of divine grace; the moral imperative is an expression of divine love. When Jesus bids his disciples before all else to seek the kingdom of God (cf. Mt 6:33), he tells them also that they are to reflect in their own lives the 'perfection' which belongs to the divine life (cf. Mt 5:48). This call to 'perfection' echoes the Lord's call to the people of Israel to participate in his holiness (cf. Lev 19:2). As such, it does not ignore human fragility, failure, and sin; but it does lay bare the full dimensions of a response that reflects the height and breadth and depth of the divine righteousness and love (cf. Rom 8:1-4).

93. Human beings are not purely spiritual beings; they are fashioned out of the dust (cf. Gn 2:7). Created in the image of God, they are shaped by nature and culture, and participate in both the glory and the shame of the human story. Their responsibility to God issues in a responsibility for God's world, and their transformation into the likeness of God embraces their relationships both to the natural world and to one another. Hence no arbitrary boundaries may be set between the good of the individual, the common good of humanity, and the good of the whole created order. The context of the truly human life is the universal and all-embracing rule of God.

94. The world in which human beings participate is a changing world. Science and technology have given them the power, to a degree unforeseen in earlier centuries, to impress their own designs on the natural environment, by adapting the environment to their own needs, by exploiting it and even by destroying it. However, there are ultimate limits to what is possible. Nature is not infinitely malleable. Moreover, not everything that is humanly possible is humanly desirable, or morally right. In many situations, what is sometimes called progress is, as a consequence of human ignorance, degrading and destructive. The moral task is to discern how fundamental and eternal values may be expressed and embodied in a world that is subject to continuing change.

95. The world in which human beings participate is not only a changing world; it is also a broken and imperfect world. It is subject to futility and sin, and stands under the judgement of God. Its human structures are distorted by violence and greed. Inevitably, conflicts of value and clashes of interest arise, and situations occur in which the requirements of the moral order are uncertain. Law is enacted and enforced to preserve order and to protect and serve the common good. Admittedly, it can perpetuate inequalities of wealth and power, but its true end is to ensure justice and peace. At a deeper level, the moral order looks for its fulfilment to a renewal of personal freedom and dignity within a forgiving, healing, and caring community.

2. Communion and the Church

96. Life in Christ is a life of communion, to be manifested for the salvation of the world and for the glorification of God the Father. In the fellowship of the Holy Spirit the Church participates in the Son's loving and obedient response to the Father. But even if, in the resurrection of Christ, the new world has already begun, the end is not yet. So the Church continues to pray and prepare for the day when Christ will deliver the kingdom to the Father (cf. 1 Cor 15.24-28) and God will be all in all. In the course of history Anglicans and Roman Catholics have disagreed on certain specific matters of moral teaching and practice, but they continue to hold to the same vision of human nature and destiny fulfilled in Christ. Furthermore, their deep desire to find an honest and faithful resolution of their disagreements is itself evidence of a continuing communion at a more profound level than that on which disagreement has occurred.

97. The Church as communion reflects the communion of the triune God, Father, Son, and Holy Spirit (cf. Jn 17:20-22; Jn 14.16f; 2 Cor 13:13), and anticipates the fullness of communion in the kingdom of God. Consequently, communion means that members of the Church share a responsibility for discerning the action of the Spirit in the contemporary world, for shaping a truly human response, and for resolving the ensuing moral perplexities with integrity and fidelity to the Gospel. Within this shared responsibility, those who exercise the office of pastor and teacher have the special task of equipping the Church and its members for life in the world, and for guiding and confirming their free and faithful response to the Gospel. The exercise of this authority will itself bear the marks of communion, insofar as a sustained attentiveness to the experience and reflection of the faithful becomes part of the process of making an informed and authoritative judgement. One such example of this understanding of the interaction of communion and authority, we suggest, is the careful and sustained process of listening and public consultation which has preceded the publication of some of the pastoral letters of Bishops' Conferences of the Roman Catholic Church in different parts of the world.

98. Communion also means that, where there has been a failure to meet the claims of the moral order to which the Church bears witness, there will be a determined attempt to restore the sinner to the life of grace in the community, thereby allowing the Gospel of forgiveness to be proclaimed even to the greatest of sinners. Anglicans and Roman Catholics share the conviction that God's righteousness and God's love and mercy are inseparable (cf. *Salvation and the Church*, 17 and 18), and both Communions continue to exercise a ministry of healing, forgiveness and reconciliation.

3. Towards Moral Integrity and Full Communion

99. Anglicans and Roman Catholics share a deep desire, not only for full communion, but also for a resolution of the disagreement that exists between them on certain specific moral issues. The two are related. On the one hand, seeking a resolution of our disagree-

ments is part of the process of growing together towards full communion. On the other hand, only as closer communion leads to deeper understanding and trust can we hope for a resolution of our disagreements.

100. In order to make an informed and faithful response to the moral perplexities facing humanity today, Christians must promote a global and ecumenical perception of fundamental human relationships and values. Our common vision of humanity in Christ places before us this responsibility, while at the same time requiring us to develop a greater sensitivity to the different experiences, insights, and approaches that are appropriate to different cultures and contexts. The separation that still exists between our two Communions is a serious obstacle to the Church's mission and a darkening of the moral wisdom it may hope to share with the world.

101. Our work together within this Commission has shown us that the discernment of the precise nature of the moral agreement and disagreement between Anglicans and Roman Catholics is not always an easy task. One problem we faced was the fact that we often found ourselves comparing the variety of moral judgements present and permissible among Anglicans with the official, authoritative teachings of the Roman Catholic Church. This feature of our discussions was inevitable, given the differences between our two Communions in the way they understand and exercise authority. Working together, however, has convinced us that the disagreements on moral matters, which at present exist between us, need not constitute an insuperable barrier to progress towards fuller communion. Painful and perplexing as they are, they do not reveal a fundamental divergence in our understanding of the moral implications of the Gospel.

102. Continuing study is needed of the differences between us, real or apparent, especially in our understanding and use of the notion of 'law'. A clearer understanding is required of the relation of the concept of law to the concepts of moral order and the common good, and the relation of all these concepts to the vision of human happiness and fulfilment as 'persons-in-community' that we have been given in and through Jesus Christ. However, Anglicans and Roman Catholics do not talk to each other as moral strangers. They both appeal to a shared tradition, and they recognise the same Scriptures as normative of that tradition. They both respect the role of reason in moral discernment. They both give due place to the classic virtue of prudence. We are convinced, therefore, that further exchange between our two traditions on moral questions will serve both the cause of Christian unity and the good of that larger society of which we are all part.

103. We end our document with a specific practical recommendation. We propose that steps should be taken to establish further instruments of co-operation between our two Communions at all levels of church life (especially national and regional), to engage with the serious moral issues confronting humanity today. In view of our common approach to moral reflection, and in the light of the agreements we have already discovered to exist

between us, we believe that bilateral discussions between Anglicans and Roman Catholics would be especially valuable.

104. We make this proposal for the following reasons.

Working together on moral issues would be a practical way of expressing the communion we already enjoy, of moving towards full communion, and of understanding more clearly what it entails; without such collaboration we run the risk of increasing divergence.

Moving towards shared witness would contribute significantly to the mission of the Church and allow the light of the Gospel to shine more fully upon the moral perplexities of human existence in today's world.

Having shared vision of a humanity created in the image of God, we share a common responsibility to challenge society in places where that image is being marred or defaced.

105. We do not underestimate the difficulties that such collaboration would involve. Nevertheless, we dare not continue along our separated ways. Our working and witnessing together to the world is in itself a form of communion. Such deepening communion will enable us to handle our remaining disagreements in a faithful and more creative way. 'He who calls you is faithful, and he will do it' (1 Thes 5:24).

19. CHRISTIAN ETHICS IN THE ECUMENICAL DIALOGUE:

ANGLICAN ROMAN CATHOLIC INTERNATIONAL COMMISSION II AND RECENT PAPAL TEACHING

Anglican–Roman Catholic Dialogue in the United States, 1995

1.   Our Churches have long recognized the need for serious engagement with Christian ethics as an important component of our endeavor to restore full ecclesial communion. The Second Vatican Council had suggested that 'on the common basis of the Gospel, dialogue can lead to a more profound understanding on both sides' (*Decree on Ecumenism*, no. 23). Although ecclesiological and other doctrinal issues took priority in the various bilateral dialogues initiated after the Council, including the international and national Anglican-Roman Catholic dialogues, it became increasingly clear that ecumenical dialogue on ethics could not be long postponed.

In 1979, addressing an ecumenical assembly of church leaders toward the close of his first U.S. visit as pope, John Paul II spoke of 'deep division which still exists over moral and ethical matters', and declared: 'The moral life and the life of faith are so deeply united that it is impossible to divide them' (7 Oct. 1979, Trinity College, Washington, D.C.). During the next decade, the perception grew that progress toward Christian unity might now be hampered by differences over current moral issues even more than by the doctrinal differences inherited from the Reformation era.

2.   That discouraging perception has now been challenged in an agreed statement on morals published by the Second Anglican Roman Catholic International Commission (ARCIC II), entitled *Life in Christ: Morals, Communion and the Church* (LC) (1994). Drawing upon the Commission's previous agreed statement, *Church as Communion* (1991), the present statement on morals emphasizes that the communion to which we are all called involves responsibilities to God, to society, and to the world we inhabit. From the outset, *Life in Christ* affirms that Anglicans and Roman Catholics 'share the same fundamental moral values' (LC, no. 1). The opening chapters set forth the shared vision and common heritage of our two Churches as regards the meaning of Christian life (nos. 4–35). Differences between us in the articulation of this moral vision—for example, concerning the respective roles of personal conscience, ecclesial tradition, and magisterial teaching in Christian moral formation—are seen and presented as a matter of varying emphasis rather than substantive disagreement (nos. 43–53).

In addressing certain specific moral issues where some measure of real disagreement is evident, *Life in Christ* endeavors to situate these differences within the context of broader areas of basic agreement between the Anglican and Roman Catholic Churches. Regarding divorce and remarriage, and also contraception, the divergent official positions of our two Churches are seen as differences over detailed moral conclusions which should not obscure our fundamental agreement on the nature of marriage as a permanent covenant open to procreation (nos. 64-80). Our differing approaches to abortion in certain difficult cases are seen as expressing diverse understandings of the status of absolute moral prohibitions in ethical discourse, a diversity which leaves intact our common reverence for the sacredness of all human life (nos. 85-86). As regards to homosexuality, *Life in Christ* acknowledges differences between Anglican and Roman Catholic pastoral practice but does not view these differences as compromising a shared appreciation of the marriage covenant as 'the normative context for a fully sexual relationship' (no. 87).

According to *Life in Christ*, therefore, it would appear that our differences concerning morals amount to relatively narrow disagreements over secondary issues, or to variations of emphasis which involve no real disagreement at all, or to matters of practice which are not seen to present a significant challenge to moral teaching. *Life in Christ* claims that the importance of all such differences has been exaggerated by the very fact of our broken communion, which tempts us to exalt our differences into church-dividing issues (nos. 53, 89). In the perspective of *Life in Christ*, none of our differences regarding morals is a valid warrant for our Churches to remain separated. On the contrary, strengthening our communion offers the best hope for resolving our outstanding moral differences and bearing more effective common witness to our shared Gospel values (no. 88).

3.   The optimistic thesis of *Life in Christ* appears to be significantly challenged, in its turn, by the papal encyclical *Veritatis Splendor* (VS), which was published only months earlier (5 Oct. 1993). We note with regret that these two documents were prepared independently of each other, and we find our Churches challenged to be more collaborative in the future. Still, now we must take account of important contrasts in outlook between the two documents and the likely implication of these contrasts for the eventual assessment of *Life in Christ* by the papal magisterium.

Whereas *Life in Christ* sees the fundamental moral question as 'What kind of persons are we called to become?', rather than 'What ought we to do?' (LC, no. 6), *Veritatis Splendor* is mainly concerned with 'What must we do?' This divergence on the primary ground of ethics—in character or in behavior—has long standing in the Christian tradition overall, and indeed it remains currently a focus of much lively discussion. Furthermore, other differences in approach between *Life in Christ* and *Veritatis Splendor* are also significant.

Veritatis Splendor is intended as a magisterial directive specifically for Roman Catholics, rather than as a contribution to ecumenical dialogue (which is the intent of *Life in Christ*). *Veritatis Splendor* bases its moral vision primarily on the concept of divine law, rather than the relationship-responsibility concept which governs *Life in Christ*. By contrast with ARCIC's acceptance of a degree of ethical diversity as compatible with healthy ecclesial communion, it is a major objective of the papal encyclical to reprove the growth of such diversity among Roman Catholics as inimical to authentic communion (VS, no. 113). Finally, while *Life in Christ* advocates closer ecumenical dialogue as the preferred remedy for moral confusion, in *Veritatis Splendor* the major remedy indicated is the firmer exercise of papal and episcopal authority (VS, nos. 114–116).

Some of the above contrasts between *Life in Christ* and *Veritatis Splendor* may very well be seen as matters of divergent emphases dictated by different specific objectives. For example, the concentration in *Veritatis Splendor* on the question, 'What must we do?' can be understood in terms of the pope's special concern to address current internal Roman Catholic controversies about how to determine moral rectitude in human actions; and this need not be taken as negating ARCIC's attribution of fundamental primacy to the question, 'What kind of persons are we called to become?' Likewise, the encyclical's preference for the 'divine law' model in articulating its moral vision could well be based on the special aptitude of that particular model for asserting absolute principles governing specific human actions. This preference need not imply a devaluing of other moral models highlighted in *Life in Christ*.

Other points of contrast are more formidable, however. As indicated above, the two documents appear to take incompatible positions concerning the impact of ethical diversity on ecclesial communion and concerning the appropriate role of ecclesiastical authority in dealing with such diversity. More specifically, ARCIC's suggestion that differing Anglican and Roman Catholic views on 'absolute moral prohibitions' are not of central importance seems hardly reconcilable with the major concern of *Veritatis Splendor*—reiterated, in part, in the subsequent encyclical *Evangelium Vitæ* (EV) (25 March 1995)—to underline the importance of such absolute prohibitions particularly as regards issues involving human life, sexuality, and marriage (VS, nos. 80–83; EV, no. 62). Nor does ARCIC's suggestion appear congruent with the intense debate among Roman Catholics themselves about the status of absolute prohibitions and about the authoritative force of various papal statements.

4.   It is the view of ARC-USA that, in light of the difficulties noted above, certain conclusions of ARCIC II as presented or suggested in *Life in Christ* stand in need of further study and refinement, so as to secure the possibility of fruitful ecumenical dialogue in relation to current authoritative Roman Catholic teaching. More attention must be given particularly to: (1) the significance of divergent Anglican and Roman Catholic positions on absolute moral prohibitions regarding specific categories of human action; (2) the contemporary influence of theological, geographical, and cultural diversity on the formulation of Anglican doctrines concerning moral questions, by contrast with the universal teaching that characterizes the Roman Catholic magisterium in such matters; and (3) the role of

ecclesiastical authority in shaping the formation of moral judgments by individual Christians and by the whole Church.

The experience of our two Churches in the United States indicates further that the specific moral issues highlighted in *Life in Christ* are considerably more conflictual—both within each of our Churches and between us—than ARCIC appears to have recognized. Even if basic areas of agreement exist as regards the sacredness of human life, the nature of marriage, and the meaning of human sexuality, our very diverse specifications and practical applications of these general principles cannot be regarded as non-essential in moral discourse, and indeed profoundly affect the extent and quality of communion. The sometimes sharply divergent specific teachings and practices of our Churches regarding divorce, contraception, abortion, and homosexuality are actually a frequently given reason why Roman Catholic and Episcopalian Christians leave one Church and enter the other.

ARC-USA welcomes and commends *Life in Christ* as a ground-breaking exploration of the ethical dimension of Christian communion. We affirm, with *Life in Christ*, that the best way to deal constructively with the differences that divide us lies in closer consultation and collaboration. At the same time, this collaborative process requires that our conflicting positions on vital issues be acknowledged openly in all their seriousness, and engaged resolutely and wisely.

20. PASTORAL GUIDELINES FOR INTERCHURCH MARRIAGES

Anglican and Roman Catholic Bishops, Canada, 1987

Differences of religious background in a marriage can be either a source of tension or an opportunity for growth in the unity to which the Church is called. With a view to encouraging cooperation between Anglican and Roman Catholic couples and their pastors, the bishops of both Churches are presenting these *Pastoral Guidelines for Interchurch Marriages Between Anglicans and Roman Catholics in Canada.*

Initially discussed at the national Anglican-Roman Catholic Bishops' Dialogue of 1985, the *Guidelines* were referred to both the House of Bishops of the Anglican Church of Canada and the Canadian Conference of Catholic Bishops for revision and approval. With each Church following its own procedures, the resulting text has been accepted by both bodies and is now being offered as a joint publication.

Over the past number of years, a growing closeness has developed between our two Churches. Building upon this ecumenical experience, these *Guidelines* do not attempt to break new ground nor to anticipate future changes but to give full expression to the possibilities present in current regulations and practice. It is to be hoped that joint discussion and increasing cooperation will extend our vision and lead to more consistent pastoral care for interchurch couples and families.

We also pray that the dialogue between Anglican and Roman Catholic Churches will, when and in the way Christ desires, bear fruit in unity of faith and life. In that dialogue, the partners in interchurch marriages may have a prophetic role to play.

✠ **BERNARD HUBERT**
President
Canadian Conference of Catholic Bishops
✠ **MICHAEL G. PEERS**
Primate
Anglican Church of Canada

ANGLICAN-ROMAN CATHOLIC MARRIAGES
Introduction

The eleventh annual meeting of representative Anglican-Roman Catholic Bishops in Canada is happy to offer this statement for the assistance of Anglican and Roman Catholic clergy and laity.

We acknowledge that until our two Churches are in full communion, the sharing of one's own faith tradition with one's partner and children would be easier if one's spouse were from that same tradition. Nonetheless, though Anglicans and Roman Catholics who marry have been baptized in different Churches, their union is a true sacrament and gives rise to a 'domestic Church'. They are called to a unity which reflects the union of Christ with his Church, and their family is bound to a witness based on that spiritual union. Our prayerful hope is that the partners in these marriages will be encouraged to deepen their own faith commitment and to grow in respect for that of the other while seeking to provide their children with a truly fruitful Christian education.

Marriage, as a covenant, builds upon the original baptismal covenant by which the believer is united to Jesus and his Body, the Church. Exercising the priesthood of their baptism-confirmation, each baptized party administers in the name of the Church the sacrament to the other, with its special sacramental grace, which perdures throughout their married life.

They 'establish between themselves a partnership of their whole life, and which of its own very nature is ordered to the well-being of the spouses and to the procreation and upbringing of children' (Code of Canon Law, Canon 1055, 1).

'The essential properties of marriage are unity and indissolubility: in Christian marriage they acquire a distinctive firmness by reason of the sacrament' (Code of Canon Law, Canon 1056).

'The Church affirms in like manner the goodness of the union of man and woman in marriage, this being of God's creation (cf. Gn 1:27-31). Marriage also is exalted as a sign (Eph 5:31b) of the redeeming purpose of God to unite all things in Christ (Eph 1:9b), the purpose made known in the reunion of divided humanity in the Church (Eph 2:11-16)' (The Anglican Church in Canada, Canon XXI, *On Marriage in the Church*, Preface, no. 2)

The blessing of the celebrant, who acts as official witness and presides over the liturgical celebration, recalls the importance of the Lord for the couple who confer this sacrament.

Role of Law

An international commission set up to study the theology of marriage as it related to interchurch marriages, set out some important insights regarding the role of law in the Anglican and Roman Catholic traditions. It pointed out that in a marriage between an Anglican and a Roman Catholic 'there is a meeting, not only of the two Churches represented by the parties, and not only of the doctrines and traditions of those Churches, but also of two jurisdictions, two societies whose lives are regulated to different extents, by law' (Anglican-Roman Catholic Commission on the Theology of Marriage, *Final Report*, 1975 [Vischer, 1984]).

For both Roman Catholics and Anglicans the way in which Canon Law is interpreted has great pastoral implications. In general terms, Roman Catholic Canon Law is based on

Roman Law: the written canons are strictly stated and are to be interpreted with all the personal adaptations contained in the law. Anglican Canon Law is based on English common law: the laws are few but to be interpreted strictly. The difficulty for Roman Catholics arises in those cultures where English common law abounds: the strict Roman-based law is interpreted with the English common law mind-set, that is, strictly!

For Anglicans marriage is regulated by each autonomous Church in the Anglican Communion, although there is a common teaching about marriage based on the Scriptures. In Canada, marriages solemnized in Anglican Churches are governed by Canon XXI of the Canons of the General Synod of the Anglican Church of Canada. While Canon XXI makes fewer specific demands on persons coming to marriage than does Roman Catholic Canon Law, it is important that the parties understand the standards set by Canon XXI. The canonical responsibilities of a pastor in preparing for and solemnizing a marriage also need to be understood by all the parties concerned.

In the Roman Catholic Church Canon Law has to be seen in the context of that Church's understanding of its pastoral responsibility for its members, to help them grow in the knowledge and love of Christ. The canonical regulation of marriage, like the dispensation of all the sacraments, generally is seen to be part of this whole. The Code of Canon Law represents the last stage in Roman Catholic modification both of discipline and of its expression. It takes account of the rapidly changing conditions of today and the development of thought reflected in such Vatican II documents as the *Declaration on Religious Liberty* and the *Decree on Ecumenism*. Interchurch marriages are seen as a fact of life and an object of pastoral solicitude; a solicitude which, in the case of Anglican-Roman Catholic marriages, is proper to both Churches involved and a proper object of sincere openness and enlightened confidence between the respective clergy.

There are several areas concerning interchurch marriages which require particular care:

- pre-marital preparation
- completing necessary forms
- promises (of the Catholic party) regarding the baptism and education of children
- worship in each other's Churches
- celebration of the marriage
- joint pastoral care
- spiritual growth of the couple and future family

The following pastoral guidelines are an attempt at this moment of our ecumenical journey, to promote our life in Christ and to live in joyful hope for the day when our Churches will be one in the richness of a legitimate diversity.

Pastoral Care of Interchurch Marriages

A. Preparation for Marriage

Article I

Anglican and Roman Catholic clergy at the local level are encouraged to get to know each other and to understand the faith and life of each other's faith community. This commitment to grow in reconciliation and seek unity by stages ought to facilitate our joint pastoral care of couples preparing for Anglican-Roman Catholic interchurch marriages.

Interchurch Couples

Although each individual situation will be different there are three types of interchurch marriage often spoken of:

1. Marriages where both parties are active and practising members of their respective Churches and wish to maintain these allegiances

It is such marriages that are most appropriately called 'interchurch' marriages. An ecumenical approach to the preparation for the marriage and joint pastoral care afterward can be of great support to such marriages. The commitment of each partner should be a source of rejoicing to all concerned, as each will bring the strengths and insights of their tradition into the marriage relationship.

2. Marriages where only one party is a practising member of either Church and the other a nominal member of the other

In such cases it seems likely that the marriage ceremony will take place in the church of the more active partner. However, it should not be too quickly assumed that there should be no involvement of a priest of the other Church. For the officiating priest to try to gauge the commitment of the person concerned would be inappropriate. People often have deep ties of loyalty and affection to the Church in which they were brought up, even though they may not attend worship. Also a Roman Catholic may become unable to receive communion if the proper procedures are not followed. Prior to the service the officiating priest should suggest that the parties contact a priest of the other Church and express a willingness to invite the other priest to participate. The relationship between the two partners will also be enhanced if the non-practising partner is encouraged to learn more about the faith commitment of the other.

3. Marriages where both parties are inactive or nominal members of their respective Churches

The couple may be coming for a church wedding out of social custom or family insistence. Equally, however, they may have a real desire to have God's blessing on their marriage. Such marriages provide an opportunity for the officiating priest to present the claims of the Gospel and to set forth the Christian understanding of marriage. The couple should be received in a spirit of evangelization rather than of proselytism. What has already been said about the emotional ties of people to the Church of their upbringing should also be kept in mind.

Relationships with Parents and Families

In many interchurch marriages there are often devout parents, and other family members, of either or both parties to be considered. This may be the case even when the couple's practice is only nominal. The priest's major pastoral responsibility is toward the couple themselves but it can be of great help to all concerned if the couple is enabled to retain the goodwill and support of their parents and family. It may be necessary for the priest to help the couple understand and respect the religious convictions of their parents.

The clergy concerned may also see it as part of their responsibility to discuss the situation with the parents and encourage them to respect the consciences of the couple. It is in this kind of situation that an ecumenical approach can prove its value.

Article 2

The priest of the church in which the marriage is to be celebrated should contact the priest of the other church so that mutual responsibilities can be discussed.

From the start, preparations for the marriage should be conducted in a cooperative manner. Wherever possible, various aspects of the preparation including investigations, instructions, ecclesial permissions and dispensations, the publishing of banns, the recording of the marriage, and the wedding ceremony itself, should be reviewed and jointly planned by the two priests involved.

Article 3

The responsibility for the preparation of the couple will be that of one or other of the Churches in the regular marriage preparation process.

Premarital instructions are to be arranged for the couple in accordance with the practice of each Church (Catholic Engaged Encounter, pre-marriage courses, Evenings for the Engaged, etc.). Wherever possible, joint marriage preparation is to be encouraged. At least one joint session involving the couple and the Anglican and Roman Catholic priests should be held. This is likely to be difficult to schedule but is important as a witness to our Churches' concern for the spiritual lives and the marriage of the couple, as well as to provide a model for a couple of the interchurch respect they are being called upon to live.

Article 4

The priests should ascertain that both parties freely and knowingly consent to the marriage with a proper understanding of its nature and without fraud, mental reservation, coercion, or mistake in the identity of the partner.

Article 5

The couple should be helped to understand that marriage is a physical and spiritual union of a man and a woman, a partnership of life and love which is entered into by mutual consent within the community of faith with the intent that it be lifelong and open to the gift of children.

Article 6

If, for any reason, a priest of either an Anglican or Roman Catholic Church refuses to solemnize a marriage and the couple then approaches a priest of the other Church for this purpose, it is strongly recommended, without prejudice to Article 10, that the two priests discuss the matter to achieve some mutual clarification.

Article 7

Care should be taken to ensure that each partner in the marriage understands the faith and values of the other partner and the other partner's community, and knows that the Roman Catholic and Anglican Churches are committed to the reconciliation of our Churches in a process of unity by stages. It should be made clear that the stage of unity presently attained does not permit reciprocal open communion (cf. Art 17), but does encourage common prayer and witness and a recognition of our baptismal unity and agreement in faith on most fundamental doctrines.

Article 8

Responsible parenthood is an essential topic in premarital instruction. Although responsible parenthood is a recognized value in both Churches, there are differences in the teachings of each. In giving instructions on this matter, both the Anglican and the Roman Catholic priests must be consistent with their own Church's teaching and aware of the other's doctrinal perspective.

Article 9

The obligation to educate children in the faith is shared by all Christians, for it arises from the movement of God within the conscience of every believer. The Catholic Church specifies that the Catholic express a promise to fulfill this religious duty. This promise 'to do all in one's power' does not rule out the similar obligations of conscience in the Anglican party, but is to say 'all one can do in the actual circumstances of the marriage'.

In practice, it is important to remind both parties that the Christian education of children is a bilateral obligation of conscience which will have to be lived out in mutual respect and support. The following hierarchy of values may be helpful in making a wise decision:

1. the mutual respect of the faith and doctrine of the partner, which must not be forced or manipulated;
2. the good of the marriage itself, which must not be placed in jeopardy;
3. the baptism and religious education of the children (Secretariat for Promoting Christian Unity, *Information Service*, no. 42, 1980/1, p. 6)

The promise made by the Roman Catholic to uphold his or her faith and pass it on to his or her children through baptism and education in the Catholic faith, is necessary in order to receive the permission of the bishop for the marriage. This promise is made in the presence of the pastoral minister; the Anglican party is informed of it. The minister concerned certifies that the promise has been made by the Roman Catholic and that the other party has been informed of this fact. (See Canons 1086, 2, and 1125.)

It is to be recognized that the obligation and desire of the Anglican parties in inter-church marriages to share their faith with their children is no less real than that of Roman Catholics.

Article 10

For the valid marriage of a Roman Catholic, the canonical form is required, that is, the marriage must take place before the local Ordinary or Roman Catholic pastor of the place or their delegate (priest, deacon, or lay person), and two witnesses. (See Canons 1108, 1 and 1112.)

The local Ordinary of the Catholic party may grant a dispensation from the canonical form for reasons such as the following: to achieve or promote family harmony, to recognize the special relationships there may be with the Anglican minister, to allow the marriage to take place within the community which has special significance for the Anglican. (See Canon 1127, 2.)

Article 11

Both Anglicans and Roman Catholics encourage the celebration of marriage within the context of a supportive Christian community although witnesses of an Anglican-Roman Catholic marriage need not be members of either Church.

Article 12

When one or both of the baptized partners have drifted away and are marginalized or nominal, then the needs of evangelization and witness (cf. Art. 1, No. 3) apply. The normal rules of ecumenical sensitivity apply, but each Church is challenged to find ways of ministering to the unchurched when they seek the services of the Church.

Article 13

Priests of both communities should emphasize love and pastoral care rather than rivalry and rigorism. If the clergy respect each other's loyalty to their own community, then it will help the couple to do so as well (cf. Art. 3).

B. Specific Procedures for Anglican-Roman Catholic Marriages

Article 14

Roman Catholic priests not already authorized by the local Ordinary will apply for either of the following:

(a) Permission for a marriage of mixed religion: for a Roman Catholic to marry an Anglican with a Roman Catholic priest or qualified celebrant officiating.

or

(b) Permission for a marriage of mixed religion; and dispensation from form for a Roman Catholic to marry an Anglican with an Anglican priest presiding.

Article 15

The Anglican priest will ensure that the requirements set out in Canon XXI, *On Marriage in the Church*, have been met, including the signing of the Declaration of Intention.

We, _____ and _____, hereby declare that we intend to enter into marriage which we acknowledge to be a union in faithful love, to the exclusion of all other on either side, for better or for worse, until we are separated by death.

We undertake to prepare ourselves for the exchange of vows at our wedding, recognizing that by this mutual exchange our union in marriage will be established.

We intend to strive thereafter to fulfill the purpose of marriage: the mutual fellowship, support, and comfort of one another, the procreation (if it may be) and the nurture of children, and the creation of a relationship in which sexuality may serve personal fulfillment in a community of faithful love.

Article 16

Where both partners are active in the life of their parish, it is pastorally important for them to have their priest, deacon, or pastoral minister present to participate liturgically in the ceremony of marriage. An effort should therefore be made to have a priest, deacon, or pastoral minister of each Communion present—even though this is not canonically required by either.

It is the responsibility of the priest in whose church the marriage ceremony is being performed to receive the marriage vows and to declare the blessing on the marriage according to the rites of that particular Church. Within the framework of this rite the assisting cleric should be given the opportunity to offer appropriate prayers and blessings, read the Scriptures, or preach.

Article 17

Owing to the present legislation regarding eucharistic hospitality, it is normally not recommended that the wedding be celebrated within the context of a eucharist.

Article 18

When the marriage is celebrated in an Anglican Church, the Roman Catholic priest is obliged to record the marriage or to have it recorded in the usual manner, in the register of the parish to which the Roman Catholic party belongs, in the baptismal register by marginal notation, and in the register of dispensations at the diocesan curia (Canons 1121, 3; 1122).

C. Participation in the Anglican or Roman Catholic Wedding

The orders of celebration for non-eucharistic Anglican and Roman Catholic wedding ceremonies are given below. Assisting clergy from the other Church may be invited to perform any part of the service which is indicated by an asterisk.

1. *The Anglican Marriage Ceremony*
   (a) *Book of Common Prayer*
       1. Entrance of clergy
       2. Exhortation and charge
       3. Marriage rite

4. Psalm and Prayers*

5. Nuptial Blessing

(b) *Book of Alternative Services*

1. Entrance of Roman Catholic and Anglican clergy

2. The greeting and charge

3. Prayer

4. Readings*

5. Sermon*

6. Rite of Marriage

7. The prayers of the people*

8. Nuptial blessing

9. The peace*

2. *The Roman Catholic Ceremony*

1. Entrance of Roman Catholic and Anglican clergy

2. Greeting

3. Prayer

4. Readings*

5. Homily*

6. Rite of Marriage

7. Petitions*

8. Nuptial blessing

9. Lord's prayer*

10. Concluding blessings*

D. Continuing Pastoral Care After the Wedding

Article 19

Each partner should be encouraged to participate actively in his (her) own faith community and to respect and take an interest in the other. Couples should try to do all together that can be done together: prayer, Bible readings, services, works of mercy, Christian commitment to justice and peace. They should also, through their mutual support, pray and long for the day when unity of faith and life of their respective Churches may more adequately mirror the unity willed by Christ.

Article 20

The parents should encourage their children to respect and understand both Church communities, even though they can fully belong to only one of them.

Article 21

Joint pastoral care should include consultation and sharing of information between Anglican and Roman Catholic clergy when this can be done without breaking a pastoral confidence.

Article 22

We strongly encourage the formation of associations of Anglican-Roman Catholic couples: that is, *The Association of Inter-Church families.*

It would certainly be most helpful for couples of Anglican-Roman Catholic marriages to meet and to share their experiences of spiritual growth as well as the challenge of living out their interchurch marriage.

As Pope John Paul II said during his visit to the City of York, England on May 31st, 1982:

> *In your country, there are many marriages between Catholics and other baptized Christians. Sometimes these couples experience special difficulties. To these families I say: You live in your marriage the hopes and difficulties of the path to Christian unity. Express that hope in prayer together, in the unity of love. Together invite the Holy Spirit of love into your hearts and into your homes. He will help you to grow in trust and understanding.* (Osservatore Romano, June 7, 1982)

Conclusion

These pastoral guidelines for interchuch marriages between Anglicans and Roman Catholics are an attempt to reflect our joint ecumenical journey in the realization that the 'domestic Church' of the Anglican-Roman Catholic family is called to exercise a prophetic role for our larger Church communities.

Given that partners in Anglican-Roman Catholic marriages have much at stake in the progress of their respective Churches towards unity, they are encouraged to be active promoters of collaboration between their two Churches in the spirit of the ecumenical principle: 'Do everything together as far as conscience permits'. Thus they will be, in the unity they live in their 'domestic Church', a prophetic sign that the unity of faith and life sought by their respective institutional Churches is a real possibility. Their family itself is called to be an image of the Church and a sign of unity for the world.

As their bishops, we encourage them to celebrate their conjugal union and their family life in Jesus Christ through mutual faith, hope, and love, enhanced by prayer and enriched by the Scriptures. Finally, we ask the Father, Son, and Holy Spirit to bless these Anglican-Roman Catholic marriages with true peace, happiness, and holiness.

21. A MESSAGE FROM THE ANGLICAN-ROMAN CATHOLIC BISHOPS' DIALOGUE TO THE CLERGY AND PEOPLE OF THE ROMAN CATHOLIC AND ANGLICAN CHURCHES IN CANADA, 1994

This marks the 30th anniversary of the proclamation by the Second Vatican Council of the Decree of Ecumenism (*Unitatis Redintegratio*). That decree, and the spirit which informed it, sparked fresh ecumenical activity all over the world. It committed the Roman Catholic Church to the ecumenical movement which had been growing through the twentieth century. It resulted in the formation, six years later, of the Anglican Roman Catholic International Commission (ARCIC) which, in its turn, brought our two Communions into a closer relationship with each other and raised the hope of reconciliation leading to full and visible communion.

Thirty years later, we hear people lamenting that, after such a promising spring, we are now in an ecumenical winter, with the harvest only partly reaped. We are confident, however, that such fears are unjustified.

Here in Canada, Churches have achieved a high level of cooperation in addressing issues of justice and peace, as well as pastoral care of interchurch marriages, work on mutual recognition of baptism, and preparation of materials for and celebration of the Week of Prayer for Christian Unity. In many of these areas, we work with other Christian Churches, frequently through the Canadian Council of Churches. We also have two structures for our Churches to work together: the Anglican-Roman Catholic Dialogue (Canada) and the annual Bishops' Dialogue. Projects of these dialogue groups have contributed to the achievements of ARCIC I and II, and have led to agreements on several pastoral questions as well as procedures for clergy moving from one of our Communions to the other. They have also created a climate of friendship and commitment to one another.

At the international level, this year saw the Vatican's welcoming of *Clarifications* on the ARCIC I statements on eucharist and ministry. We can be confident that our theology of these questions no longer constitutes a barrier to unity, even though we differ on the question of who may be ordained. ARCIC II is continuing to work at reconciling our understandings of authority and its exercise, which underlie the questions regarding ordination. ARCIC has also offered us a vision of 'Church as Communion'.

The basis of our search for Christian unity is that, through baptism, we are already one in Christ Jesus. Though our unity is not complete, it is already real. The term 'communion' is frequently used in ecumenical dialogue to speak of 'the richness of our life together in Christ—community, sharing, fellowship, participation, solidarity'. Because we experience communion with God the Holy Trinity, we do not meet as strangers. Roman Catholics and Anglicans are related to each other; we are part of a family. Together we share in God's self-giving love; together we seek to share that reconciling love with the world through our commitments to faith and justice and peace. Together we are called to make that communion visible and complete.

We now commit ourselves, and call all our people to commit themselves with new vigour to the unity for which Jesus prayed. We declare, *There is no turning back*, either from the goal of visible unity or from the single ecumenical movement that unites concern for the unity of the Church and concern for engagement in the struggles of the world'.[1]

'There can be no ecumenism worthy of the name without a change of heart'.[2] It is not enough to have cordial relations, to work together on community issues, and to pray with each other from time to time. Response to Christ's vision calls for conversion, a change of mind and heart in both persons and institutions. Whenever we make decisions about our work and our mission, we need to uphold the prophetic vision of the Lund principle that calls us: 'to act together in all matters except those in which deep differences of conviction compel us to act separately'.

As we journey toward full communion, we challenge Anglicans and Roman Catholics to take the initiative to engage in specific projects at the local level, inviting Christians from other Churches to join us. We invite all congregations, dioceses, regions to take concrete steps within the next twelve months to make our unity more visible. We offer some examples:

- to explore common approaches to preparation and provision of support for families in interchurch marriages
- to hold joint retreats and parish missions
- to speak together on current social issues such as aboriginal concerns, immigration, the social safety net, medical ethics, or issues arising in the local context
- to encourage youth to pray and work together on common issues
- to encourage neighborhood groups to undertake joint Bible study
- to share resources for the development of parish programmes
- to make joint use of church facilities
- to pray and worship together whenever possible, especially when marking an event of significance to the wider community

May there be no turning back. Let us set out with new determination on the pilgrim road to that city where all reconciled creation rejoices in the love and unity of God. Let us strive with renewed vigour to make the vision of that city a reality in our communities by praying and working together, by reconciling our differences, and by rejoicing in each other's gifts of grace.

November 25, 1994

Since 1974, representatives of the Anglican and Roman Catholic Bishops of Canada have met in dialogue once a year. In 1994, the dialogue met at St. Paul Seminary in Ottawa from November 3-5, with Cardinal Edward Cassidy, President of the Pontifical Council for Promoting Christian Unity, in attendance.

NOTES

1   Message to the Churches from the Santiago Fifth World Conference on Faith and Order.
2   Decree on Ecumenism, Article 7.

APPENDIX I
PUBLICATIONS AND MAJOR EVENTS

SURVEY OF ANGLICAN-CATHOLIC EVENTS AND LITERATURE

1965   Meeting of representatives of the Ecumenical Commission of the Episcopal Church and of the Bishops' Commission for Ecumenical Affairs of the Roman Catholic Church in the United States, June 22

1966   Meeting of the Roman Catholic Bishops' Commission for Ecumenical Affairs and the Joint Commission for Ecumenical Affairs of the Episcopal Church in the United States (subsequently to be known as the Joint Commission on Anglican-Roman Catholic Relations, usually informally abbreviated as ARC USA), February 2-4

   Common Declaration by Pope Paul VI and the Archbishop of Canterbury, March 24

1967   ARC USA, Statement on the Eucharist

1968   The Anglican/Roman Catholic Joint Preparatory Commission, *The Malta Report*

   Letter from Augustin Cardinal Bea to the Archbishop of Canterbury, proposing Joint Commission, June 10

   Lambeth Conference 1968 recommends setting up a Permanent Joint Commission

1970   ARC USA, VII Report

1971   ARCIC, *Eucharistic Doctrine* (Windsor)

1972   ARC USA, statement *Doctrinal Agreement and Christian Unity: Methodological Considerations*

1973   ARCIC, *Ministry and Ordination* (Canterbury)

   ARC Canada, *Ministerial Priesthood in Relation to Christ and the Church*

1974   ARC Canada, *An Examination of Vatican II's Dogmatic Constitution on Divine Revelation* (two papers)

1975   Correspondence between the archbishop of Canterbury and the pope on the ordination of women, July 1975-March 1976

ARC USA, *Agreed Statement on the Purpose of the Church*

1976   ARC Canada, *Papal Primacy: An Anglican Perspective*

ARC USA, *Pro and Con on the Ordination of Women* (published papers)

ARC USA, *Statement on the Ordination of Women*

ARCIC, *Authority in the Church I* (Venice)

1977   *Common Declaration* (Pope Paul VI and the Archbishop of Canterbury), April 29

ARC USA, *Twelve-Year Report: Where We Are: A Challenge for the Future*

1979   ARCIC, *Eucharistic Doctrine: Elucidation* (Salisbury)

ARCIC, *Ministry and Ordination: Elucidation* (Salisbury)

ARCIC, *Authority in the Church: Elucidation* (Windsor)

1981   ARCIC, *Authority in the Church II* (Windsor)

ARCIC, *The Final Report* (Windsor)

1982   ARC Canada, *Canadian Agreed Statement on Infallibility*

'Congregation of the Doctrine of the Faith Comments on ARCIC Final Report' (*Origins* 11 [April 15, 1982]: 703 f) (*Origins* 11:47 [May 6, 1982]: 752-56 and *Ecumenical Bulletin* 54)

Statements and Common Declaration of Archbishop Runcie and Pope John Paul II at Canterbury, May 29

1983   EDEO/NADEO, *Five-Year Report*

ARC USA, *Images of God: Reflections on Christian Anthropology*

1984   U.S. National Conference of Catholic Bishops, 'Evaluation of the ARCIC Final Report' (*Origins* 14:409 f)

ARC Canada, *Building Bridges: A Canadian Study Guide to The Final Report of ARCIC I*

ARC Canada, *Remarks on the Congregation of the Doctrine of the Faith's 'Observations on The Final Report of ARCIC I'*

1985   Report of the Standing Committee on Ecumenical Relations to the General Convention of the Episcopal Church, including Resolution on ARCIC *Final Report* (*Ecumenical Bulletin* 71)

ARC Canada, *The Promise in Mixed Marriages, Midstream*

ARC Canada, *Reception of The Final Report of the Anglican Roman Catholic International Commission by the Anglican-Roman Catholic Dialogue of Canada*

1987   ARCIC II, *Salvation and the Church*

The Emmaus Report, chapter 3: 'The Anglican Roman Catholic International Commission', including analysis of responses to ARCIC *Final Report* by 19 of 29 Provinces of the Anglican Communion

ARC Canada, *Growth in Communion: A Schema*

ARC Canada Bishops, *Pastoral Guidelines for Interchurch Marriages Between Anglican and Roman Catholics in Canada*

1988   ARC USA, *Roman Catholic Views on Authority in The Final Report*

Lambeth, *Response to Final Report*

ARC USA, *Anglican Orders: A Report on the Evolving Context of Their Evaluation in the Roman Catholic Church*

ARCIC II, *Church as Communion*

1989   Pope John Paul and Archbishop Runcie meeting in Rome, *Common Declaration*

1990   ARC Canada, *A Call to Perseverance in Ecumenism: Observations of the Anglican/ Roman Catholic Dialogue in Canada on the Meeting of the Archbishop of Canterbury and Pope John Paul II*

1991   ARC Canada, *Reflection on the Experience of Women's Ministries*

ARC Canada, *Comments of the Anglican–Roman Catholic Dialogue of Canada on the Observations of the Congregation for the Doctrine of the Faith on Salvation and the Church*

ARC Canada Bishops, *Pastoral Guidelines for Churches in the Case of Clergy Moving from One Communion to the Other*

'Response to ARCIC I Final Report by the Roman Catholic Church' (*Origins* 21 no. 28 [December 19, 1991])

1992   ARC USA, *Statement of Recommitment*

1993   Statement of Bishop Theodore Eastman and Archbishop Rembert Weakland

ARC USA, *How Can We Recognize 'Substantial Agreement'?*

ARC Canada, *A Reply to the Vatican Response to the ARCIC I Final Report*

1994   ARC Canada, *A Response to the Belonging Together Document*

ARC USA, *Five Anglican–Roman Catholic Affirmations on the Eucharist as Sacrifice*

ARICIC II, *Life in Christ: Morals, Communion, and the Church*

ARC USA, Bishops' Pilgrimage to Canterbury and Rome (*One in Christ*, 1995)

1995   ARC USA, *Christian Ethics in the Ecumencial Dialogue*

ARC Canada Bishops, *A Message for the Anglican–Roman Catholic Bishops' Dialogue to the Clergy and People of the Roman Catholic and Anglican Churches in Canada*

APPENDIX II
DIALOGUE
PARTICIPANTS

ANGLICAN ROMAN CATHOLIC INTERNATIONAL COMMISSION (DOCUMENTS 1, 5, AND 18)

Anglicans

Mark Santer, Bishop of Birmingham, UK *(Co-Chairman)*

John Baycroft, Suffragan Bishop of Ottawa, Canada

E. D. Cameron, Assistant Bishop, Diocese of Sydney, Australia (until 1988)

Henry Chadwick, Master of Peterhouse, Cambridge, UK (until 1989)

Julian Charley, Priest-in-charge of Great Malvern, UK (until 1988)

Kortright Davis, Professor of Theology, Howard University Divinity School, Washington D.C., USA (until 1988)

E. Rozanne Elder, Professor of History, Western Michigan University, USA (1990-)

David M. Gitari, Bishop of Mount Kenya East, Kenya (until 1989)

Christopher Hill, Canon Residentiary of St. Paul's Cathedral, London, UK (to 1991, *previously Anglican Co-Secretary*)

Jaci Maraschin, Professor of Theology in the Ecumenical Institute, Saõ Paulo, Brazil (1990-)

John Muddiman, Fellow and Tutor in Theology, Mansfield College, Oxford, UK (1990-)

Michael Nazir-Ali, Bishop of Rochester, UK (1990-)

Oliver O'Donovan, Regius Professor of Moral and Pastoral Theology, University of Oxford, UK (until 1988) *(Consultant 1991)*

John Pobee, Programme on Ecumenical Theological Education, World Council of Churches, Geneva, Switzerland (until 1988)

Nicholas Sagovsky, Dean of Clare College, Cambridge, UK (1990-)

Charles Sherlock, Senior Lecturer, Ridley College, Melbourne, Australia (1990-)

Mary Tanner, Secretary, Council for Christian Unity of the General Synod of the Church of England, London, UK (until 1988)

Arthur A. Vogel, Retired Bishop of West Missouri, USA (until 1988)

J. Robert Wright, Professor of Church History, General Theological Seminary, N.Y., USA (until 1988)

Secretary:

Christopher Hill (until 1990)

Stephen Platten, Archbishop of Canterbury's Secretary for Ecumenical Affairs (1990-1994)

Donald Anderson, Anglican Consultative Council (1994-1996)

Morals Consultants:

Peter Baelz, retired Dean of Durham and formerly Professor of Moral and Pastoral Theology, University of Oxford, UK

Oliver O'Donovan, Professor of Moral and Pastoral Theology, University of Oxford, UK

Observer:

Donald Anderson, Anglican Consultative Council, London, UK

Roman Catholics

Cormac Murphy-O'Connor, Bishop of Arundel and Brighton, UK (*Co-Chairman*)

Abraham Adappur, SJ, Staff Member, Lumen Institute, Cohin, India (until 1988)

Peter Damian Akpunonu, Rector, Catholic Institute of West Africa, Port Harcourt, Nigeria (until 1988)

Brian Ashby, Bishop of Christchurch (1983-1984)

Mary Cecily Boulding, OP, Lecturer in Systematic Theology, Upshaw College, Durham, UK (until 1988)

Peter Butelezi, OMI, Archbishop of Bloemfontein, South Africa (until 1988)

Sara Butler, Associate Professor of Systematic Theology, University of St. Mary of the Lake, Mundelein, Ill., USA (1990-)

Peter Cross, Professor of Systematic Theology, Catholic Theological College, Clayton, Australia (1990-)

Adalbert Denaux, Professor, Faculty of Theology, The Catholic University, Leuven, Belgium (1990-)

Pierre Duprey, Titular Bishop of Thibare, Secretary, Pontifical Council for Promoting Christian Unity, Vatican City

Brian V. Johnstone, CSSR, Professor, Academia Alphonsiana, Rome, Italy (1990-1995)

Patrick Kelly, Archbishop of Liverpool, UK (1996-)

Raymond W. Lessard, Bishop of Savannah, USA (until 1988)

Brendan Soane, Spiritual Director, Pontifical Beda College, Rome, Italy (until 1988)

John Thornhill, SM, Lecturer in Systematic Theology, Catholic Theological Union, Hunters Hill, NSW, Australia (until 1988)

Jean M. R. Tillard, OP, Professor of Dogmatic Theology, Dominican Faculty of Theology, Ottawa, Canada

Bernard J. Wallace, Bishop of Rockhampton, Australia (1986-1988)

Liam Walsh, OP, Professor of Dogmatic Theology, University of Fribourg, Switzerland (1990-)

Edward Yarnold, SJ, Tutor in Theology, Campion Hall, Oxford, UK (until 1988)

Secretary:

Richard L. Stewart, Staff Member, Vatican Secretariat for Promoting Christian Unity (1983-1985)

Kevin McDonald, Pontifical Council for Promoting Christian Unity, The Vatican (1985-1993)

Timothy Galligan, Staff Member, Pontifical Council for Promoting Christian Unity, The Vatican (1993-)

Morals Consultants:

Enda McDonagh, Professor of Moral Theology, St. Patrick's College, Maynooth, Ireland

Bruce Williams, OP, Professor of Moral Theology, Pontifical University of St. Thomas Aquinas, Rome, Italy

World Council of Churches Observer

Günther Gassmann, Director, Faith and Order Commission, WCC, Geneva, Switzerland (until 1996)

ANGLICAN-ROMAN CATHOLIC DIALOGUE CANADA (DOCUMENTS 3, 7, 10, 15, 17, AND 20)

This dialogue group has varied in size from an initial seven members on each side, plus staff (1971-1977), to eleven, plus staff (1977-1982), and back to seven, plus staff (1982-present).

Anglicans

Donald Anderson, General Secretary Canadian Council of Churches (1982-1986)

Alyson Barnett-Cowan, Trinity College, Toronto (1977-1980); Staff member of Anglican General Synod (1991-)

John Baycroft, Bishop of Ottawa (1977-1985, *Co-chair* from 1985-)

Robert Black, Chaplain, Trinity College, Toronto (1996-)

Jim Boyles, Staff member of Anglican General Synod (1975-1981)

Eugene Fairweather, Professor, Trinity College, Toronto (1971-1995)

Richard G. Flemming, Dean, Diocese of Ontario (1971-1975)

Lewis Garnsworthy, Bishop of Toronto (1971-1973), deceased

John Gibaut, Director of Anglican Studies, St. Paul University, Ottawa (1990-)

Paul Gibson, Staff member of Anglican General Synod (1990-1991)

Alan Hayes, Professor, Wycliffe College, Toronto (1986-1989)

Henry G. Hill, Bishop of Ontario, Kingston (1975-1981)

John Hill, Rector, Church of St. Augustine of Canterbury, Toronto (1990-)

Lettie James, Rector, St. Hilda's, Montreal (1983-1987)

Eric Jay, Professor, Faculty of Divinity, McGill University, Montreal (1971-1977)

Jacob Jocz, Professor, Wycliffe College, Toronto (1971-1982), deceased

Patricia Kirkpatrick, Professor, Montreal Diocesan Theological College (1989-)

William McKeachie, Toronto School of Theology (1974-1978)

Thelma Anne McLeod, SSJD, Retreat and Music Director (1981-1989)

Helen Milton, Professor, University of Windsor, Ontario (1977-1985)

Linda Nicholls, Rector, Holy Trinity Church, Thornhill, Ontario (1990-)

Oliver O'Donovan, Professor, Wycliffe College, Toronto (1979-1982)

Geoffrey H. Parke-Taylor, Suffragan Bishop of Toronto (*Co-chair* 1976-1985)

Reginald Pierce, Bishop of Athabasca (*Co-chair* 1971-1975)

Brian Prideaux, Staff member of Anglican General Synod (1982-1990)

H. L. Puxley, Director, Ecumenical Institute of Canada, Toronto (1971-1975)

Ronald Reeve, Professor, Bishop's University, Lennoxville, Quebec (1982-1989)

John Simons, Principal, Montreal Diocesan Theological College (1996-)

Don Thompson, Principal, College of Thorneloe University, Sudbury, Ontario (1978-)

Reginald M. Turpin, Executive Officer, Diocese of Montreal (1976-1983)

Bill Zion, Professor, Queen's Theological College, Kingston, Ontario (1974-1975)

Roman Catholics

Irenée Beaubien, SJ, Director, Canadian Centre for Ecumenism, Montreal (1971-1982)

MacBeth Brown, CSB, Associate Director, Canadian Centre for Ecumenism (1981-1984), deceased

Jacques Chenevert, SJ, Professor of Theology, Trois-Rivières, Quebec (1971-1975)

Catherine Clifford, University of St. Michael's College (1993-)

Brian Clough, Judicial Vicar, Toronto Regional Marriage Tribunal (1992-)

Wilfrid Dewan, Professor, University of St. Michael's College, Toronto (1973-1974)

Gérard Dionne, Bishop of Edmonston, New Brunswick (*Co-chair* 1976-1982)

Renée Fortin, Associate Director, Canadian Centre for Ecumenism, Montreal (1984–1986)

Donna Geernaert, SC, Staff member of Canadian Conference of Catholic Bishops (1984–)

Marcel Gervais, Archbishop of Ottawa (*Co-chair* 1982-1985)

Joseph Hardy, Pastor, Diocese of London, Ontario (1971-1983)

John Keating, CSP, Office for Ecumenism, Toronto (1971-1975), deceased

Bernard Hubert, Bishop of Saint Jean Longueil, Quebec (*Co-chair* 1992-1995), deceased

Emmanuel Lapierre, OP, Associate Director, Canadian Centre for Ecumenism, Montreal (1996-)

Jean-Marc Laporte, SJ, Professor, Regis College, Toronto (1975-1992)

Robert Lebel, Bishop of Valleyfield, Quebec (*Co-chair* 1975-1976)

Josephine McCarthy, RSCJ, Staff member of Canadian Conference of Catholic Bishops (1979-1981)

Gertrude McLaughlin, SNJM, Canadian Centre for Ecumenism, Montreal (1977-1983)

Harry McSorley, Professor, University of Saint Michael's College, Toronto (1974-1993)

Attila Mikloshazy, SJ, Professor, St. Augustine's Seminary, Toronto (1975-1989)

Michael O'Connell, Staff member of Canadian Conference of Catholic Bishops (1975-1977)

Margaret O'Gara, Professor, University of St. Michael's College, Toronto (1977-1993)

Harold O'Neill, Professor, St. Augustine's Seminary, Toronto (1975-1982)

Veronica O'Reilly, CSJ, Staff member of Canadian Conference of Catholic Bishops (1982-1983)

Marc Pelchat, Professor, Université Laval, Quebec (1993-1996)

Terrence Pendergast, SJ, Auxiliary Bishop of Toronto (1989-)

Johann Pristl, PB, (1971-1974)

Thomas Ryan, CSP, Director, Canadian Centre for Ecumenism, Montreal (1986-1995)

Jean M. R. Tillard, OP, Professor, Collège Dominicain, Ottawa (1971-)

Edward Troy, Bishop of Saint John, New Brunswick (*Co-chair* 1986-1992)

Diane Willey, NDS, Associate Director, Office for Ecumenism, Toronto (1971-1974)

Joseph Windle, Bishop of Pembroke (*Co-chair* 1971-1974)

United Church Observers

Janet Cawley, Pastor, Toronto (1984-1988)

Edward Furcha, Professor, United Theological College, Montreal (1993)

Joseph McInnis, Pastor, Saint Laurent, Quebec (1994-1995)

Hugh Rose, Pastor, Toronto (1972-1984)

Martyn Sadler, Pastor, Sawyerville, Quebec (1989-1991)

ANGLICAN ROMAN CATHOLIC CONSULTATION USA, ANGLICAN ORDERS (DOCUMENT 14)

Roman Catholics

John F. Whealon, Archbishop of Hartford (*Co-Chairman*)

Mary Ann Fatula, OP, St. James Convent, Columbus, Ohio

F. Joseph Gossman, Bishop of Raleigh

Frederick M. Jelly, OP, St. Mary's Seminary

Ronald Lawler, OFM Cap., Holy Apostoles Seminary, Cromwell, Conn.

Jon Nilson, Loyola University of Chicago

George H. Tavard, AA, Brighton, Mass.

James C. Turro, Seton Hall University

Episcopalians

A. Theodore Eastman, Bishop of Maryland (*Co-Chairman*)

R. William Franklin, St. John's University, Collegeville, Minn.

Bruce Griffith, Christ Church, Oyster Bay, N.Y.

Frank T. Griswold, Bishop of Chicago

Elizabeth T. Kennan, Mount Holyoke College

Eleanor McLaughlin, Mount Holyoke College

Charles P. Price, Virginia Theological Seminary

Philip Turner, The General Theological Seminary

Participants Ex Officio

Thaddeus Horgan, SA, deceased

William A. Norgren, staff

Joan Monica McGuire, OP, National Association of Diocesan Ecumenical Officers

J. Robert Wright, The General Theological Seminary

Drafting Committee

R. William Franklin and George H. Tavard

Consultants to the Drafting Committee

James O'Connor, Dunwoodie Seminary, and William Stafford

ANGLICAN ROMAN CATHOLIC CONSULTATION USA, 1992 – (DOCUMENTS 4, 11, 13, AND 19)

Roman Catholics

John J. Snyder, Bishop of St. Augustine (*Co-Chairman*)

Raymond Barton, Church of the Holy Comforter, Charlottsville, Va.

F. Joseph Gossman, Bishop of Raleigh

Michael Himes, Boston College (1992-1994)

Mary E. Hines, Emmanuel College, Worcester, Mass. (1994-)

Fredrick M. Jelly, OP, Mount St. Mary's Seminary, Emmitsburg, Md.

Jon Nilson, Loyola University of Chicago

Joanne M. Pierce, College of Holy Cross

George Tavard, AA, Marquette University

Bruce Williams, OP, St. Dominic Priory

Ecumenical Officer:

Jeffrey Gros, FSC

Episcopalians

Frank T. Griswold, Bishop of Chicago (*Co-Chairman*)

Paula D. Barker, Seabury-Western Theological Seminar

Ashton J. Brooks, The General Theological Seminary

Marsha L. Dutton, Hanover College

William Franklin, The General Theological Seminary

Charles P. Price, Virginia Theological Seminary

Ellen K. Wondra, Bexley Hall, Rochester Center for Theological Studies

Theological Consultant:

J. Robert Wright, The General Theological Seminary

Ecumenical Officers:

Christopher Agnew (1992-1994)

David Perry (1994-1995)

ANGLICAN-ROMAN CATHOLIC BISHOPS CANADA (DOCUMENT 21)

This dialogue meets once a year and includes nine bishops from each Church. Membership rotates with some members continuing and some members changing each year. During 1993-1995, the following bishops have participated in the dialogue.

Anglicans

John Baycroft, Bishop of Ottawa

Anthony Burton, Bishop of Saskatchewan

James Cruikshank, Bishop of Cariboo

Barry Curtis, Bishop of Calgary, Archbishop of Rupert's Land

Terence Finlay, Bishop of Toronto

John Hannen, Bishop of Caledonia

Donald Harvey, Bishop of Eastern Newfoundland and Labrador

Michael Ingham, Bishop of New Westminister

George Lemmon, Bishop of Fredricton

Peter Mason, Bishop of Ontario

Michael Peers, Archbishop and Primate of Canada

Bruce Stavert, Bishop of Quebec

Roman Catholics

Bertrand Blanchet, Archbishop of Rimouski

Gilles Cazabon, Bishop of Timmins

John Knight, Auxiliary Bishop of Toronto

Robert Lebel, Bishop of Valleyfield

Brendan O'Brien, Bishop of Pembroke

Gilles Ouellet, Archbishop Emeritus of Rimouski

Cornelius Pasichny, Eparch of Saskatoon

André Vallée, Bishop of Hearst

Gerald Wiesner, Bishop of Prince George

Neil Willard, Auxiliary Bishop of Montreal

James Wingle, Bishop of Yarmouth

APPENDIX III
BIBLIOGRAPHY

Anglican Consultative Council. *The Emmaus Report*. London: Anglican Consultative Council, 1987.

Australian Study Guide Committee. *Traveling Together: Australian Study Guide for the ARCIC Final Report*. Eastwood, New South Wales: Australian Study Guide Committee, 1984.

Bird, David, et al. *Receiving the Vision: The Anglican–Roman Catholic Reality Today*. Collegeville, Minn.: Liturgical Press, 1995.

Bishops' Conference of England and Wales. *Response to the Final Report of ARCIC I*. London: Catholic Truth Society, 1985.

Buchanan, Colin Ogilvie. *ARCIC and Lima on Baptism and Eucharist, including The Lima Eucharistic Liturgy*. Grove Worship Series, 86. Bramcote, Notts.: Grove Books, 1983.

Burgess, Joseph and Jeffrey Gros, eds. *Building Unity*. New York: Paulist Press, 1989.

———. *Growing Consensus*. New York: Paulist Press, 1995.

Catholic Press Association of the Diocese of Rockville Center. *ARCIC I Revisited*. Hemstead, N.Y.: Catholic Press Association of the Diocese of Rockville Center, 1985.

Coleman, Robert, ed. *Resolutions of the Twelve Lambeth Conferences, 1867–1988*. Toronto: Anglican Book Center, 1992.

Episcopal Diocesan Ecumenical Officers and National Association of Diocesan Ecumenical Officers. *Companions in the Struggle: Church Unity & Ethical Issues*. Richmond, Va.: Episcopal Diocesan Ecumenical Officers and National Association of Diocesan Ecumenical Officers, 1996.

Faculty of General Theological Seminary. *Response of the Faculty to the ARCIC Final Report*. New York: General Theological Seminary, 1984.

Faith and Order Advisory Group of the Church of England. *The Church of England's Response to BEM and ARCIC: Supplementary Report to GS 661*. London: Board for Mission and Unity, 1986.

Falardeau, Earnest, ed. *ARC Soundings: A U.S. Response to ARCIC I*. Lanham, Md.: University of America Press, 1990.

Franklin, William R., ed. 'Anglican Orders: A Century of *Apostolicæ Curæ*. Essays on the Centenary of *Apostolicæ Curæ*, 1896-1996'. *Anglican Theological Review* 78:1 (Winter 1996) (also London and Oxford: Mowbray).

Gaither, Linda L. 'Competing Notions of Reception in the ARCIC Dialogue Process: An Analysis through Reader-Response Criticism'. Washington, D.C.: The Catholic University of America, 1993.

Geernaert, Donna. 'Canadian Anglican-Roman Catholic Dialogue'. *Ecumenism* 88 (December 1987): 28-30.

Gros, Jeffrey. 'Anglican-Roman Catholic Dialogue, U.S.A.'. *Journal of Ecumenical Studies* 143 (Winter 1993): 143.

———. 'Episcopal-Roman Catholic Bishops Pilgrimage Witnesses Commitment and Realism'. *Ecumenical Trends* 24:1 (January 1995): 1-14.

Hill, Christopher and Edward Yarnold, eds. *Anglicans and Roman Catholics: The Search for Unity*. London: SPCK-CTS, 1994.

Huffman, Bryon L. 'Anglican-Roman Catholic Dialogues: Mutual Recognition of Ministries'. *Journal of Ecumenical Studies* 30:2 (Spring 1993): 157.

Latimer House. *Rome and Canterbury: The Final ARCIC Report. A Study Guide*. Oxford, U.K.: Latimer House, 1982.

Lehmann, Karl and Wolfhart Pannenberg, eds. *The Condemnations of the Reformation Era, Do They Still Divide?* Minneapolis: Fortress Press, 1990.

Locke, Geoffrey. *Just Before God?: Justification and ARCIC II. A Study Guide to the Debate*. Bramcote, Notts.: Grove Books, 1989.

Martineau, Suzanne. *Les Anglicans*. Turnhout, Belgium: Editions Brepols, 1996.

McGrath, Alister E. *ARCIC and Justification: An Evangelical Anglican Assessment of 'Salvation and the Church'*. Latimer Studies 26. Oxford: Latimer House, 1987.

National Conference of Catholic Bishops. 'Evaluation of the ARCIC Final Report'. *Origins* 25 (December 6, 1984): 409-413.

Neuner, J. and Jacques Dupuis, eds. *The Christian Faith in the Doctrinal Documents of the Catholic Church*. Bangalore, India: Theological Publications of India, 1991.

Nilson, Jon. *Nothing Beyond the Necessary: Roman Catholicism and the Ecumenical Future*. New York: Paulist, 1995.

———. 'Vatican Responds to Talks with Anglicans'. *The Christian Century* 109:11 (April 1992): 324.

Norgren, William A., ed. *Ecumenism of the Possible: Witness, Theology and the Future Church*. Cincinnati: Forward Movement Publications, 1994.

Norgren, William A. and William G. Rusch, eds. *"Through Full Communion" and "Concordat of Agreement"*. Lutheran-Episcopal Dialogue, Series III. Minneapolis: Augsburg, 1991.

————. *Implications of the Gospel*. Lutheran-Episcopal Dialogue, Series III. Minneapolis: Augsburg, 1988.

————. *Toward Full Communion*. Lutheran-Episcopal Dialogue, Series III. Minneapolis: Augsburg, 1991.

O'Gara, Margret. 'Another Step on the Road to Unity'. *Ecumenism* 103 (September 1991): 3-4.

'One in Mind and Heart: a Pilgrimage of Anglican and Roman Catholic Bishops'. *One in Christ* 31:2 (1995): 171-184.

'Ordained Ministry in the Catholic Response to ARCIC'. *Ecumenical Trends* 21:10 (November 1992): 149.

Platten, Stephen. 'Anglicanism and Roman Catholicism: The Continuing Story of Two Communions'. *One in Christ* 30:3 (1994): 229-255.

Purdy, William. *The Search for Unity*. London: Geoffrey Chapman, 1995.

Ratzinger, Joseph. 'Anglican-Catholic Dialogue: Its Problems and Hopes', in *Church, Ecumenism and Politics: New Essays in Ecclesiology*. Trans. Frideswide Sandemann. New York: Crossroad, 1988: 65-88.

Ryan, William. 'Anglican-Roman Catholic Dialogue in the U.S.A.'. *Journal of Ecumenical Studies* 32:2 (1995): 300.

Santer, Mark, ed. *Their Lord and Ours. Approaches to Authority, Community and the Unity of the Church*. London: SPCK, 1982.

Stott, John R. W. *Evangelical Anglicans and the ARCIC Final Report: An Assessment and Critique*. Bramcote, Notts.: Grove Books, 1985.

Tanner, Mary. 'The ARCIC Statements in the Context of Other Dialogues', in *Their Lord and Ours*, ed. Mark Santer. London: SPCK, 1982.

Tanner, Norman. *Decrees of the Ecumenical Councils*, vols. I, II. Washington, D.C.: Georgetown University Press, 1990.

Tavard, George H. 'ARCIC I on Authority', in *Communion et Reunion. Mélanges Jean-Marie Roger Tillard*. ed. G. R. Evans and M. Gourgues. Leuven, Belgium: Leuven University Press, 1995: 185-198.

————. 'Apostolicæ Curæ and the Snares of Tradition', in *Anglican Orders: A Century of Apostolicæ Curæ. Essays on the Centenary of Apostolicæ Curæ, 1896-1996*. ed. R. William Franklin. (*Anglican Theological Review* 78:1 [Winter 1996] and London and Oxford: Mowbray, 1996): 30-47.

Tillard, Jean-Marie. 'Hope from ARCIC'. *The Tablet* 246:7939 (October 3, 1992): 1243.

Towards a Church of England Response to BEM Baptism, Eucharist and Ministry (World Council of Churches) and ARCIC, The Final Report of the Anglican Roman Catholic International Commission. London: CIO Publishing, 1984.

Vischer, Lukas and Harding Meyer, eds. *Growth in Agreement: Reports and Agreed Statements of Ecumenical Conversations on a World Level*. New York: Paulist Press, 1984.

Wright, J. Robert, ed. *A Communion of Communions: One Eucharistic Fellowship*. New York: Seabury Press, 1979.

———. 'Fundamental Consensus: An Anglican Perspective', in *In Search of Christian Unity: Basic Consensus/Basic Differences*. ed. Joseph A. Burgess. Minneapolis: Fortress, 1991: 168-184.

———. 'The Problem of Tradition in the Definitive Response of the Vatican to the Final Report of the ARCIC I', in *The Quadrilog: Tradition and the Future of Ecumenism. Essays in Honor of George H. Tavard*. ed. Kenneth Hagen. Collegeville, Minn.: The Liturgical Press, 1994: 223-238.

———. *Quadrilateral at One Hundred*. Cincinnati: Forward Movement Publications, 1988.

———. 'The Reception of ARCIC I in the USA: Latest Developments', in *Communion et Re-union*. Leuven, Belgium: Leuven University Press, 1995: 217-230.

Wright, J. Robert and Joseph Witmer, eds. *Called to Full Unity: Documents on Anglican-Roman Catholic Relations, 1966-1983*. Cincinnati: Forward Movement Publications, 1985.

———. 'Report of the Anglican/Roman Catholic Joint Preparatory Commission', in *Called to Full Unity: Documents on Anglican-Roman Catholic Relations, 1966-1983*. Cincinnati: Forward Movement Publications, 1985.

Yarnold, Edward. *An ARCIC Catechism: Questions and Answers on the Final Report of the Anglican Roman Catholic International Commission*. London: Catholic Truth Society, 1983.

———. 'Tradition in the Agreed Statements of the Anglican Roman Catholic International Commission', in *The Quadrilog: Tradition and the Future of Ecumenism. Essays in Honor of George H. Tavard*. ed. Kenneth Hagan. Collegeville, Minn.: The Liturgical Press, 1994: 239-254.

INDEX

as discerning the mind of Christ, 195
of human sexuality, 202-203
natural, 190
preconceptions about, 200-201
shared vision of, 187-195
See also theology, moral
Mulieres Dignitatem, 170
multiculturalism, 151. *See also* diversity

'Observations' (CDF), status of, 52
orders, Anglican, 125-147
and ARCIC I, 136-138
early history of, 125-126
new context for, 125, 141, 143
and the Preparatory Commission, 133-135
and Vatican Council II, 126-128
orders, holy
institution of, 90-91, 118-119
reordination on moving to another
communion, 182
See also ordination
orders, religious, in Canada, 155-157
ordination
Catholic rite of, 140
irrevocability of call to, 90, 119
relation to Christ, 118
and sacraments, 89-90
of women. *See* women, ordination of
See also episcopate; ministry; *Ministry and
Ordination*; orders, holy; priests
orthopraxies, as test of orthodoxy, 111
O'Hanlon, Daniel, 133

Parker, Matthew, 139
Paul IV and Anglican orders, 126, 127, 128,
133, 138, 139-141
Paul, St., and unity, 8-9
penance, sacrament of, 199
and salvation/sanctification, 47, 55-56
personhood, 188-189. *See also* anthropology
Peter, role of, 73. *See also* ministry, Petrine
Pius V, 127
Pius XII, 140
Plumptre, Canon, 153
plurality and unity, 24-25
Pole, Reginald, 126, 129
Pontifical Council for Promoting Christian
Unity
response to ARCIC I, 69-77
poor, concern for, 15

Portal, Fernand, 132
priests
moving to another communion,
177-183
shortage of, 154-155, 167
See also ministry; orders, holy; ordination
privilege, Pauline, 206
procreation, 209
Purdy, Canon, 133

Rampolla, Cardinal, 130
Ramsey, Michael, 133
reception of doctrine, 94-95, 111
reconciliation, 15
Rerum Novarum, 151
righteousness, 33. *See also* justification,
salvation
Roman Catholic Church. *See* Catholic Church
Rubric, Black, 87, 101 n. 45
Runcie, Robert
Common Declaration of, 4-5, 19
and ordination of women, 169
meeting with John Paul II, 26-27, 30

sacraments and ordination, 89-90
Sacramentum Ordinis, 140
Sæpius Officio, 130-131
salvation
agreement on, 32-33
assurance versus certitude of, 46, 53-54
and the Church, 34, 39-41, 44, 48-49,
55-57
and faith, 33, 34-35, 43, 46, 54
and good works, 33, 37-39, 44
gratuity of, 54
historical contention about, 32
and interior transformation, 45
and justification, 35-37
New Testament language for, 35-36
of those without explicit belief in Christ,
31
See also justification, righteousness,
sanctification
Salvation and the Church
ARC Canada on, 52-62
history of, 1-2
Lambeth Conference on, 66
observations of Vatican on, 43-51
text of, 30-42

sanctification
    sacramental dimension of, 47
    and justification, 36-37
Scannell, T. B., 129
Scripture
    canon of, and the Church, 12
    interpretation of, 76, 91, 97-98
Second Vatican Council. *See* Vatican Council II
sexuality, 202-203
sin, 194
    impairing communion, 7-8
    and justification, 53
Sisterhood of St. John the Divine, 156-157,
    160
sisters. *See* orders, religious
Sisters of the Church, 157
Smith, Fr. J., 134
social activism, in Canada, 150-151
spirituality, sharing between Anglicans and
    Catholics, 19
stewardship, 40
substantial agreement, 108-109, 112
succession, apostolic, 14, 75-76, 92-93, 119-
    120, 138

theology, moral, 198-199
tradition
    as living word of God, 12, 13
    and morality, 189, 190-191
    need for attention to, 50
transubstantiation, 86, 116-117
trust, in dialogue, 57-59

Unitatis Redintegratio, 26, 232
unity
    need for, and evangelization, 81
    and plurality, 24-25

and the Roman pontiff, 97
as gift of God, 23
utilitarianism, 201

Vachon, Archbishop Louis-Albert, 163, 164
van Beeck, Franz Josef, 133
Vatican Council II
    and women, 154
    acknowledgment of special relationship
        with Anglican Church, ix
    and sacramentality of the episcopate,
        138-139
Vatican
    and *The Final Report,* 28
    See also John Paul II; Congregation for the
        Doctrine of the Faith; Pontifical
        Council for Promoting Christian
        Unity
Veritatis Splendor, 218-219
vocation, signs of, for ordained ministry,
    180-181
war, 187
Weakland, Archbishop Rembert, 23-25
Willebrands, Cardinal Jan, 137, 141, 169-170
women
    affirmation of gifts of, 163-164
    circumstances of, in Canada, 150-155
    ordination of, 2, 20-21, 66, 75, 92, 120,
        161-162, 166-174
    role of, in Church, 154
    scholarship on, 154
Women's Auxiliary, 157
works, good, and salvation, 33, 37-39, 44
world, openness to, 191-192
worship, sharing between Anglicans and
    Catholics, 19
Württemberg Confession, 32